IDEOLOGY AND CULTURAL PRODUCTION

IDEOLOGY AND CULTURAL PRODUCTION

Edited by Michèle Barrett, Philip Corrigan,
Annette Kuhn and Janet Wolff

ST. MARTIN'S PRESS NEW YORK

All rights reserved. For information write:
St. Martin's Press Inc., 175 Fifth Avenue, New York,
N.Y. 10010
Printed in Great Britain
First published in the United States of America in
1979

Library of Congress Cataloging in Publication Data
British Sociological Association.
    Ideology and cultural production.
    Selected papers originally presented at the 1978
conference of the British Sociological Association.
    Bibliography: p.225
    Includes index.
    1. Arts and society. 2. Popular culture.
I. Barrett, Michèle. II. Title.
NX180.S6B74 1979   301.2'1   78-26901
ISBN 0-312-40451-4

CONTENTS

ACKNOWLEDGEMENTS

We would like to acknowledge the enormous assistance given to us by Ann Dix in the preparation of this volume and the organisation of the conference which gave rise to it. We also wish to thank all those people who contributed to the conference, and the Calouste Gulbenkian Foundation for giving financial assistance in the provision of cultural events and media access. Our literary agent, Frances Kelly, helped us in all the stages of planning and publication of the book. Finally we would like to acknowledge the support we have given each other, as conference organisers, editors and authors: much enjoyment and educational reward has come from the friendship and mutual support generated in the process of working together.

Michèle Barrett
Philip Corrigan
Annette Kuhn
Janet Wolff

August 1978

1 REPRESENTATION AND CULTURAL PRODUCTION

Michèle Barrett, Philip Corrigan, Annette Kuhn and Janet Wolff

The areas indicated by terms such as 'culture', 'ideology' and 'representation' have in recent years been the subject of extensive and increasing analysis and debate. As the editors of this collection of essays we aim at offering a contribution to this debate, not so much by taking up a position, but by attempting to locate problems and outline developments. The papers published here were originally given at the 1978 conference of the British Sociological Association, the theme of which was 'Culture'. As organisers of this conference we were faced with the problem of defining the area of work which would be embraced by that vexed and ambiguous term. This problem of definition led us to consider the more fundamental question of the relationship between work in the area of 'cultural studies' and the traditional concerns of institutionalised academic sociology. Given the virtual non-existence of any sociology of culture we were confronted by a field that was largely unmapped: consequently in selecting papers for the conference, we were unable to adopt a strategy either of reflecting 'the state of the art' or of providing a showcase for the 'best' work being done in the field. In defining the theme we were therefore necessarily forced to take up a position on what we considered to be important points of development and lines of future work.

The definition of 'culture' made public in our various statements for contributors was not in fact reflected in the range of work presented at the conference. This is by no means a matter of local interest to the several hundred people who attended the conference, but is much more generally symptomatic of the uneven development of work on culture, its diverse institutional bases, and the contradictory directions currently taken in such work. The conference did not seek to address the conventional anthropological notion of 'culture', nor did it seek to reflect the traditional emphasis in sociological work on the analysis of literature (the latter being extensively covered in the annual conferences held under the auspices of the Literature department of the University of Essex). Instead we wished to contribute to broader theoretical debate and to emphasise work on the material and ideological bases of

9

cultural production in modern society, drawing on a wide range of instances such as film, television, the media, visual art and music. In relation to this, we wished to promote discussion of the 'cultural' aspects of current debates in the areas of language, science and sexuality, and to address the politics of gender, race and class in cultural production. In assigning a high priority to questions of gender and race through discussion of representations of gender difference and sexuality and by raising questions of cultural imperialism and racial stereotyping, we necessarily endorsed the recent break with conventional sociological and Marxist approaches in which culture and ideology are theorised as superstructural reflections of class contradictions at the economic level.

The notion of culture which we would advance hinges on the concept of production. We see cultural products and practices in terms of the relations between their material conditions of existence and their work as representations which produce meanings. In other words, our concern is both with modes of production and with modes of signification. It is also clear that, thought in this way, studies of 'culture' may constitute a challenge to the traditional subject boundaries of academic institutions and discourses: they are by their nature interdisciplinary. Indeed it is no coincidence that much of the work done under the rubric of 'cultural studies' emerges from relations of production which are profoundly subversive of the individualistic notions of authorship common in much academic work. Various degrees of collective or collaborative work underpin a good part of the contents of this book. This was even more evident in the structure of the conference itself, with its emphasis on open workshop sessions, its inclusion of work from a variety of disciplines, and its attempt (while recognising the dangers of a simplistic elision of theory and practice) to challenge conventional barriers between those who produce critical and theoretical work and those who see themselves primarily as 'practitioners'.

The seven papers which follow are not intended in any way to be a 'representative sample' of the conference proceedings.[1] Indeed many of the contributions we would have wanted to include could not be transposed into the medium of a book. Several sessions constituted informal presentations of work in progress, many depended upon visual, auditory or dramatic material, and others aimed to open up debate through brief contributions from a panel of speakers. Some of the themes raised in these panel sessions (on culture and ideology; language and discourse; cultural imperialism; debates in TV news research; Marxism, feminism and cultural practice; the state, culture and patronage) have, where possible, been drawn into this introductory essay. We have chosen to publish these particular papers because they focus the issues which we regard as central in constructing work around 'culture' defined as the socially and historically situated process of production of meanings. In saying this, however, we are not suggesting that the articles are to be seen in any way as exemplary, for to embrace such notions of excellence would be to suggest a closure which we would expressly regard as impossible at the present moment. However, they each raise and attempt to address some of the difficult and unresolved issues faced by studies of culture, and indicate the ways in which these issues were taken up at the conference.

There are, as we have already suggested, some acute problems in existing sociological work on culture. Bird, in 'Aesthetic Neutrality and the Sociology of Art', points to the general poverty of attempts to found specific theories of various cultural forms (such as literature). A tendency neither to engage with the major problems of social forma-tion, class structuration and ideological configurations, nor to recognise the validity of critical judgements constituted within the instance being investigated, has led to analyses which regard cultural products as illustrations of the consequences and effects of determinations which are located externally. Some of these approaches are markedly reductive in a sense which is different from the normal use of that term. The term 'reduction' commonly indicates an attempt to deny the autonomy (even if relative) and the specificity (even if structured externally) of cultural practices. But there is another reduction which simply privileges the artefact itself, divorced from its conditions of production and existence, and claims that it alone provides the means of its own analysis. In the work of Leavis, for example, this surfaces in the notion of a correct *reading*. Other positions exist which, although fundamentally unlike that of Leavis, still take the text and its reading as the end, as well as the obvious beginning, of analysis.

The theoretical inadequacy of much sociological work on culture can only be combated by rigorous, historically informed analysis of cultural and ideological relations and practices. For only such work can resist the tendency to theoreticism so evident at present, and which indeed recalls Marx's comments on the 'violent abstraction' and 'meta-physical speculation' of many of his contemporaries (Sayer, 1979a, 1979b). One aspect of this theoreticism — the mobilisation of theory for its own sake — is ironically that it is not in Marx's terms theoretical enough: it has not grasped the phenomena. The general tendency towards theoreticism in work in the areas of culture and ideology is inextricably and integrally related to similar problems in the wider field of sociological debate. One particular manifestation of it is discussed below when we deal with the various polarisations of position which have been created and maintained to the detriment of constructive and rigorous debate. These polarisations, or dichotomies, are frequently assumed as means of mounting an easy attack; one has only to accuse another of 'culturalism', or 'historicism', or 'economism', or 'Althusserianism' (to name a few examples) to render engaged debate unnecessary. Such general, and often false, oppositions have been drawn from the most universalistic tendencies in current theoretical debate.

Three years ago, Raymond Williams presented a useful overview of 'Developments in the Sociology of Culture' which was later published in the BSA's journal *Sociology* (Williams, 1976c). There he began by noting both the 'specialized and marginal' way in which the sociology of culture was seen, and argued that it was also evidently underdeveloped. Williams then went on to list the contributions to the debate from sociology and from 'cultural studies': 'studies of *effects*, of explicitly structured *institutions*, and of intellectual *formations*' from sociology, and '*traditions*, . . . *forms* and . . . the exceptionally complex relations between "forms" in this intellectual, literary and artistic sense and "forms" and "formations" in more familiar social senses' (1976c, pp. 498 and 500; italics in original). Williams then went on to note the centrality of the Marxist contribution to studies of culture and ideology, citing in particular the work of Althusser and also work in anthropology and linguistics. He concluded with the suggestion that future work would focus upon the materiality of signs, arguing that

> the success of various kinds of formalism is due mainly to their correct emphasis on sign systems as the radical elements of all cultural process. It is not surprising that work of this kind is replacing *criticism* which still residually dominates humanistic studies but which can now be seen more clearly as the theoretical and practical generalization of specifically bourgeois uses of culture (the concepts *criticism*, *literature* and *art*, in their currently available forms, are all contemporaneous with bourgeois society, and are the theoretical forms of its cultural specialization and control) [1976c, p. 505].

Significant developments have taken place in the study of culture since that article was written, some of which we discuss below. But it is important to note that some of the tensions and contradictions which have recently emerged more clearly within cultural studies are actually implicit in these earlier formulations. Immediately prior to the publication of his book *Marxism and Literature* (1977a), Williams made it clear that he distanced himself quite radically from 'specialised literary studies' on the grounds that cultural studies embrace a much wider area. They do so in the concrete sense of what they cover, namely

> all other forms of writing . . . the related non-written activities of communication which extend from the new media as Art in the conventional sense to the new media not seen as art [Williams, 1977c p. 14].

This is true for the methodology and epistemology of cultural studies. Williams condemns formalism, and calls upon cultural studies to recognise the fundamental historicity of social life. In distancing himself from formalism, Williams specifically cites semiotics as profoundly non-historical or even anti-historical because of its roots in structuralism.

Such criticisms understand semiotic analysis as grounded in Saussure's formulation of a science of signs in society — semiology — in a synchronic rather than a diachronic linguistic theory (Saussure, 1974). Less commonly voiced is the criticism that semiotics is fundamentally idealist in that it is based on the Saussurean conceptualisation of the signified as a mental construct rather than as a material referent. Neither of these lines of criticism however takes account of various other tendencies in structural linguistics on which semiotics has drawn. In this context we could take as examples the work of Jakobson (1972) and Benveniste (1971), in which notions of *address* in language are mobilised. These arguments are founded on the notion that *parole* — the speech act as opposed to the underlying code (*langue*) — necessarily inscribes a source and an object of address. This operates notably through the personal pronoun, an observation which has led to the proposition that determinate conceptions of self and other are produced in language. As Benveniste argues:

> it is by identifying himself as a unique person pronouncing *I* that each speaker sets himself up in turn as the 'subject' . . . [1971 p. 220].

Considered in this way, language — or more specifically, the speech act — is the historically situated site of the creation of subjectivity. Indeed

Lacanian psychoanalysis bases itself on the notion that a prior and necessary condition of the institution of subjectivity is the self-other split implied in the pronouncing of *I* and *you* (Lacan, 1968; Coward and Ellis, 1977). It is clear that in such a semiotics the question of the autonomy of the signification process becomes crucial. On the one hand, the Saussurean notion of the 'arbitrary' character of the signified in relation to any material world which might be posited as pre-existing the subject seems to lead to an extreme non-determinist position. On the other, questions as to the degree and character of that autonomy and its external structuration remain the subject of contentious debate.

It is relevant to note here that the inscription of notions of subjectivity, address and context into a semiotics founded on structural linguistics does permit a move away from the formalist variant of semiotics which restricts itself to the specificity of textual practices. Williams' critique of this tendency is complemented by Hill's contribution to the present volume, 'Ideology, Economy and the British Cinema', in which it is argued that around 1970, *Cahiers du Cinéma* took up a position in which filmic and ideological specificity is considered independently of its determinations. Hill's critique is perhaps representative of the arguments which were levelled against semiotic approaches during the course of the conference, in the sense that the object of criticism is the earlier and more formalist version of the problematic. Discussion around more recent developments in semiotics tended to founder on the difficulty of the language in which such analyses are commonly couched. Although we would agree with some of the criticisms made at the conference of the inaccessibility of some of the theoretical language used, we would argue that a distinction should be made between the obscurantist tendency of theoreticism and the necessary conplexity involved in a precise analysis of language itself. Since thought and language are inseparable, innovation must necessarily involve a challenge to the limits historically set in language. The tendency to ascribe obscurantism to every theoretical presentation which demands considerable work from the reader or listener is a dangerous one.

Another, and related, development of structuralism — discourse theory — has also been drawn upon in the attempt to establish a general analysis of signification and signifying practices. Examples of this work may be found in journals such as *Ideology and Consciousness* and in the work of Hindess and Hirst (Cutler *et al.*, 1977, 1978). However although this work has been the topic of considerable debate within sociology, there were relatively few contributions to the conference which took it as a model. In spite of the fact that there was considerable and constructive discussion of developments in discourse theory as they relate to the analysis of subjectivity (as, for example, in the presentations by Colin Mercer and Cora Kaplan in a panel session on language and discourse), there were few echoes of Hirst's argument of a 'necessary non-correspondence' between the ideological and other levels. Hirst advances his argument through a critique of Althusser's essay 'Ideology and Ideological State Apparatuses' (hereafter the ISAs essay) (Althusser, 1971), and arrives at a total, rather than a relative, autonomisation of all social realms. In this idealisation of social existence nothing exists outside of discourse. Arguing that the signified does not exist prior to its signification (Hirst, 1976b, p. 411), Hirst denies the materiality of language and the historicity of the determinations which make possible or impossible certain kinds of practices to which we refer as cultural. It is perhaps not surprising to find that such an approach has had limited purchase, at least in its most radical form, in work in the field of cultural studies.

A major debate which brought together a number of these issues took place recently in the magazine *Screen*, which has been influential in promoting work on semiotics and psychoanalysis. Rosalind Coward's article, 'Class, "Culture" and the Social Formation' (Coward, 1977a), argues against a view of culture held to be operational in cultural studies in general and in the work of the Birmingham University Centre for Contemporary Cultural Studies in particular. The reply from the Centre (Chambers *et al.*, 1977) and Coward's subsequent response provide useful texts for establishing some of the major theoretical oppositions which dominated the conference and structure the field. Coward's original article is distinctive for its critique of the assumption of a non-contradictory subjectivity in work which mobilises the concept of 'culture'. This assumption involves the notion that the subject is the vehicle or site of the operation of social/historical forces, and does not acknowledge the subject as being in its own right a process of production and therefore a site of contradiction. This argument has been understood as one informed by a Hirstian anti-historicism, although in a more recent article Coward does in fact appeal to an understanding of the conditions of existence of discourses on representation and sexuality. In this later piece she argues that representations have to be analysed

in terms of the practices which work to produce definitions . . . This

begins a move away from an analysis in terms of direct correspondence with an economic formation but it does not reduce the imperative of understanding the conditions of existence of these discourses
[Coward, 1978, p. 17].

Such an injunction suggests a movement towards theoretically
informed historical work. As Raymond Williams argued in 1973:

We should look not for the components of a product but for the
conditions of a practice. When we find ourselves looking at a
particular work, or a group of works, often realising as we do so their
irreducible individuality, we should find ourselves attending first to
the reality of their practice and the conditions of the practice as it
was then executed [Williams, 1973, p. 16].

This move towards specific historical work — which is in no sense a
retreat from theoretical questions — has wider implications. It would
first constitute a challenge to many of the arid dichotomies and false
oppositions which seem to be a feature of theoreticism. Secondly, the
kinds of theoretical work done in the past ten years or so have tended to
accompany certain aspects of academic life, to be reinforced within, as
it were, the relations of knowledge production and curricula in higher
education. To pose the specificity of cultural practices is also to
challenge the kind of theoretical 'imperialism' which has been a norm
of such academic discourse. Icons and (significantly) Heroes have been
promoted and equally rapidly disgraced with a bewildering ease which,
curiously, leaves their earlier acolytes and epigones somehow more
assured in their theoretical correctness. This process has been instrumental in the making of a series of individual — predominantly male,
white, middle-class — reputations.

By contrast, as well as arguing for specific types of work we would
also argue that different styles of work may be (and indeed fruitfully
have been) adopted under the rubric of cultural studies. We recognise,
for instance, the need for a period of extensive consolidation in which
different working groups familiarise themselves with a range of work.
Although this consolidating task may involve the risk of repetition, we
would argue that it is a necessary stage for the development of a
genuinely reflexive body of work on ideology and culture. The women's
movement, and some methods of work within socialist groupings, in some
publishing collectives and distinctively at the Centre for Contemporary
Cultural Studies, have shown the necessity for this consolidation, to

combat the reproduction of individual and oppressively dominant 'master-minds'. From these movements has emerged some of the best theoretical historical work we have.

It is significant that the kind of informed attention paid to historical analysis that we have suggested is in keeping with certain shifts within cultural practices themselves; these shifts, speaking very broadly, have made the construction of the work visible in its final representations. In relation to this the 'Conclusion' written by Frederic Jameson to the debates collected in *Aesthetics and Politics* (1977) is extremely relevant. He warns against the dogmatisation of particular theoretical positions, dogmatism which follows from the suppression of the conditions of their original construction. Some of his remarks on the 'aesthetic of novelty' inform us of certain distortions in modes of working on culture and ideology: have we not seen 'ever more rapid rotations on its own axis' (Jameson, 1977, p. 211) in theoretical work? We would agree with Jameson's strategic conclusion:

> To take an attitude of partisanship towards key struggles of the past does not mean either choosing sides, or seeking to harmonize irreconcilable differences. In such extinct yet still virulent intellectual conflicts, the fundamental contradiction is between history itself and the conceptual apparatus which, seeking to grasp its realities, only succeeds in reproducing their discord within itself in the form of an enigma for thought, an aporia. It is to this aporia that we must hold, which contains within its structure the crux of history beyond which we have not yet passed [Jameson, 1977, p. 213].

It is clear that the analysis of cultural products and practices presents a number of problems and complexities, which at present manifest themselves in several ways — in differences, for instance, in how the notion of production as applied to culture is to be thought, and in the degree to which textual practices are to be treated as autonomous of economic practices. These differences signal what is perhaps the most crucial issue here, and one on which a variety of positions are adopted: that is, the character of *determinations* surrounding cultural products and practices. Even the terminology adopted here indicates particular positions. To speak of 'conditions of existence' is to imply a degree of relative autonomy for different levels and instances of the social formation, culture (if such a term be used) and ideology included. According to such a view, it is quite legitimate to focus analysis on the internal structures of texts themselves, to examine how texts work as meaning-producing practices in their own right. It may be thus possible to indicate ways in which textual practices may operate 'unconsciously' in contradiction with their own conditions of existence. The analysis by *Cahiers du Cinéma* of John Ford's film *Young Mr. Lincoln*, which is cited by Hill in his contribution to this volume, pivots on the argument that some texts may be riven by internal contradictions which subvert their apparent ideological closure, and that it is the work of analysis to bring these contradictions to light. However the *Cahiers* analysis, as Hill points out, is grounded on the autonomous operation of the film as text and fails systematically to consider the implications of the fact that *Young Mr. Lincoln* is a Hollywood studio product of a certain conjuncture, in spite of a nod in the direction of the economic and political conditions surrounding its production. However, this is not to say that material conditions of existence are necessarily ignored or set aside in work which seeks to treat textual practices as productive, in their own right, of representations. Bland, McCabe and Mort, whose contribution to this volume 'Sexuality and Reproduction' constitutes an examination of various discourses of the state — official and semi-official reports — dealing with the family and with sexuality, demon-strate the ways in which, both within and between the texts they deal with, there exist a number of mutually contradictory positions, and more significantly, positions which might actually appear to go against the interests of the capitalist state. It is perhaps symptomatic that it is the position of women which emerges as the site of many of these contradictions. For example, in the 1950s during a period of increased demand for unskilled and semi-skilled labour which could not be met from the male workforce, married women — who constituted virtually the only internal source of reserve labour — were drawn into the labour market in large numbers. At the same time official discourses of the state (articulated particularly, during the 1950s, in reports dealing with the education of girls) were based on the assumption that women's primary lifelong role would be a family-centred one. When birth rates later began to show a distinct falling off, such positions continued to be held, and were evident notably in justifications of the failure to re-examine the position of married women with regard to social security benefits and income tax (McIntosh, 1978b; Beechey, 1978).

In their paper, 'Ideology and the Mass Media', Golding and Murdock here address themselves to the economic determinations framing the process of cultural production. In holding to the notion of determina-tion as opposed to conditions of existence, the authors are suggesting a more direct determination of representations by the economic level, in this instance the commercial (as opposed to the state monopoly) imperatives of free-enterprise broadcasting. They criticise work which privileges the operation of texts on the grounds that such work has failed to explore with any degree of thoroughness the question of economic determinations. At the same time, however, Hill puts forward a critique of an earlier piece of work by the same authors (Murdock and Golding, 1977a) on the grounds that their position is founded on an abandoning of the specificity of the operation of the text, 'for imagery is not only the end product of an economic process, but the product of a work of signification as well, with its own internal dynamics and operations'. This debate around determination constitutes the crux of many of the difficulties facing work on culture: it is obviously a very important issue, and one on which much work remains to be done. But at the same time, we are aware that the debate is bedevilled by what we call 'dichotomous theorising' — a tendency to present two positions, often in a highly oversimplified or abstract form, as mutually exclusive (in this instance, 'economism' versus 'structuralism'), with the implied injunction that it is necessary to choose one or the other. In pointing to this tendency we are not advocating agnosticism: rather we want to consider the ways in which certain approaches to theoretical work may in the end not actually be very productive for the progress of work on culture.

Dichotomous theorising is distinguished by a high level of abstraction: as such, it is a part of that retreat from the specificity of cultural production which we have already discussed. It tends to operate by means of an all-consuming series of elisions, in which different practices and positions are collapsed into readily recognisable 'Ghosts and Monsters', which can then be exorcised by the application of the correct theoretical salt, a tendency which Johnson considers here in his discussion of 'Histories of Culture/Theories of Ideology'. It is perhaps relevant to note that Marx was alive to this even in the 1840s in his sustained argument against all forms of metaphysical speculation. In *The German Ideology* Marx and Engels argue against 'theoretical bubble blowing' and against those 'learned gentlemen' for whom

it is altogether simply a matter of resolving this ready-made nonsense they find into some other freak, i.e. of presupposing that all this nonsense had a special *sense* which can be discovered; while really it is only a question of explaining these theoretical phrases from the actual existing relations [Marx and Engels, 1846, p. 56].

That this was not some quirk of Marx's early years can be seen from even the most cursory inspection of later works such as *Capital Volume III* and *Theories of Surplus Value*, or in the more pointed *Notes on Adolph Wagner* in which the critique of speculative subjectivism is particularly in evidence.

In examining the arguments which underlie the 'economism/ structuralism' split, we have already pointed to the debate around determinism. In arguments which pose the two tendencies as opposites 'economism' is held to be distinguished by its emphasis on the determination of ideology or representations by the economic, and 'structuralism' by its renunciation or bracketing of determinism in favour of a kind of fetishism of the text. Of course, things are never quite as simple as this; for example, an examination of Marx's notions of base and superstructure, often mobilised in support of economism, indicates how complex the situation actually is. We have to be clear from the start that the notions of 'base and superstructure' (the apparent obviousness of the 1859 'Preface' notwithstanding) were used by Marx as metaphors, as condensed and shorthand devices. A closer reading of the 1859 'Preface', taken with what Marx tells us it is held to condense — Chapter One of *The German Ideology* and other works of the 1840s — shows that politics and ideology operate as *fetishised representations*. That is to say, that the relations of production (political, cultural, moral, ideological, as much as economic, forming an 'economic structure', not because of some essentially economic qualities, but because they are entailed in production in a certain way) manifest themselves in particular forms, phenomena which by their emphasis upon their own unique features determine their appropriation as apparently separate areas which have then to be 'connected' back to production. Marx's language supports this clearly: he speaks of an 'ideological superstructure' and of 'forms' in which people become 'conscious'. But if we move away from the much-quoted 1859 'Preface' and examine, as Stuart Hall suggests (1977b; 1977d), *The Eighteenth Brumaire* or the drafts and text for *The Civil War in France*, we find that it is impossible to sustain the normal base/superstructure distinction and its direction of 'causality' as the basis of Marx's analysis.

Central to this whole debate is the question of how the notion of *production* is to be understood. The inadequate way in which production is very commonly thought makes it possible to understand the 'base' simply as economics plus technology, in such a way that political, cultural, ideological and moral relations are considered to be outside the authentic realm of production and related to it as both external and determined. This is disastrous for analysis of any kind, but it is crippling when that image of production is taken, as metaphor, to inform studies of cultural practices. Within such a problematic they can only be understood in a quite deforming way: their materiality is frequently reduced to the property relations and economic contexts within which they are situated, and this location means that they cannot be understood as having their own specific relations of production. In this way areas of analysis which could be fruitfully brought together are often kept apart.

The ways in which cultural production operates specifically are a matter for empirical and historical investigation. Supra-historical theories and abstractions cannot be used to make historical analyses. The outline we have drawn from Marx provides guidance in what to look for: the real analysis has then to engage with what actually is there — novels, films, painting, music — and to employ very sensitive judgements drawn from previous historical and theoretical work to make sense of how that cultural product was produced, and what are, in Williams' terms, the conditions of its practice.

The problem of culturalism versus structuralism, another recurring dichotomy, is addressed at some length in Johnson's contribution to this volume, and it features in many of the other papers; it was also dominant during the conference. In this area too, major errors arise through elision. We would argue that there is no coherent and monolithic body of 'culturalists' or of 'structuralists', nor is there, in any meaningful sense, any group of 'Althusserians', 'Thompsonians' or 'Hindess-and-Hirstians'. Such labels serve merely to polarise positions and reduce the possibility of constructive engagement in debate. This point can be made with some force in relation to the highly influential case of Althusser. Althusser celebrates as Marx's great scientific revolution the opening up of 'the third great continent: the continent of History' (1972, p. 166). After distancing himself from dabbling in structuralism, Althusser continues:

> The continent (of history) was opened up a hundred years ago. The only people who have ventured into it are the militants of the revolutionary class struggle. To our shame, intellectuals do not even suspect the existence of this continent, except to annex and exploit it as a common colony.
>
> We must recognise and explore this continent, to liberate it of its occupiers . . . [p. 186].

How many of those who praise, attack, follow Althusser would now
understand that celebration? How many, furthermore, would recognise
the Althusser who stresses that:

> *There is no such thing as a process except in relations (sous les
> rapports)*: the relations of production . . . and other (political,
> ideological) relations [ibid] .

This anomaly has arisen because a certain kind of Althusserian
structuralism, and the ISAs essay in particular, has been appropriated
to academic sociological discourse (Clarke, 1977a, 1977b). What this
appropriation has done, however, is simply to leave behind — as quite
indigestible to the delicate bourgeois palate — precisely the cutting edge,
politically speaking, of the analysis. The Althusser 'on offer' in sociology is a kind of Parisian functionalist. We do not seek here to re-
elevate the fallen idol of Althusser, but simply to remark on the uneven
reception of his work. In particular the ISAs essay has been very
partially taken up, and has frequently been combined with other
analyses which dilute, if not actually defeat, what Althusser was
attempting in his overall project. Some aspects of this partial appropriation were discussed at the conference, notably the influence of the first
part of the ISAs essay, which has become dominant to the exclusion of
any serious consideration of the essay's concluding section on the
interpellation of the subject in ideology.

The shortcomings of the first part of the ISAs essay are perhaps now
more clearly recognised. Althusser's formulation that the reproduction
of the relations of production takes place (descriptively) in the superstructure and (theoretically) by the operation of the State Apparatuses,
has tended to displace the material reality of the process of reproduction, a point made clear in the contribution to this volume by Bland,
McCabe and Mort. Secondly, despite our emphasis earlier that elsewhere in his work Althusser attaches due weight to historical analysis, it
cannot be denied that in the ISAs essay he does fail to examine the
operation of ideology in its historical specificity: and if we drain our
analysis of history we are freezing the categories of analysis (and to
some extent the object analysed). As Sayer has argued, Marx's critique
is completed (and made possible) by historical analysis, since in Marx's
words:

> from the moment that the bourgeois mode of production and the
> conditions of production and distribution which correspond to it are

recognised as *historical*, the delusion of regarding them as natural
laws of production vanishes and the prospect opens of a new society
. . . to which capitalism is only the transition [1863c, p. 429].

We have indicated one kind of absence in our discussion of how an
impoverished notion of production in general has been used as
metaphor and model to distort the understanding of cultural production. But within this there is a particularly glaring absence — how are
meanings made? This is often, quite simply, never considered — theories
of cultural production concentrate upon certain steps in cultural production and declare them to be explanatory of the whole. This often
entails either aesthetic mysticism or a commitment to a notion of
individual creativity. The work done in making cultural products meaningful and the work of their 'publication' and 'exchange', and equally
the work through which audiences make meanings, is frequently ignored
(Hohendahl, 1977; Jauss, 1970). It is true that authorial figures may
attempt to restrict the variety of meanings taken from their works —
and we can see from the papers by Hill and Thompson how
complicated are the 'authorial figures' operating within certain codes
(as for example in film), employing subcodes (such as those of a genre)
and their own distinctive repertoire (through which we may distinguish
the paintings of Picasso from those of Ernst, for example). This restriction, however, can never be complete. Totalitarianism within cultural
practices always remains the limit case — never reached.
    This question relates to a general failure in work on cultural produc-
tion to analyse historically the sign-systems, codes and styles which are
available for authorial and audience groups to make meanings with.
What matters about a given technological development, such as steam
printing, a new kind of paint, or a 'better' lens, is that it is already
'spoken of' within certain relations of production, although it may
quickly transcend or at least challenge those relations. In this context,
the final paper, 'Ideology and the Mass Media' by Golding and
Murdock, leads us back to the problem of locating cultural production
within wider systems of ownership, control and production. The position that we should work on a political economy of culture has been
abandoned in some quarters because it is seen to embody a simplistic
view of cultural transformation whereby it is thought to be guaranteed
simply by taking control of the cultural means of production. However,
it is now clear that what is also entailed is a conscious attempt at the
transformation of cultural practices — that there is, in other words, a
politics of images and equipment which must challenge the apparent

dominance of the technological means of production and transform their restrictions. While Thompson, in advancing the notion of 'Television as Text', puts forward precisely this view in his contribution, Golding and Murdock suggest on the other hand that the abandonment of a political economy of culture has been too complete and that the real problems of control have been surrendered in other forms of analysis. Indeed it is true, as Perkins argues here in the context of a re-examination of the process of stereotyping, that the transformation of cultural imagery is no simple task. The option of inversion does not exist. Many stereotypes, for example, operate through a precise if partial 'anchoring' in real, material, experience, and their transformation can only come about with the transformation of the material grounds which sustain them. The struggle against stereotypes is thus always prosecuted at more than one level. But whilst Marx was correct to emphasise that liberation was an historical and not a mental act, we should not forget that 'the transformation of circumstances and people' of which he spoke must also involve profoundly important changes at the level of consciousness.

Since these difficulties, which underpinned a good deal of the work of the conference, are in our view a reflection of the current state of work on cultural production, we have felt it necessary to discuss them in some detail here. Veering from the view that representation is an unmediated reflection of material conditions of existence to the view that representation is necessarily totally autonomous of those conditions, analysis has taken the ultimately futile path of theoreticism. We hope that in future work such dangers can be avoided through the analysis of the meaning production in its historically specific conditions of existence.

Notes

1. Chapter 1 was written especially for this book, while Chapters 2 to 8 are all versions of papers originally given at the conference. Some of the other material presented at the conference has now been published elsewhere: see, for example, Liz Brown 'The two worlds of Marrakech', *Screen*, vol. 19, no. 2, 1978, pp. 85-118; John Berger 'Ways of remembering', *Camerawork*, no. 10, 1978, pp. 1-2.

2 AESTHETIC NEUTRALITY AND THE SOCIOLOGY OF ART

Elizabeth Bird

In this chapter I want to look at some problems which cluster around the concept of a 'sociology of art', in particular those problems which stem from attempts to define how sociology can properly concern itself with certain cultural products which have already been staked out by the disciplines of 'literature', 'art history', 'music', 'drama', and so on. I don't want to suggest that these problems are merely the result of inter-disciplinary or inter-faculty rivalries, for there are considerable theoretical issues involved which transcend mere political factions within educational institutions. However, to some extent the problems are compounded by the tendency of academic organisations to contrive and maintain subject areas and their boundaries. I want to look at attempts made, on the whole from within sociology, to define a 'sociology of art', and at how these attempts have resolved, or tried to resolve, the question of aesthetic or critical evaluation of the work of art. I will suggest that the solution that argues that sociology, or sociologists, should not involve themselves in critical judgements but maintain a position of aesthetic neutrality is in itself untenable, as it can be shown to be both theoretically unsound, and impossible to apply in an empirical investigation. I will be using a research project which looked at the production of art in Glasgow (which was carried out by myself and one other colleague over three years of active research and funded by the Social Science Research Council), as an example of an empirical piece of work which, implicitly, if not explicitly, depended upon the principle of aesthetic neutrality.

Before proceeding to develop this outline of the chapter, I should like to comment upon the somewhat archaic nature of some of the arguments I shall be discussing. Many of the attempts made to define a 'sociology of art' are to be found randomly scattered about the sociological literature of the 1950s and '60s, although they survive longer in the United States and may be said still to be the subject of debate there. However, within Britain, the problem of how to define a specifically *sociological* approach to art, has, I think ceased to be discussed (it never was the subject of much debate), although there has been a fairly spectacular increase in the number of courses offered in at least the sociology of literature to students of both sociology and literature. The reason why it has been possible to develop this area of study without having to define the specifically sociological way of studying literature (or art in general) seems to me to be explained by a number of separate trends within both sociology and the arts-based disciplines. Firstly, sociology itself has lost its way, in that the theoretical premises of the 'fifties — objectivity, scientific study of the facts, and the testing of theories against the accumulation of evidence — have been swept away in the attack on positivism. Thus, it is much harder to maintain that there is a specifically sociological method. Sociology has rather become a focus, a lens, a pair of spectacles, whatever metaphor you wish, a way of looking at the world, and as such it has infected the neighbouring disciplines of literature, art history and music. The second trend thus involves a convergence of disciplines, with the arts-based subjects becoming more interested in both the social and the scientific. Within art history, for example, there is more and more work being done on patronage and the economic support for artists, and there has also been some attempt to analyse the ideological components of paintings, as in Tim Clark's work (Clark, 1973a and 1973b) on Courbet and other mid-nineteenth-century French painters. Within art criticism there has been an extension from literary criticism of the methods of structuralism and semiology into the specific analysis of the image. Structuralism and semiology are attempts to develop a more rigorous, schematic and thus scientific way of textual or visual analysis. Barthes (1957 and 1977) has looked at visual images found in advertising, but, to date, there have been no substantial semiological analyses of paintings. The most extensive application of structuralist and semiological methods has been in the theory of the film, and much of this work has taken place under the banner of cultural studies. The rapid growth of cultural studies, wherein culture can be studied autonomously, is a third trend which has obviated the need to develop a specifically sociological theory of art. Cultural studies have the advantage as a banner that it implies no one disciplinary allegiance, but is able to gather in followers recruited from all kinds of camps, although such recruits may often have to contend with the disapproval of their generals and officers. Cultural studies defy definition in that culture itself has proved difficult, if not impossible, to define. They have often been able to flourish by dealing, at least initially, with those cultural products which have been rejected by the academic establishment: pulp fiction, comics, pop music, films, television. These products all have some claim to a place within the study of literature, art history, music and drama and indeed they now may be being reclaimed and incorporated into the academic establishment as that establishment responds, albeit slowly, to social change. Within cultural studies, however, the products of the mass media can be studied alongside their consumers; for example, not rock music as rock music but as the expression of a sub-culture, as a product which is rooted in the processes of production and consumption of a cultural commodity. Like that other banner under which I fight, women's studies, cultural studies have been able to establish themselves, tenuously, in polytechnics and institutes of higher education, if not in universities. Like women's studies, cultural studies can bring together sociologists, psychologists and others 'trained' in social sciences both with those who have graduated in arts subjects, and, perhaps more importantly, with those whose interest comes not from studying culture, but from producing it — artists, television producers, playwrights, journalists, filmmakers.

I would suggest that because these three developments have taken place alongside each other, that is, the shifting of emphasis within both sociology and the arts-based disciplines combined with the development of cultural studies, the debates about what constitutes a sociology of art have largely become irrelevant. Why then revive them here? I think it is important to revive them if only to lay the ghost (with any luck for once and for all) though this I doubt. Because the debate about what constitutes a sociology of art has never been fully discussed, remnants of the old debates recur at regular intervals, partly because knowledge is still divided into lots. Cultural studies exist marginally within a university. The Centre for Contemporary Cultural Studies at Birmingham, for example, was founded in 1964 by Richard Hoggart as a research grouping within the English department at the university. It is housed in the arts faculty and students are not automatically eligible for SSRC studentships. The formation of the centre, to quote Stuart Hall, its current director, (Hall, 1971) 'required us to trespass across boundaries traditionally well-defined and well-patrolled in normal academic life'. Such trespassing, although not met by prosecution, has not been easy. Only now, some fourteen years after the founding of the Birmingham centre, is it becoming possible to think of taking a degree in cultural studies, and such a possibility is more likely in polytechnic courses, the universities remaining wedded to traditional disciplines. Sociology, although perhaps less well-patrolled than other disciplines, still has boundaries. Sociologists (or others) who choose to apply to the SSRC, wishing to do research into those cultural products which are still within the arts-based disciplines, may find it difficult to gain funding. And even if you gain such funding, where do you publish your findings? The journals are still tied to disciplines, and are likely to pose the same old questions — is it truly a contribution to sociology? Is it a contribution to literature or art history? Not to mention higher degrees, undergraduate anxieties (I surely cannot be the only person to teach the sociology of literature who encounters anxious queries from students about whether their work is truly sociological), external examiners, boards of studies, the whole panoply of institutional constraints which result, all too frequently, in my experience, in the resuscitation of the old question, what is a *sociology* of art? As one of the few who have received a grant from the SSRC for research into an area which might be considered to belong more properly to art history, I feel a certain obligation to give an account of that research, and to put forward some of the reasons for the research failing to produce the sort of findings expected by the SSRC. In addition, the increasing numbers of students in both sociology and the arts-based disciplines, who wish to find out what the sociology of art is, are doubtless searching through the literature as I did, turning up those articles from the 1950's, seizing on such references as Adolf S. Tomars' *Introduction to the Sociology of Art* (1940), in search of the answers to what now seems to me to be a fundamentally misplaced question: how can art be examined in a specifically *sociological* way? For all these reasons, I hope that this paper will meet some need, and serve as an encouragement to those who wish to unload themselves of the burden of the sociologists' stone.

Constituents of the Sociological Model

Although it would be possible to review the variety of attempts made to construct a sociology of art, such a review is not intended here. Rather, I wish to identify a set of premises which are held to be essential for a sociology of art being developed in such a way as to establish the sociological *bona fides* of the enterprise, and to avoid competing or conflicting with the disciplines of literature, art history, and so on. These premises are not to be found in any one work or article. I have derived them from a number of articles and essays, which seem to me to have a sociological basis, either being published within the sociological literature, or written from the standpoint of sociology. They include Albrecht (1968), Barnett (1958), Barnett (1959), Silbermann (1968), Sewter (1935) and Watson (1968). A collection of essays which seems to me to typify this particular approach to art and literature, which I am calling the *sociological* approach, is that entitled *The Sociology of Art and Literature* compiled by three Americans,

Albrecht, Barnett and Griff (1970).

To label such an approach as *the* sociological model requires some justification. Francastel (1940-48 and 1970), Duvignaud (1967 and 1965), and Goldmann (1967), have all written works entitled more or less 'The Sociology of Art', and have attempted definitions of sociological approaches to art, but I am excluding their work from my 'sociological model'. The difference between the predominantly American school on the one hand, and the predominantly European one on the other, is not one of geographical location, it is more one of intellectual tradition. Francastel, Duvignaud and Goldmann are all heirs to a broad humanistic approach to culture, and their work has been situated within non-sociological disciplines. Their commitment to sociology is a commitment to the *a priori* relevance of social forces in both the creation of cultural forms and their subsequent acceptance and maintenance. It is also somewhat misleading to refer to a 'school', for all three writers, while sharing certain aims, have very different approaches. The work of Lucien Goldmann is well known and has been both translated into English and discussed in Britain. Questions of objectivity and the need for a 'scientific' study of culture are dealt with by Goldmann, but they are raised within the context of Marxism, not of postivisim. Francastel and Duvignaud are much less known. A translation of Francastel's work into English is long overdue (one is currently being prepared). His work does not fall readily into any school or discipline; like Duvignaud he has been strongly influenced by Durkheim and in what is perhaps his most interesting book, *Peinture et Société*, he develops the Durkheimian concept of 'social space' in a comparison of the construction of rational Euclidian space of the Renaissance, which he sees as being tied into individualism, with the fragmented non-perspectival space of modern European painting. Duvignaud, whose major work *Sociologie du Théâtre* has also not been translated, is more thoroughly Durkheimian in his analyses of drama as ritual, and of culture as part of the 'collective consciousness'. All three writers in their definitions of the sociological utilise such concepts as the 'world view' or the 'collective consciousness' in order to locate cultural expressions within a societal framework. Culture is assumed to be an integral part of society, and its analysis is thus bound up with the analysis of social change. Society itself is not a problematic concept. One might argue that this results in rather vague generalisations, often intuitive rather than scientific, being offered as explanations of the relationship between art and society (such a criticism cannot be made as easily of Goldmann). The important distinction between these writers

and what I am calling the sociological model is that for them the
analysis of culture is inevitably bound up with that of society because
creation is a social act, whereas for Albrecht, Barnett and others,
there has to be a justification for sociology to turn its attention to particular cultural products, namely those products enshrined within 'high'
culture, and which are properly the study of the humanities, not the
social sciences. For the sociologist ('sociologue' does not have the same
force) the key problems are those of scientific objectivity and predictive
force.

In outlining how a sociological study of art would differ from any
other way of studying art the following premises for the sociological
model are frequently suggested:

1. The formulation of general laws regarding the production of art —
   under what conditions and circumstances do certain types of art
   appear — and the testing of these laws against the facts of the
   production of art, in the past, present and future.
2. The necessity of aesthetic neutrality: the sociologist should not be
   concerned with the value (impact, effect) of the artistic product, as
   such a value can only be subjectively determined. The sociologist
   must limit himself or herself to the objective facts of production, and
   consumption.
3. The objective facts are to be found in the social relations governing
   the production of art: 'the socialisation and careers, the social
   position and roles' of artists, 'the distribution and rewards systems',
   'tastemakers and publics', to cite the headings in the Albrecht reader.

The research which was carried out in Glasgow was entitled the 'Socio-
economic context of artistic creation', and it relied upon a socio-
economic model of art production largely derived from the above
premises. I should like to spend some time in expanding these three
premises of the sociological model, before moving on to describe the
Glasgow research.

The Formulation of General Laws

It seems extraordinary that such an ambitious scheme should ever have
been proposed, or that sociology could be deemed capable of showing
what conditions and circumstances would result in the production of
certain types of art, but this is from the standpoint of disillusionment.
One finds, in an early article of 1935:

The task which the sociologist of art sets himself [sic] is to attempt to discover the principles or laws which underlie the relations of types and variations in the arts with other social manifestations . . . to attempt to measure correlations between the arts and other social variables [Sewter, 1935, p.444].

Admittedly this comes from a later art historian rather than a sociologist, but it is one of the few articles to be found within the mainstream sociological journals. Such ambitious endeavours have also been undertaken, in works such as those by Sorokin (1937), Read (1936) and Kavolis (1968), although the types of variables which are considered are not always obviously social. Such an ambition, although not stated so clearly, is also to be found in the original objectives of our Glasgow study. The emphasis upon general laws and the search for a model which can explain all the varieties of artistic production can also be found in Weber's *Rational and Social Foundations of Music* (Weber, 1958). In this essay, which is unfinished, Weber proposes that the different development of music in the west and the east can be explained by the dominance of the principle of rationality in Western development. The development of harmony and counterpoint in Western music is the result of the working out of the principle of rationality, and this same principle can be discerned in the development of technology, which in turn influences the type of music. Weber's essay is not widely known, but it has been developed by sociologists of music such as Silbermann and Adorno. For Silbermann 'this fragment is a model for any study of the sociology of art, both as regards methodology and epistemology' (Silbermann, 1968, p. 579). The actual achievement of being able to formulate general laws, despite the attempts mentioned above, has yet to be realised, but the objective is that the accumulation of systematic study of the social relations of art will enable these general laws to be formulated, and to be subsequently tested. It could be said that it is the lack of such systematic studies which has prevented the sociology of art from advancing, and to a certain extent this is true, given that, compared with other fields of investigation, there has been very little sociological study of art; it is more arguable however, that the aim is itself misplaced, and that art is rather more resistant to general laws of explanation than other phenomena. Whether sociology has proved itself more able to provide explanations in the form of scientific laws for other phenomena is not our concern here.

The Necessity of Aesthetic Neutrality

It is this premise which is constantly emphasised when the possibility of a sociology of art is discussed. For example:

> Whoever wishes to study the sociology of art must start from objective, impartial premises, and study the facts impartially. The facts constitute the raw material of art but are not in themselves its substance. The raw material must first be processed, analysed according to sociological method and reduced to abstractions; only then can laws be formulated and tested [Gurvitch, 1956, p.169].

> The art sociologist is therefore not interested in analysing the painting, music or literature as such, for he recognizes that it would be attempting the impossible to try to apprehend the so-called irrational content of painting, music or literature as if it were a definite object, or a palpable fact [Silbermann, 1968, p.586].

The principle of aesthetic neutrality is observed by Weber also, both in his *Rational and Social Foundations*, and also in his other references to artistic phenomena. Freund (1968) puts Weber's position thus: 'no science — and the sociology of art is an empirical science — can by its procedures assert that one finished work is artistically superior to another'. (Freund, 1968, p.268.) The sociologist should confine himself to the 'empirically discernible relationships between different art-styles or between different orientations of the same art' (Freund, 1968, p. 268). Such a principle is merely an extension of the principle of ethical neutrality (that the sociologist should not make moral judgements) into the field of aesthetics. The consequences of the principle of aesthetic neutrality are two-fold: firstly, the sociologist should not attempt to evaluate the art that he or she is studying, and that includes not seeking to rank art in aesthetic terms. Secondly, by extension of this principle, the sociologist should not study the art at all, but confine him or herself to the study of the objective facts. This renouncing of aesthetic evaluation raises a further question, which is how does the sociologist choose which art to study, if aesthetic judgement is ruled out? In fact, as I shall argue below, the choice of *what* to study, must involve an aesthetic judgement. It is sometimes argued that the study of 'bad' or minor art may prove more rewarding to the sociologist of art. This argument is put forward on a number of grounds, but it is clearly related to the principle of aesthetic neutrality, the underlying assumption being that the content of minor or 'bad' art is somehow either easier to ignore than that of 'great' art, or more easily reducible to the arena of 'palpable fact'. The argument that the sociologist should not look at the work of art is not adopted by 'content-analysis' where the text has been subject to detailed scrutiny. Content analysis is a predominantly American method, and it has been used in basically two ways. One method is to quantify the recurrence of certain words or phrases, and the results may be used to resolve authorship disputes, or be applied within a general linguistic analysis. The other method is to impute certain values to statements or phrases in the text; these values are then quantified. An example of the latter method is Albrecht's 'Does Literature Reflect Common Values?' (Albrecht, 1956) where he identified ten approved values about the family, together with ten alternative values. The content of a sample of short stories from large circulation magazines was then analysed by means of coding those statements which indicated one or more of the approved or alternative values. Statistical criteria of objectivity and representativeness were adhered to in drawing up the sample, and the findings of the research were that literature (in this case magazine fiction) did indeed reflect common values. The problems of imputation are not considered by Albrecht; for example no quantitative distinction was made between values found in authors' statements, descriptions of characters' thoughts and behaviour, and plot resolution, which would seem to ignore the common literary devices of irony, fantasy and allegory. The bulk of work in this second type of content analysis has been done on popular or 'minor' art, notably magazine fiction, which is in line with the assumption that such texts can be reduced to quantifiable facts because they are not aesthetically significant.

The Socio-Economic Model

What then are the objective 'facts' which are to provide the sociologist of art with his or her raw material? As was discussed above, these facts are the relations of production whereby the artist can be located in the social structure. Silbermann (1968) lists two different sets of facts relating to artists and the public. For artists:

> the description and analysis of artists' social position and relation-
> ships — facts such as social origin of certain groups of artists — inform-
> ation concerning their ethnic, economic and educational background,
> data on their style of living, their leisure activities, their working

habits, their social contacts and also their potential and actual attitudes [Silbermann, 1968, p.586].

For the public:

> Groups — individual behaviour during the consumption of art, art fashion, motives and patterns of behaviour during listening, beholding or reading, artistic taste, the economics of art, art policy, and art education. [Silbermann, 1968, p.587].

Albrecht, (Albrecht *et al.*, 1970) who defines art as an institution and thus open to sociological analysis, suggests that this institution has eight major elements — technical systems (technology); traditional forms of art, for example, the song or sonnet; artists, their socialisation and training; disposal and reward systems; art reviewers and critics; publics and audiences; formal principles of judgement; broad cultural values sustaining art in society. The last two elements are to be studied in conjunction with the whole as part of the study of 'distinct networks of relations and processes' (Albrecht *et al.*, 1970, p.8). It is in this area of the gathering of facts that the bulk of what we can call studies in the 'sociology of art' have been done. Such studies may range from the analysis done by Burke (1974) of the biographies of 600 Renaissance artists, philosophers and so on, (making up what Burke terms the 'creative elite') in order to see whether there were observable correlations between such factors as birthplace, father's occupation, geographical mobility and so on, to the application of models of professionalisation and socialisation found among art-school students (Griff, 1970). Where such studies are based on contemporary material they are fairly clearly within sociology (who else would attempt to do such a study?) but where they relate to the past then there are obvious overlaps with history, artistic or literary. The 'facts' in themselves do not constitute a sociology. They have then to be used within the formulation of hypotheses about the social determinants of artistic production. An example of such a study would be that done on the French Impressionists by the Whites who took the relevant 'facts' from a standard historical work, and used them to argue that the development of impressionism was linked to institutional change in the 'French Painting World' (White H. and C., 1965), namely the development of the dealer. Although I am taking the majority of my examples from studies done on the visual arts, there are similar studies within other fields, studies of authorship, publishing, the professionalisation of the writer, social background of the writer, all of which have been attempts to establish the 'facts' surrounding artistic production.

The three premises, that is, the aim of formulating general laws, the principle of aesthetic neutrality, and the search for 'facts' within the socio-economic framework of production and distribution, correspond roughly to the model of sociology as a positive science, where the sociologist must maintain a position of scientific objectivity. With the exception of attempts at content analysis mentioned above, this sociological method results in the virtual exclusion of the cultural product from the field of study. I should like to emphasise that such a method is by no means the only possible way for sociology to look at 'art'. On the contrary, where sociologists or others have tried to adhere to these premises, the results have shown that such methods are inappropriate to the understanding of the creative process, and have led to attempts within this methodological framework being severely criticised, especially from within the established, arts-based and opposing, disciplines.[1] As Janet Wolff (1977, p.19), has argued:

> a sociology of literature (or art) . . . must be the result of a three fold exercise. It must comprise the understanding (i) of the works of literature in their own right and on their own terms; (ii) of these works as expressions, in some sense, of a world view or ideology of a social group or of a society; and (iii) of that ideology, here expressed in aesthetic form, as originating in social processes, class relations, and structural features of society.

Such a stricture echoes that pronounced by Leavis (Leavis, 1962, p. 198) some twenty-five years earlier — 'no "sociology of literature" and no attempt to relate literary studies with sociological will yield much profit unless informed and controlled by a real and intelligent interest — a first-hand critical interest — in literature'. There is no doubt that the sociologist of art must be competent to study and to understand both social structures and processes and the meaning of artistic phenomena. That such a task is difficult does not mean that it cannot or should not be undertaken.

I shall return at the end of this paper to discuss the kind of ways in which artistic processes and phenomena can be more fully understood by methods which include a sociological understanding but which do not conform to the scientific, objective sociological model. I should like now to describe the aims and objectives of the study of Glasgow in which I took part, and to show how these aims and objectives adhere to the objective model. I will then demonstrate some of the problems which arose in trying to apply this objective model, and in particular the impossibility of maintaining a position of aesthetic neutrality.

The Glasgow Study

The research proposal which was submitted to the SSRC, and which resulted in a grant being given to the Department of Sociology, University of Glasgow in order to carry out a three-year programme of research, was written and submitted by A.F. Wells, who was at that time Head of Department. I was appointed as Research Assistant after the grant had been given, and at the time of taking up the post, did not realise that Glasgow had ever been a centre of significant artistic activity. I knew about Charles Rennie Mackintosh, of course, but was ignorant of the Glasgow School of painters, of Glasgow's importance as the home of a number of collectors of advanced taste, of the city's interest in Whistler, and of the very fine collections of paintings held by the municipal galleries. Alan Wells had been in Glasgow for some years, and had done a lot of preliminary historical research into the artistic institutions of the city from about 1850 onwards. This enabled him to draw up the research proposals, and they reflect his own interest in social institutions, as demonstrated in his book (Wells 1970), which includes a chapter on artistic institutions. The research aims and objectives were thus the work of Alan Wells but this does not mean that I did not agree with them when starting the research. The problems which we encountered were in the specific application of the aims and objectives set by the research, and in the difficulty in reaching any concrete or quantifiable findings. We also had difficulties, or at least I had, in meeting the 'sociological' criteria of the SSRC who were worried that such publications as I produced were more 'art historical' than 'sociological'.

The objectives of the research as set out in the proposal were as follows:

(a) (Theoretical): An analysis of the concept of patronage; for example testing the views of such writers as Henning on patronage in the arts; relating the nature of art-patronage to patronage in other fields.
(b) (Theoretical): The construction of a model of the social organisation of art production, or perhaps a series of models related to different socio-economic contexts.
(c) (Empirical): An account of developments in a particular sub-system of Scottish society. In this connection, it is very relevant to

note that studies of any aspect of Scottish society are relatively few, compared with studies of English society; also that no study of this kind has yet been carried out for any section or period of British society.

The methods were described thus:

> The methods to be employed will be the normal methods of historical research in the field of social relations: that is, the directed search for an evaluation of relevant data, and the construction from them of a picture of the social system of art production at the time.

Other important statements from the original proposal are:

> The value of the project lies in the fact that, while the visual arts form an unquestionably significant part of human culture, few detailed empirical studies of the social organisation of artistic activity exist.

and

> As such it (Glasgow) would appear to be an appropriate place in which to investigate some of the central issues of the sociology of art, such as the structure and functions of artistic groups; interrelations of artist and public; the social relations of artistic styles. It is not pretended that a study of Glasgow will provide general answers to problems in the sociology of art. It should provide data which in themselves are specific, but may be capable of generalised interpretation; and may act as models for comparable studies of other regions.

The empirical areas of investigation were then set out in much the same format as the examples given above of the socio-economic model:

1. The Artist: social and geographical origins of the artists working in Glasgow in the period; recruitment to the artistic professions; training; example and inspiration (other artists, groups, leadership); related occupations ('commercial' artists, teaching jobs); recognition; professionalism.
2. The Buyers of the Work of the Artist: who were they – local or foreign, individuals or corporations, social origins and occupations

of buyers; prices paid; correlations with wider economic trends; 'patronage' and its influence; other forms of support for artists; new technologies for reproduction and diffusion and their effects on sales.

3. Intermediaries:
   (a) Agencies for sale of work — dealers, exhibiting societies, and so on.
   (b) Critics and art-politicians.
   (c) Experts, for example, art gallery personnel, university.

4. The Public: government and local government organisation; art education; knowledge of art; artists' attitudes to the public; artists' attitudes towards stylistic, political and ideological trends.

5. Change during the period.

Although the above is of necessity a résumé of the objectives and areas of investigation, the fundamental assumptions of the research seem to me to be in line with what I have described above as the scientific, objective sociological model. Firstly, the possibility of being able, ultimately, to arrive at the formulation of general laws governing art production is contained within the hope that the research may provide data which are 'capable of generalised interpretation; and may act as models for comparable studies of other regions', and the lack of any empirical studies is seen as a hindrance to the development of a sociology of art. The aim is that this study, when added to others, will contribute towards the formulation of general laws; that it may be possible to arrive at conclusions as to what combinations of the factors of education, patronage, public interest in art, economic trends, local or national identity, will lead to creative activity. Thus, if we are able to provide an answer to the question of why all this flowering of the visual arts took place in Glasgow at that point in time, in terms of a set of socio-economic factors, then we may also be able to answer the question of why the Italian Renaissance happened where and when it did in terms of socio-economic factors, or even more, we may be able to make policy recommendations which will bring about a *future* flowering of creative activity. Secondly, the products of this creative upsurge are not included within the areas of the study. As is quite clear above, the fields of investigation are *contextual*, they are the objective 'facts' surrounding the production of art, but the artistic product, which cannot be reduced to a set of facts, is not to be studied. The principle of aesthetic neutrality is further maintained by the non-critical definition to be used of the artist, which also entails a non-critical or non-evaluative definition of art. The only definition given of the artist is 'this term is intended to include painters, designers, and architects, but to exclude, for example, those concerned with literature or music'. This assumes that 'the artist' is a non-problematic concept, but, as I shall show below, such an assumption cannot be justified. The third premise, that a sociology of art should only look at objective facts, and that these facts are to be found in the social relations governing the production of art, is, perhaps, the dominant premise of the research proposal as it stands. The kind of facts, or data, which are to be looked for, are listed under institutional headings, and these institutions are seen as the context in which artistic creation takes place. Although mention is made of non-institutional factors, such as artists' attitudes, inspiration, the public's knowledge of art and so on, these are all firmly located within a particular institutional framework. The product of the artists' work is not to be studied, although the 'social relations of artistic styles' are referred to as one of the 'central issues of the sociology of art'.

I do not wish to be critical of the research proposals as such. They follow an accepted methodology within the sociology of art, indeed they conform to the premises which I have suggested are seen to be essential for a properly 'sociological' study, within the framework of a particular kind of sociology, namely the aims of scientific objectivity, and of positivism. It was no doubt because of this conformity (although this can only be a speculation) that the SSRC agreed to fund the research. It was only when I came to do the research, that the drawbacks of this methodology became apparent. I think there is still a tendency, perhaps not so much within sociology as within the social history of art, to assume that it is only because of deficiencies in historical data that we are unable to arrive at a definitive model of, for example, the process of patronage. Thus if we had all the information about an artist's sales, his or her commissions, the buyers, how much they paid, then there would be no problem in showing how artistic style is determined by the demands of the patronising class. The experience of the Glasgow study, where considerable amounts of information were amassed, demonstrates that 'facts' in themselves do not provide explanations of cultural forms, and leads to a sceptical view of the determining character of socio-economic factors. Let me now turn to the research process itself.

I want first to describe how I went about the research and the kinds of problems I encountered. I then want to see to what extent those problems could not be resolved without fundamentally questioning the premises of objectivity and aesthetic neutrality, and then, finally, to consider what can be gained from our research, both in a positive sense of being able to produce some findings, and in a negative sense, of lessons about the perils of positivism.

The research method, happily described above as 'the normal methods of historical research in the field of social relations, that is, the directed search for an evaluation of relevant data', turned out to be somewhat more problematic. The original research proposal was to cover the period 1880-1950, and a significant part of the project was intended to deal with the decline in artistic activity which took place following the First World War, in an attempt to explain that decline. In the event, the amount of relevant material made this time-span impossible, and at an early stage it was reduced to 1880-1930. In fact, little systematic research was done into the years following 1920. The amount of material to be investigated is not, of course, an absolute, as it depends upon the parameters of the research, which leads to the fundamental question of the definition of 'artist' employed. The research proposal does not define the term 'artist', other than to confine this term to the visual arts, design, and architecture. But the term itself is not unproblematic, just as the concept 'art' itself cannot easily be defined. There are problems about 'professional' and 'amateur' artists, about trained and non-trained, or self-taught, artists. Although the research had defined historical and geographical limits, there were still problems of exclusion and inclusion here; were we looking only at artists born in Glasgow, or at those who died there? What of the artist born in Edinburgh, who lived in Edinburgh, but was friendly with a group of Glasgow artists? What of the artist whose major body of work fell outside the historical period but who was still exhibiting in the period? These problems of definition point out the inadequacies of an institutional framework when the subject to be studied — art — goes beyond the institutions in which it is created. As an example, if Cubism were to be defined as an art form which was produced in Paris by French artists, then not only would two of its major practitioners — Picasso and Gris — be excluded, but so would the development of Cubism in Prague, Moscow, London and elsewhere. The analogy is not a fair one for we were not studying the Glasgow *style*, but the production of art *in* Glasgow. However, the lack of any stylistic criteria, as we shall see, resulted in immense problems of definition.

Given that we were looking at the production of art in Glasgow, how did we arrive at a definition of Glasgow artists? There were several possibilities. One, which would have resulted in the smallest number of artists, would have been to use the indices of artists cited in reference books about Scottish art. The problem here is that, firstly, there are very few such books about Scottish art. The only comprehensive work (Caw, 1908), stops in 1908. To have used this work alone would have resulted in a list of about fifty artists (it would not have provided a list of architects or designers), with an unavoidable bias towards those artists considered significant by the author. Secondly, only those artists who worked in Glasgow were relevant, and further information would have been needed to work out which were the relevant artists. There are several books (Brown, 1908; Martin, 1897; Scottish Arts Council, 1968) on the Glasgow School of painters, but these refer to only one group among many other artists, namely those who painted in the style which became known as the Glasgow School, or the Glasgow Boys, and there is considerable argument over which painters belonged to the school anyway. Peter Burke (1974) in his study of the Renaissance mentioned above, draws his selection of the 'creative elite' from five standard reference books. By relying on reference books to provide a sample of artists, one is only substituting the value-judgements of a consensus view of which art is significant for personal 'subjective' value judgements. The whole problem of how some artists and some artistic products are valued and preserved while others are forgotten is glossed over. Burke argues that the main danger lies in being biased rather than arbitrary, but his problem of being biased towards Florence could not be overcome, precisely because there is more information available on Florence, because Florence has been seen as more important. It is impossible to see how the circularity of such arguments can be avoided, other than to say that Florence's importance as an artistic centre was originally due to a 'real' superiority over other centres. I am aware that this explanation is also unsatisfactory and I shall return to the problem in my conclusion. As far as the Glasgow study is concerned, Glasgow has not been seen as an important centre of artistic activity, nor have Glasgow artists been highly valued; consequently historical evidence has not been collected, sifted, assessed and re-assessed in the way that historical material from the Florentine Renaissance has been. One cannot even pretend to summon the 'impartial judgement of history' to give evidence. The 'index' method was thus not possible. Another method, which would have resulted in the largest number, would have been to use the Glasgow Trade Directories, which included categories of artists, architects, designers and art dealers. The problems here would have been – a total lack of any concept of artist (some of the entries in the artists section read .... (in Hair) or .... (Fireworks)); a number of names about which nothing was known, nor could ever be found out; and numbers ranging from 100 to 300 in each year. The method which was finally adopted was to use the exhibition catalogues of the Glasgow Institute. This was the major exhibiting body throughout the period (it was founded in 1861). There was a complete set of catalogues of annual exhibitions (some of them illustrated), and the names and addresses were listed at the back. We selected artists who had Glasgow addresses for at least four years and exhibited more than one work a year. This had the added advantage of tying in with one of our major sources — the sales records of the Institute from 1870 to 1906. This method was backed up by checking with the list of members of the Glasgow Art Club. Designers were harder to identify, or define, and the majority of designers for whom we gained information came from the Glasgow School of Art. There was a good reference book available for architects, but in the end we did not fully investigate architects, owing to the constraints of time.

The buyers category was derived from people who had bought from the Institute, and that their names entered in the sales records (buyers were not always recorded), and from information from loan exhibitions where works by Glasgow artists might be lent by named owners. However, such people often had a collection which was not primarily of work by Glasgow artists. This does not mean that their support for non-Glasgow art was unimportant. It might include work which influenced the Glasgow artists (for example Burrell's Whistlers), and their purchasing activities sustained the large number of practising dealers, and the exhibiting societies and other artistic institutions whose existence enabled the local artists to survive, and created the ambiance of a lively art market. Thus the institutional activities were inter-related but not necessarily derived from Glasgow artists.

The above methods resulted in a total number of 428 artists and 443 buyers being identified. However, the attempt up to that point to devise an objective list became a meaningless exercise because it was quite impossible to regard these 428 and 443 as in any sense homogeneous. Some artists on the list would merely be names, addresses, and a list of titles of their works shown at the Institute. For others, there was a wealth of material, including substantial biographies, catalogues raisonnés, and unpublished manuscripts. Similarly, for buyers, there might be merely a name and two recorded transactions, or a museum full of *objets d'art* and paintings, as in the case of Burrell. The selective processes of history itself and the ascription of historical significance resulted in a bias in information. Unfortunately, in some circumstances, importance did not necessarily mean a wealth of information, as in the case of the dealer Alexander Reid, possibly one of the most important figures in terms of influence. Very little is known about him, and we were not able to find out any more. The historical sources for our study might seem to be finite, but in fact they approach infinity, once they are not limited by aesthetic criteria. It might have been possible to find out a bit more about the people who were merely names, but at the cost of reading all the daily papers, all the evening papers, all the weeklies, let alone combing the Records Office for wills, dates of birth and death, changes in address, etc. At times I felt more like an American searching for records of my great-great-uncle, than a sociologist of art. I don't want to spend more time on describing the research process, but I hope I've said enough to show how problematic premises of objectivity and aesthetic neutrality can be.

A number of conclusions can be drawn from our experience, both about the possibility of applying what I have called the 'sociological' model, and the findings about Glasgow itself. Firstly, the necessity for differentiation between different kinds of artists, art products, and art consumers makes it impossible to draw up any general model of art production. It was possible to suggest that some institutions and some kinds of buyers were especially important in Glasgow, but this would not necessarily apply to anywhere else. The Glasgow study on its own was not able to indicate why Glasgow had enjoyed the flowering of artistic activity, and why not Edinburgh, or Liverpool, or Birmingham. It would be possible to do studies of other centres for comparison, but there would be similar problems with uneven information, and the ascribing of significance. There is no guarantee that the products being studied would be any more comparable than, say, the output of an unknown, totally undistinguished Glue-pot artist,[2] with the work of Charles Rennie Mackintosh. Secondly, the premise of aesthetic neutrality is, as I have shown, impossible to maintain, because the historical process itself assigns a value. The specific problem with Glasgow is that there were a number of known styles or art movements, together with an undifferentiated mass of unknowns, and that the styles themselves have an uncertain historical value. Tastes shift and change in such a way that some artists in the study were international household names in the 1890s, totally unknown in the 1940s and '50s, and are now in the process of becoming known again today. In some cases, we have no way of knowing what the paintings or products looked like. I must confess that the question of significance became the greatest obstacle for me in that I found myself increasingly wondering just why I was tracking down lost and long-forgotten artists. Glasgow art raises interesting questions about the vagaries of taste. The whole phenomenon of the creative activity in Glasgow between 1880 and 1914 sits unhappily between artistic and social history. To make an aesthetic judgement, the mass of art produced in Glasgow is not interesting enough from the standpoint of art history to justify pro-longed analysis or historical investigation; as a social phenomenon there are other aspects of Glasgow's social history which both attract and justify more attention — sanitation and housing, public health and the water supply. The history of Glasgow's bourgeoisie is yet to be written and it is perhaps there that our work belongs, rather than in the 'sociology of art'. It will be apparent that our study stuck most assiduously to the third premise of looking for the 'facts' surrounding the production of art. However, without some definition of art (which will in itself entail aesthetic evaluation) the relevant facts will be infinite. The study produced the paradox of an abundance of facts of doubtful significance with a lack of significant facts.

The aims and objectives of the research as outlined in the proposal were both empirical and theoretical. The study did result in a large amount of empirical material of the 'facts' variety being acquired, and this material is on file for consultation in the Department of Fine Art at the University of Glasgow. There is obviously some value in using the material to produce a straightforward historical account of art in Glasgow from 1880 to 1930. It is difficult to see how such an account would be *sociological* other than to emphasise the institutional frame-work within which the art was created. I would not wish to suggest that such an account would be of no interest, but I do not think that it would provide an answer to methodological problems in the sociology of art. It is also worth mentioning that there have been many attempts from within art history to write an account of Glasgow's artistic achievements but, so far, all have come to grief, which suggests that others may have had difficulty in deciding upon the significance of the art which was produced, and how it fits into European developments.

Of the two theoretical aims of the research, I have suggested that the second one of constructing a model of the production of art cannot be accomplished without some way of differentiating between the various artistic products. A series of models might therefore be more appro-priate, and it would be possible to devise several categories of artistic products and suggest that each category presented a slightly different model of production. In order to devise such categories however, one would *either* have to rely on the aesthetic judgements of a few people, *or*, and this would be more satisfactory, draw up a set of stylistic criteria which would be the basis for the assignation of products to different styles. One would then look at the artists who worked in those styles, who bought their work, how it was distributed, what was its ideological meaning for both producers and consumers, and from the answers to these questions arrive, perhaps, at a series of models. Such an enterprise would necessarily involve the sociologist in both looking at the works of art and making some judgements about them, though these judgements would not be of the order of 'good' or 'bad' art, but rather 'French landscape' style or 'German art nouveau' style. I would thus conclude that it is possible to construct a series of models of art production in Glasgow, provided that these models are based on an analysis of the products themselves, and that here the task of the sociologist is essentially similar to that of the art historian or art critic, and will depend upon developments in the analysis of the image, whether in semiology, structuralism or anywhere else. One has to add the proviso that examples of the art products have to be available in order to both devise stylistic categories, and assign products to them, and if your artists are so unrecognised that nothing by them can be identified, then all you can do is place them in a category of 'unknowns'. Such a category would be interesting in itself for it would throw some light on the process whereby some artists are recognised and others forgotten. A recent study of the acquisitions policy of the Tate Gallery (Brighton, 1977) raises similar questions about the processes of inclusion and exclusion of practising contemporary artists, and it is only by a close examination of these processes that we can resolve the problem of aesthetic circularity that 'great' art is 'great' because it is 'great' referred to above. Once an artist, or his or her work, makes it into the reference books, then history does the rest, although it is always possible for history to be re-written. Works of art, like other cultural products, persist over time, and far outlive the economic structures in which they were produced. This persistence is problematic for the proponents of straight reflection theory who maintain that culture directly reflects the economic relations of the base. It is less problematic if we accept that cultural products are not just commodities, but also contain meanings which are constantly being re-interpreted. The persistent quality of the work of art is derived from the present, not the past, and it is bound up with the process of cultural transmission which includes the process whereby aesthetic values are transmitted via art galleries and museums, the educational system, reproductions, art historical monographs and so

on. The interesting question then becomes what qualities in the work
of art are valued and why, which leads us back to the ideological
components of the visual image. We can ask a further question, what
qualities are valued and by whom? This leads us into the nature of
patronage.

The first theoretical aim of our research, it will be recalled, was to
analyse the concept of patronage, and the example of patronage will
also serve to demonstrate the relationship between the facts in themselves and how they can be used. Patronage has been seen as the 'key'
to the social determination of artistic style in a number of studies
(Henning, 1960; Antal, 1947; Hauser 1962; Hadjinicolaou, 1978). The
theory of patronage is stated generally by Henning to be that the power
held by patrons enables them to determine the style in which the artist
will work. The most extensive empirical study of patronage is Antal's
work on the Florentine Renaissance. Antal argues that the stylistic
differences between the work of, for example Masaccio and Gentile da
Fabriano, can be explained by the fact that Masaccio was sponsored by
the emerging bourgeois class while Fabriano was supported by the
declining aristocratic class. Fabriano painted in a formal courtly style,
seen as reactionary when compared with the progressive 'realism' of
Masaccio. Hauser employs a similar theory but extends it to the whole
history of western art, arguing that in any period the progressive or
emergent class will sponsor progressive styles. Hadjinicolaou argues that
the different styles found within the work of *one* artist can be explained
in terms of the fact that different styles were painted for different
sections of a class. Thus various theories can be seen to hang on the
crucial question of who bought this painting, or who commissioned it,
which brings us to the facts of consumption and distribution. It is in
this area of patronage studies that one comes across the tendency to
which I referred earlier, that somehow all will be explained if only one
can retrieve the facts, and that it is only the deficiencies of historical
data which prevent such explanations being achieved. The results of
our research suggest several conclusions about the theory of patronage.
On the one hand, a study I undertook of patronage of the Glasgow
School painters could be said to confirm Antal's hypothesis in that the
buyers of the Glasgow School works (which were seen at the time to be
innovatory) although they all belonged to the bourgeoisie, came predominantly from those sections of the bourgeoisie engaged in new
forms of enterprise — retailing, ship-owning, and the like. On the other
hand, this conclusion is based on very partial evidence for we were not
able to retrieve information about even the majority of original sales. It

also depends upon a quantitative judgement rather than a qualitative one for there were one or two very important buyers who were entrepreneurs in declining industries. Thus, the hypotheses of Antal and others may be valid, but the results of the Glasgow study show that it is impossible to prove or disprove such hypotheses by empirical means even in a period where the 'facts' are relatively retrievable. Patrons undoubtedly can influence the style in which an artist paints but that is not to say that they *determine* the style. I think we have to recognise that the process by which an artist comes to paint in a particular style is a complex one, as is the process by which his or her work comes to be recognised. We have to consider the set of meanings attached to style and the variety of factors that contribute to the formation of those meanings. Here again the sociologist has to work within the general field of culture, drawing on the contributions made by other disciplines in an attempt to construct the ideological meaning of the work of art, literature or whatever, in a way which recognises the complexity of the ideological meaning of cultural products, and does not reduce them to such simplistic categories as 'bourgeois naturalism' or 'proletarian realism'.

What then can we conclude about the possibilities of a 'sociology of art'? As I suggested at the outset we have to consider whether such an attempt − defining a specifically sociological approach to art − is not fundamentally misguided. Certainly the kind of approach that results in what I have called the sociological model has many weaknesses. I have tried to indicate the sorts of problems which such an approach encounters when it is applied to an empirical area, and I consider that the major problem for our research in Glasgow was the fact that such a model did not allow for aesthetic discrimination in how we defined what we were studying, nor did it allow room for a study of the cultural products themselves. I would argue that the premises of the sociological model reflect an anxiety about the 'proper' sphere of sociology which results in a restricted, and consequently impoverished, analysis of artistic or cultural forms. If the only proper way for sociologists to study the paintings of the Impressionists is to find out how much money Degas received from his father, or what kind of contract he had with Durand-Ruel, then such a study can never be more than peripheral. It can only be about the context of creativity, and can only provide partial answers to the important questions of why did Degas paint as he did, and what is the significance of his work, both then and now. The 'facts' surrounding cultural production are important. They are necessary but not sufficient for an understanding of cultural forms. It has to be remembered that such 'facts' are not considered by some art historians or literary critics to be at all necessary for an understanding of the cultural product and the emphasis placed by sociologists on the socio-economic context of artistic creativity is a vital corrective to the view that creativity takes place independently of any social or economic forces. One cannot claim that this corrective has been effective in all quarters but the convergence of the arts-based and social science disciplines has resulted in the development of ways of analysing culture which are predicated upon the belief that culture is inextricably bound up with social and economic forces. The problem is now not whether art or literature is related to society, but how they are related. The question of whether culture is determined, or determining, or both, is a sociological question, but it is not one which *sociology* has to answer, for it is a question which transcends the boundaries of any one discipline.

Notes

1. For example, Gombrich's review of Hauser's *Social History of Art* (Gombrich, 1963) and Leavis's attack on Schücking's *The Sociology of Literary Taste* (Leavis, 1962).
2. The artists of the Glasgow School referred to the older generation of Glasgow artists as 'Glue pots'. This was a reference to their liberal use of varnish or 'megilp', similar to the 'Sir Sloshua' epithet applied to Reynolds by the Pre-Raphaelites.

HISTORIES OF CULTURE/THEORIES OF
   IDEOLOGY: NOTES ON AN IMPASSE

   Richard Johnson

Introduction

This chapter examines a particular form of a more general problem.[1]
The problem belongs to the sphere of the study of culture/ideology,
assuming, for the moment, that these terms share the same object.
The difficulties are best focused by considering the problem in its
practical state: how to study culture/ideology as an aspect of
particular situations; how to construct accounts of particular
cultural/ideological relations as part of a larger historical analysis. By
'historical' in this context, we do not mean 'past', but neither do
we exclude it. This would be to accept the common-sense distinction
of past (the object of 'history') and present (the object of
contemporary analysis), a notion somewhat surprisingly reproduced
in otherwise very sophisticated texts. (Hindess & Hirst, 1975,
esp. pp. 308 ff). The analysis of 'historical' and 'current' situations
is in principle the same and poses the self-same problems.[2] To
divorce the two is to render 'history' trivial and political analysis super-
ficial.

The study of the cultural and ideological dimensions of 'relations
of force' (Gramsci, 1971) has been rendered problematic in two
main ways. As the couplet culture/ideology suggests, certain sets of
relations have come to be thought of very differently within different
styles of analysis. In addition to 'culture' and 'ideology' (and the
other older term 'consciousness'), we have a plethora of newer terms
which are sometimes held to have replaced the old: 'subjectivity',
'signification', 'representation' and 'discourse'. One difficulty of
commencing an analysis, then, is how to situate oneself within
increasingly fractured sets of theoretical problematics.

While theory has been over-developed and has tended to acquire
a dynamic of its own, studies at a lower level of abstraction have
tended to be neglected. While theoretical starting-points are legion,
it is not easy to point to models of close, careful but fully
conceptualised concrete studies. Indeed, current debates have
sometimes helped to drive a wedge between theory and the
analysis of current situations. At a very general level, this paper is an

attempt to work through, by a particular route, both these sets of difficulties.

We shall have a better chance of success if we consider the actual provenance of these problems, though a proper history of how they arose cannot be attempted here.[3] We might start by noting that the concern with culture/ideology/consciousness has been a marked feature of intellectual work and politics in most Western countries since the later 1950s. These movements were diverse and belong to histories that are distinct. But they did have features in common. One might list the emergence from English literary and historical traditions of two allied tendencies in the analysis of culture: Raymond Williams' literary criticism and Edward Thompson's socialist-humanist history; the theories of ideology, science and epistemology associated with French structuralist Marxism; Jean Paul Sartre's attempt to reconcile existentialism and historical materialism; the more general revival of interest in the early Marx, especially in more 'experiential' texts and categories, like the *1844 Manuscripts* and the category 'alienation'; the cross-Atlantic development of the Marxism of the Frankfurt School with its concern with subjectivity and the ideological work of the media; and the re-discovery (in England) of the work of second-generation Marxist theorists, notably Gramsci and Lukacs, both of whom were thought (rightly) to have much to say on cultural/ideological questions.

These questions have been most urgently posed within Marxism, partly because it was there that they had been so plainly neglected before, and with such disastrous consequences. But in the heartlands of conventional sociology, there was a not dissimilar and plenteously self-recorded revolt. The revival of phenomenological philosophy in Europe was matched by new sociologies in the USA which were concerned (often exclusively) with the processes of making sense of the social world, or even with its inter-subjective construction. A similar tendency can be seen in sectoral or sub-sociologies. These have often in the last twenty years passed through a similar succession: from various functionalisms, through a focus on symbolic or cultural interactions, to some kind of combination of the concern with culture or knowledge with a re-worked Marxism. A path like this can be traced, for instance, for the sociologies of deviance and education. The parallels between these intellectual currents and the newer forms of popular politics of the 1960s — the early 'new left', the student movement, black power, the counter-cultures and

Women's Liberation — have often been noted: both have focused, in different ways, on the inwardness of experience and of apprehension of the world, usually in opposition to a sociology, a Marxism (or a world) that has been seen as oppressive, mechanical, reductive or deterministic.

This move into the experiential occurred in different ways across countries and intellectual traditions. In Britain, it is useful to distinguish between two main phases. We might define the first as the moment of 'culture'. This includes the break made with elitist and (in part) with literary notions of 'culture' in the work of Richard Hoggart and Raymond Williams (Hoggart, 1957; Williams, 1958, 1965) and the work of the English communist historians from Dona Torr's *Tom Mann and his Times* (1956) and *Democracy and the Labour Movement* (1954) to Edward Thompson's *Making of the English Working Class* (1963), E.J. Hobsbawm's *Primitive Rebels* (1959), and the later work of Christopher Hill (see Hill, 1972, as a classic 'culturalist' text). What is sometimes referred to as 'new left history' was formed in a break from orthodox marxism-leninism, from traditional 'labour history' and to some extent, though the picture here is very complex, from the younger historians' own mentors, notably Maurice Dobb.[4] Although, following Dobb's *Studies in the Development of Capitalism* (1945), most of this generation of marxist historians worked on aspects of the long transition from feudalism to capitalism; they work in a manner very different from that of Dobb himself, stressing class and culture rather than mode of production and economic transition. The new history of the 1960s was especially concerned with the attitudes and forms of communal action of 'the people', concentrating on 'primitive rebels' rather than the post-1850 proletariat. Politically, this phase coincided, of course, with the crises and secessions of 1956, with the formation of the 'new left' and with a kind of communist or socialist populism which was heavily influenced by historical analyses in which modern communism was seen as inheriting the popular democratic struggles of the past (see Torr, 1956; Saville [ed.], 1954).

If the choice of paradigm now lay between sociological or literary views of culture or an orthodox Marxism on the one hand and the problematics of Williams, Thompson or Hill on the other, the choice would be very easy. The moment of culture was a time of great creativity, but it was followed by another and quite different kind of intellectual explosion. One feature of this second phase — we might call it the moment of Theory — was the establishment of a kind of common market in Marxist ideas, promoted by particular centres, but especially by the newer editors of the *New Left Review*. Having established (to their own satisfaction) that the English were parochial, the working class inert and Marxist culture absent, the new left reviewers set about repairing these deficiencies by the systematic importation of books. This priority was pursued at the cost of any real connection with a popular politics and was completely at odds with the earlier left tendency of the 1950s and early 1960s. The debates between Perry Anderson and Tom Nairn and Edward Thompson in the mid-1960s were centrally about this matter — not just the 'peculiarities' but also the potentialities of the English (Anderson, 1964, 1966 and 1968; Nairn, 1964a, 1964b; Thompson, 1965). But the whole *New Left Review* project undoubtedly worked, helping to transform the nature of Marxist discussion in Britain. Unfortunately we can only deal here with some of the results, not with the conditions of this success.

Not all the importations were equally incompatible with the existing Marxisms. In history and in cultural theory (as in politics) first Lukacs and then Gramsci were assimilated with relative ease, though in Gramsci's case particularly, often at the expense of their originality. The least digestible elements, in an incredibly foreshortened set of receptions, derived from French structuralist and Marxist structuralist traditions, especially from the work of the French communist philosopher, Louis Althusser. Althusser's own work has been followed by a series of tendencies, many of them from the same Parisian milieu. In Britain there have developed strong neo- or post-Althusserian tendencies, especially among the more theoretical of social scientists. One effect of all this — to risk a mild chauvinism — has been to render British Marxist discussion somewhat less parochial than its continental counter-parts, but also somewhat less comprehensible than before to the majority of people in Britain.

It is at this point that it is necessary to narrow the field and to look at the problem in its particular form. Many of us who had become used to working on 'culture' or on history within the earlier British tradition, have had to face the challenge, particularly, of the work of the Althusserians. The problems have thus come to be posed in the relations, apparently over-whelmingly antagonistic, between two broad tendencies in the analysis of culture/ideology. Both traditions are 'Marxist' or Marx-influenced and together, in their oppositions, and in the absence of major rivals, they have come to define the field of 'cultural studies'.[5]

In stating the matter thus there is a danger of rendering the two opposing traditions rather more homogeneous than they really are, yet, in the end, the oppositions are real ones. On the one hand there is the older British tendency, formed in breaks from Leavisite literary criticism and economistic Marxism, concerned primarily with the analysis of the history of cultural traditions, class experiences or literary forms. Though Edward Thompson describes himself as an historian within the Marxist tradition and Raymond Williams denotes his latest position a 'cultural materialism' (Williams, 1977a, p. 5), these two key representatives of the first tendency are, especially in their opposition to the second, very close together indeed. For the purpose of ease of reference, not to invent or hypostatise a position, we term this tendency a 'culturalist Marxism'.

The other tendency is still more diverse than the first. The contributory streams include the linguistics of Saussure, the structural anthropology of Lévi-Strauss, the epistemological concerns of traditional French philosophy (including 'absent' figures like Spinoza), and a 'philosophical' reading of the Marx of *Capital*. More hidden debts are owed to Lacan's adaptation of Freud's categories and a somewhat formalistic appropriation of Gramsci's work on state and civil society. We will refer to this tendency as 'structuralist', following a common practice. Subsequently it will be Thompson, Williams and Althusser himself who are mainly discussed.

The most obvious thing about these two traditions is their formal difference. *Reading Capital* and *The Making of the English Working Class* are very, very different kinds of books! The Althusserian enterprise is philosophical, formalistic and pitched, unrelentingly, at a high level of abstraction; most 'culturalist' texts take the form of specific histories and are not, in this sense, very 'theoretical'. Perhaps it is the case, then, that the two traditions just differ and are not strictly comparable at all: the one quintessentially English, the other unrepentantly French! Perhaps they belong, as it were, simply to different intellectual universes, or higher or lower levels of the stratosphere. If so, why on earth don't historians of culture simply carry on, more or less as before?

This unheroic response is, in fact, quite common, but there are several symptoms to suggest that the underlying evasion — for such it is — is not really believed. For one thing, there is much mutual criticism across culturalist and structuralist positions. The commonest form of critique has been of 'culturalist' texts from structuralist critics: Eagleton on Williams (Eagleton, 1976); Hindess and Hirst on the historians (Hindess and Hirst, 1975; Hirst, 1975); Ros Coward on *Resistance*

Through Rituals (Coward, 1977a), to cite some of the most interesting. Attacks on structuralist positions by culturalists are rarer, but the widespread ignoring of Althusser and Hindess and Hirst by historians does not extend to Thompson or to Williams themselves. Barely an occasional piece of Thompson's passes without a pot-shot or two at 'some structuralist philosophers' (e.g. Thompson, 1975; 1976 esp. pp. 18-20) and a major riposte is, at the time of writing this piece, on the way (Thompson, 1978). In the meantime, Williams' *Marxism and Literature* (1977a) conducts a principled and sustained quarrel with many structuralist formulations (see also his 1977c).

This is evidence enough that the two traditions do not merely coexist but actively interrupt each other. Structuralism, in particular, interrupts culturalist practices and it is easy to see how this occurs. Though culturalist accounts are much less abstract than structuralist theory (and this is, in part, a virtue), they are nonetheless written on the basis of definite pre-suppositions of an epistemological and theoretical kind: they presuppose a view of how historians can know about the past and some general assumptions about the nature of social relations or societies as a whole. There is, in other (Althusserian) words, a culturalist problematic which actually informs the detailed histories, which is implicit in them and can be abstracted and compared with others. If this is done, as it is done below, it becomes clear that the culturalist and Althusserian problematics are in radical opposition to the extent that on some essential matters it is necessary to choose between them. If Thompson's identification of the Althusserian demon is somewhat melodramatic and involves much misrecognition, his sense of the conflict between his own practices and Althusser's prescriptions is perfectly correct. Some working-through of this opposition cannot then be avoided by anyone concerned with the study of particular cultural formations.

It is worth stating, at the outset, some general orientations to the problem even if, at this stage, these have to consist of quite dogmatic statements. Neither of the two traditions is adequate taken on their own. *Neither culturalism nor structuralism will do!* It is not possible to develop an adequate theory of the field (still less study particular forms) from Althusserian or neo-Althusserian or even post-Althusserian positions. It is simply not fruitful to develop more and more sophisticated structuralist, semiological, linguistic or psycho-analytic *theories*, nor to engage in one-sided critique. What present themselves as structuralist critiques of culturalism, for instance, are often no more than explorations of the differences between the two positions. As such they have a clarificatory function, but since they too rarely have reference to the analysis of particular situations, they do no more. The appearance of supercession — of culturalism by structuralism — is, more than anything, the product of a particular mode of critique. The object is to show that a text is organised around a specific problematic. Certain problematics are held to be fundamentally flawed. If such a tendency is present — especially Althusser's own trio of historicism, humanism or empiricism — it is held to exhaust the whole content of the text. The text falls. The procedure is a kind of intellectual lumber-jacking, very exhilarating, especially when the target is some great big classical tree that has stood in the forest many years. Down goes Weber! Down go the Marxist historians! Down goes Marx! (Hirst, 1976a; Hindess and Hirst, 1975; Cutler, Hindess, Hirst and Hussain, 1977). But this mode of critique is almost wholly destructive and therefore non-accumulative: it 'problematises', but rarely provides another substantive account, still less one that incorporates what was rational in the first. It tends to produce a search for 'originality'. It differs very much in these respects from more creative modes, of which Marx's treatment of political economy might stand as a model.

These features of contemporary Marxist debates help to explain several current weaknesses: the ephemerality of much discussion; the proliferation of 'materialist' positions; and the relative paucity of major synthetic or substantive works that do not merely criticise orthodoxies, but actually *stand in their place*. We have in mind work of the stature of the history of Thompson, Hobsbawm, Hill or Hilton which everyone in a particular field has to negotiate.

On the other hand culturalist intellectual practices *are* extremely vulnerable to the Althusserian critique. There *are* limitations, for concrete analysis, in 'humanist' or 'empiricist' assumptions. There *is* a failure adequately to theorise the results of concrete studies and to make starting-points quite plain. There is a tendency to vacate the ground of determinations that do not show up in the experience of actors. Culturalist practices do suppress two essential aspects of an adequate social science which are central to Marx's procedures: the process of systematic and self-conscious abstraction; and the notion that social relations are structured in particular ways and operate in part 'behind men's backs'. It is precisely because Althusserianism recovers, in a non-economistic form, genuinely 'structuralist' elements in Marx's own mature work that it provides so powerful a position from which to criticise culturalisms of all kinds.

There are, then, two main routes out of this particular impasse. It is possible to continue to work on specific topics within the older paradigms, acknowledging their vulnerability and feeling the way, through the practice itself, to better formulations. This is in many ways the privileged method, involving no theoreticist detour. A second approach, however, accepts the necessity of direct theoretical clarification. What seems to be needed here is to slow the pace of speculation a little, be less destructively critical and consider, once more, some of the key texts in the two traditions, especially in relation to what they have to say on some determinate sets of problems. In this way we may avoid one-sided or formalistic modes of critique. We can ask what are the differences between the two traditions in terms of their ability to deliver specific analyses? In what ways are they opposed — apart from what we know already, that they represent different problematics? How could we construct more adequate accounts of, say, the culture of a subordinate class, drawing on elements of one or both traditions? Are there points that the two traditions share — weaknesses even? Questions like these have a limited, subordinate, clarificatory function, somewhat short of a fully 'theoretical' enterprise; but they nonetheless, as we hope to show, have their uses.

The exploration that follows is organised in the following way. First, as a solvent to a one-sided critique, we note some similarities between culturalism and structuralism, identifying some of these as the ground on which we, too, wish to commence analysis. Secondly, we conduct a critique of culturalism that draws on the strength of the structuralist position. This represents those criticisms which a culturalist practice must take into account if it is to produce more adequate analyses. Thirdly, we note some of the elements of a culturalist historiography which it is important to preserve, which, indeed, represent a very important moment in the post-war development of both history and Marxism. Fourthly, we recapitulate, very briefly, some of the most important criticisms that have been made of Althusserian theories of ideology. Fifthly, we note what we wish to retain from this system. Finally, via a detour to Marx and Gramsci, we hope to reach some general pointers towards a more adequate (that is, usable) theory of culture-ideology.

Common Ground

Common origins do beget some similarities. Both tendencies derive from a similar moment differently experienced in England and France. Both were forged in the political opposition to Stalinism and in theoretical opposition to 'economism'. It is instructive to compare

Althusser on 'the theoretical impasse into which history had put us' (Althusser, 1969, p.21) with Thompson on the immediate political context of the writing of *The Making of the English Working Class*. The terms of their rejection of economism are likewise very similar:

> If we take Marx's famous comments on the hand-mill, the water-mill and the steam-mill literally or out of context, this is their meaning . . . This temptation results in the radical reduction of the dialectic of history to the dialectic generating the successive *modes of production*, that is, in the last analysis, the different production *techniques*. There are names for these temptations in the history of Marxism: *economism* and even technologism [Althusser, 1969, p.108].

> *The Making of the English Working Class* undoubtedly arose from a two-sided theoretical polemic. On the one hand it could not have been written without the extremely firmly, intellectually very well-based, discipline of economic history. . .It is a tradition largely contaminated with capitalist ideology . . . On the other hand it was in a sense a polemic against abbreviated economistic notations of Marxism, which had become very clearly disclosed in the arguments around, inside and outside of the Communist movement, from 1956 onwards to the creation of the New Left. In this tradition the very simplified notion of the creation of the working class was that of a determined process: steam power + the factory system = the working class. Some kind of raw material, like 'peasants' flocking to the factories was then processed into so many yards of class-conscious proletarians. I was polemicizing against this notion . . . (Thompson, 1976, pp. 4-5).

Already many of the differences are also expressed in these words: a 'scientific' as against a 'literary' ambition; a stress on 'mode of production' rather than 'class' for instance. It is also true that the two founding moments differed: structuralism had a double foundation — it was defined against economism *and* humanism (in the shape, mainly, of Sartre's existentialism). Thompson, by contrast took as his object two forms of the same basic problematic: the reductionism of bourgeois economic history and an economistic Marxism. Yet both men sought to vindicate Marxism out of a peculiarly hostile cold war climate and they both did this by developing (in very different ways) Marxist work on non-economic questions. Thompson's abiding concern remains what it was at the beginning: 'a real silence in Marx' on the subject of 'value-systems' (Thompson, 1976, p. 23). All his work has centred on the analysis of culture, consciousness and, especially, on the experience and forms of communal action of the popular classes in the eighteenth and early nineteenth centuries. In later work, from the 'The Moral Economy of the English Crowd in the Eighteenth Century' (1971) onwards, he has focused especially on cultural relations of authority in the eighteenth century, drawing heavily on a particular (culturalist) appropriation of Gramsci's 'hegemony' (see, most explicitly, Thompson, 1974). These emphases have been paralleled in almost all of the real points of growth of the new history since the late 1950s. But the 'ideological and political instances' have also been the characteristic concern of the Althusserians. Althusser's most influential work has been on various aspects of ideology (Althusser, 1969, 1970, 1971). In the work of Poulantzas the political-ideological work of the state (Poulantzas, 1973) and the political-ideological constitution of classes (Poulantzas, 1976) has been more fully theorised. Hindess and Hirst are a partial exception to this but Hirst has often been at his iconoclastic best in discussing ideology in relation (or not in relation) to other levels (Hirst, 1976b.). In general, Althusser's essay on Ideological State Apparatuses (Althusser, 1971) has been massively influential, defining, for many readers, the actual terrain of 'materialism'.

This point about similarities can be pushed a good deal further, first in relation to some common inadequacies, secondly in relation to shared strengths. We might compare with advantage the relative places of 'culture' and 'ideology' in these two accounts of the social world. The obvious similarity lies in the catholicity of the two terms. From the corpus of English usages of 'culture', Hoggart, Williams and the historians, absorbing anthropological conceptions *en route*, expand the term to mean 'way of life'. 'Cultural studies' inherits this conception and expands it further so that it contains matters as heterogeneous as language-in-general, the specific output of the mass media, the literary text, the values implicit in forms of working-class collective action, the styles of sub-groups, and the general political discourse. Culture certainly primarily denotes the cognitive and affective, with nothing like so epistemological a connotation as 'ideology', but it can also be extended to include practices other than thinking and feeling, domains other than that marked out generally by Marx as 'consciousness'. 'Way of life' has this clear implication. But 'ideology' too covers a vast terrain. There is a logic in Althusser's view of the social formation that assigns everything that is not economic production to 'ideology'. Whole institutions — schools or families — may, apparently, be assigned to this instance (Althusser, 1971 esp. pp. 136-49). Most of the meanings of ideology that accumulate through Althusser's various treatments — ideology as not-science, ideology as an instance in the social formation, ideology as a form of condition for the reproduction of relations of production, ideology as a 'representation of the imaginary relationship of individuals to their real conditions of existence' (Althusser, 1971, p.152) — retain an ideational basis for the concept. The genuine insight — that 'an ideology always exists in an apparatus, and its practice or practices' — becomes, however, the reckless hyperbole that 'ideology has a material existence'. There is a very similar slide here as in the culturalist 'way of life' which threatens to make both concepts too general for usefulness in analysis. Against the slides of 'material' and 'way of life' we would want to insist, in a thoroughly orthodox manner, on the distinctively 'mental' character of culture/ ideology, their broad equivalence to Marx's general term 'consciousness' (see esp. Marx, 1970, p. 65; 1976, pp. 283-4). At this stage in the argument we should note that even within this indispensable boundary culture/ideology embrace vastly dissimilar processes and that neither culturalist nor structuralist analysis supplies us with the concepts (or even words) to distinguish the orders and types of these. We might also note — a feature to which we shall return in the critique of culturalism — that both systems tend either to a reduced view of economic relations, or to render ideological relations more or less autonomous from economic production.

More positively both 'culture' and the 'materiality' of ideology are ways of countering the reduction of consciousness to a mere reflex of economic relations. Both traditions insist that culture/ideology have a determinacy or autonomy of their own. Yet at the same time, both systems insist on the *relation* between cultural-ideological and other processes. Both are opposed to an idealism. Finally, and more controversially, both Althusser and the culturalist Marxists identify their object of study as 'history' or as 'historical'. This is uncontroversial in the case of Thompson, clear enough in the manner in which Williams often writes (his histories of words for instance), but has to be argued for in relation to Althusser. It is, however, important to distinguish between Althusser and some Althusserians who have, indeed, apparently abandoned the historical path (Hindess and Hirst, 1975 esp. pp. 308ff.). Althusser himself has rightly been concerned to question 'history' as a taken-for-granted or, in Marx's term, 'chaotic' abstraction, yet 'history' is questioned in the name of an historical science. Historical

materialism is understood as 'the science of the history of social formations' (see Althusser, 1970, pp. 92-144). Against this it might be
argued that Althusser's commitment to history is formal only. It is
perfectly true that philosophy, not history, dominates the whole
project. Yet Althusser provides more than a general justification of
historical materialism: he also supplies us with notions that enrich historical understanding and our ability to analyse specific situations,
notably the notion 'conjuncture', the de-construction of unified evolutionary 'time', and, in general, the theme of complex, structured and
contradictory unities. His critique of simple or essential unity, though
it is very abstract, has major implications for historical interpretations.[6]

These points of implicit agreement constitute, at root, the claims of
both these traditions to be 'Marxist'.The premises we have noted are
Marx's major premises too: the 'rationalist' premise (thought/conscious-
ness is distinctive); the 'materialist' premise (thought expresses social
relations); and the 'historical' premise (the concern with historical
specificity, transformation or rupture). The main point of contention
lies, as we shall see, in the domain of Marx's fourth major premise which
we might indeed term 'structuralist'.[7]

Culture and the Structuralist Critique

Not all the criticisms that follow are derived directly from Althusser's
work. In general, however, they do reveal the vulnerability of familiar
positions to a critique informed by structuralism. These are points that
have to be taken into account in a revised practice of the study of
culture. The problems are of three main kinds: they concern culturalist
method and epistemology, an implicit or explicit view of the social
formation, and a 'humanist' and 'culture-bound' view of class.

Many of the difficulties arise from an over-riding moral and
political imperative with theoretical effects. The main imperative is to
respect the authenticity, rationality or validity of the experiences or
cultures that are addressed. This basic pre-supposition is common to a
large family of sociologies and histories and is, perhaps, a feature of
literary studies too, but there are two main distinguishing characteristics of a Marxist culturalism. First, experiences are understood fundamentally as class experiences; second, there is a primary concern with
the cultures of subordinate or oppressed classes which are seen as having
a particular authenticity and dignity and yet are in need of recovery
within the historical record. All this would apply to many of the popular histories or histories 'from below', including much oral history and
what we might term the History Workshop movement; in relation to

gender rather than class it also applies to much women's history. But the most consistently Marxist popular history is to be found in the work of Edward Thompson and Eugene Genovese, Marxist historian of the slave South. Together their work represents a sustained and often very polemical enterprise in socialist-humanist history. Thus, in the well-known preface to *The Making of the English Working Class* Thompson insists on the validity, according to their experience, of the utopian, millenarian or insurrectionary aspirations of groups within the early English working class, and seeks to 'rescue' them from 'the enormous condescension of posterity' (Thompson, 1963, pp.12-13). Similarly, Genovese asserts the priority of attending to the cultural achievements of the slaves over any 'theoretical advance' which their experience might suggest (Genovese, 1974, p.xvi). This kind of statement, prefacing or concluding a work, is typical of the new history of the late 1950s and 1960s (see, for example, Hobsbawm, 1959, introduction to Appendix; Hill, 1972, pp.363-4).

This basic moral stance was generated, in the first instance, in a knowledge of the political effects of deformed and mechanical Marxist orthodoxies. It also produced histories of great vitality in which previously flattened or forgotten experiences were brought to life, with all their contemporary potentialities. But the other side of the stress on 'experience' is a particular attitude to abstraction or 'theory'. A moral and political stance is often extended into a theoretical and epistemological principle. Abstraction is held to destroy authenticity, detaching the object from its real surrounding sets of relations. Abstraction is 'violent' because it imposes no check on speculation. The use of externally-derived concepts — all kinds of 'platonism' — Leninist, Structuralist, Structural-Functionalist — are bound to distort, forcing real historical materials into theoretical pre-occupations (Thompson, 1965; 1976). If the characteristic method of the Althusserians — the 'reading' — is interventionist (and has, indeed its own perils) the historian of culture or experience 'listens' (Thompson 1976, p. 15).

It is evident that in a practice so described, theory or abstraction can have little place. It may be present in very particular forms, heuristically as 'hypothesis' or informed guess (Thompson, 1973) or as critique or polemic (Thompson, 1976, p.21). But this practice has no place for the making of determinate abstractions of the kind that formed the tissue of Marx's *Capital*. The differences are caught in two brief quotations:

In all serious Marxist analysis the categories (base and superstructure) are of course not used abstractly [Williams, 1977, p. 79].

In the analysis of economic forms neither microscopes nor chemical reagents are of assistance. The power of abstraction must replace both [Marx, 1976, p. 90].

But the best example of the difference is the refusal to abstract in speaking of societies or social formations in general. It is a culturalist feature that, on principle, no distinctions are made between levels or instances. The base-superstructure metaphor is rejected and culturalism prefers to speak of an undifferentiated human praxis or of 'culture' and 'economics' as 'two sides of the same coin' or of a 'dialectic' between being and consciousness. As Williams puts it, 'it is not "the base" and "the superstructure" that need to be studied, but specific and indissoluble real processes' (Williams, 1977a, p. 82). Quite so, but the problem is *how*.

The epistemological difficulties with these formulations are those that arise with most 'empiricisms': the actual practice is itself inadequately described; the method provides no real demonstration of the validity of results; and recourse is often made to secret or 'guilty' theoretical premises. Historians of culture, for instance, while denying the validity of abstraction, must themselves abstract: they make, from material appropriated from their 'sources', a complex, 'chaotic' abstraction of 'experience'. Similarly, the knowledge-effect of interrogating 'sources' with your 'own' questions is erected into an epistemology in which 'theory' or 'model' is tested against 'grand facts' (Thompson, 1973, p.47; 1965, pp. 349-50). Since 'facts' have to be thought, before such a comparison can take place, what is described is a circle (and a dilemma), not a proof. The way the method actually works in, say, *The Making of the English Working Class* seems rather different. What is interrogated, over-whelmingly, is other people's conceptions of their lives. Yet the very importance of subjective experience as a court of appeal of human science poses the problems of relativism. In judging our conception of their world against our reading of their conceptions, we may have solved one set of problems — of the imposition of an externally-derived view-point — but are immediately into another set. We are no nearer the facticity of either account, especially since past accounts differ and we need criteria of discrimination. In practice, Thompson does arbitrate between accounts by trusting the accounts of the oppressed as more authentic than the 'ideological' character of the writings of a Dr Kay, and Andrew Ure or the average run of Blue Books. He may be right to do so, but, in the process, some fairly intrusive moral and theoretical principles have been applied. At the very least, this suggests that the theory of no-theory cannot be sustained.

But the same or similar difficulties are best illustrated on the ground of alternative conceptions of the social formation. As we have seen, it is characteristic of a culturalist position that certain abstractions are refused: base/superstructure or cultural/economic production for instance. A sense of the totality and necessary inter-connectedness of practices and social relations is preferred. At a stretch — and it is a kind of concession — consciousness and being are distinguished and set in a 'dialectical relationship'.

The weight of these formulations is addressed to economism, with which structuralisms are sometimes confused. Against economism, this position is very powerful. One typical culturalist move, for instance, that has fundamentally undermined all economistic reductions, is to insist that the cultural actually enters into economic or market relations, or that far from being 'natural', economic rationality of capitalist kind is historically and culturally constructed. Examples of this kind of insight include Thompson's work on conceptions of time and Hobsbawm's on customary elements and the determination of the wage (Thompson, 1967; Hobsbawm, 1964).

Yet, in the longer term, the refusal to make abstractions seriously weakens this position and renders its general conceptions vague and confused. Moreover, as 'values' and 'economics' are always seen as consonant, bound organically together in real situations, there is a danger of a return to those determinisms from which the whole move was designed to escape. 'Dialectical relation' is an attempt to avoid this problem, but is not a coherent or usable conception. To give it some explanatory purchase we would have to be able to specify the conditions of the dominance of the one set of relations over the other — of consciousness over being or vice versa. Otherwise all such formulations remain, notoriously, evasive.

These problems arise because abstraction is understood as a *result* and not as part of a method, as a form of closure rather than a means to more complete knowledge. Marx abstracts certain key (economic) relations, moves from the concrete to the abstract, in order to return to the 'concrete' as the product of many determinations. Abstraction is a moment in the process of inquiry and presentation. It can be seen in the structure of *Capital* itself, especially in Vol.I. For *Capital* is constructed as inter-related levels of abstraction, all the way 'down' from simple, formal and universal categories (the labour process in general; consciousness) to densely re-created specific histories (the so-called 'primitive accumulation'; the history of class struggles and the Factory Acts). To read *Capital* as a history book is to miss the prior determinate abstractions on which these historical accounts are based.[8]

The Althusserian protocols about the nature of social formations have at least the virtues that derive from an appropriately high level of abstraction. They have a clarity and adequacy to the purpose (an alternative to economism) that all culturalist formulations lack. The problems arise, however, when notions like 'determination in the last instance' or 'relative autonomy' acquire the status of *a priori* truths. Then indeed, culturalist fears of *a priorism* and 'violent abstraction' may be justified.

The third set of difficulties concerns culturalist conceptions of class. Class is indeed the central category of socialist-humanist history; it tends to displace mode of production and economic transition from its central place within the same British Marxist tradition, and is in marked contrast, too, to the structuralist stress on mode of production/ social formation. There are three main criticisms to be made of this central category. First, class is thought of as a set of relations between human beings. Classes are groups of people in relations of oppression or exploitation. This delivers a superbly historical and relational view of class, much superior to sociological conceptions (for the classic statement see Thompson, 1963 pp. 9-12). But as class relations are understood as essentially inter-personal, as relation*ships* essentially, there is little stress on what these relationships are *over*, which must include *things* (means of production and a surplus) as well as people. As Althusser has argued, most recently in *Essays in Self-Criticism*, Marx's central category of relations of production cannot be properly grasped in 'anthropological' or psychological terms, through, in short, a 'theoretical humanism' (Althusser, 1976, pp. 201-2).

Allied to the failure to think 'relations of production' in a complex way is the tendency to a reduced view of economic social relations as a whole. It is not that 'the economic' never appears in these histories. Typically, in Thompson's work, it is present all the time, but by a kind of proxy: not in its own right as a particular kind of relation, but in a form mediated by 'experience'. In the chapter on 'Exploration' in *The Making of the English Working Class* for instance, exploitation is present in the feelings and perceptions of working-class groups and individuals, but never analysed as a socio-economic process. In this chapter as in the book as a whole, the argument returns continually to a cultural mode — to the *perception* and *symbolic representation* of exploitation by contemporaries (Thompson, 1963, pp. 189-212 and compare, for this critique at more length, Johnson, McLennan and Schwarz, 1978 pp.43-52).

It could, of course, be argued that the economic is simply not the object of books like Genovese's *Roll Jordan Roll*, or Thompson's *Making*. These are 'social' histories; the necessary *lacunae* are supplied elsewhere by historians working, as a kind of collective, within the same tradition but on more economic themes. (For this argument see, for example, Thompson, 1976, p.25 where the specific reference is to the work of Saville and Hobsbawm). But this argument is not convincing for several reasons. First, we are not speaking here of an orthodox historiography with the usual parcellated sub-disciplines, but of a Marxist tradition that has always sought to grasp totalities. Secondly, since in practice they work within quite different problematics, it is not convincing to say that Thompson plus Hobsbawm equals a Marxist *histoire globale*! Third, socialist-humanist histories do not merely tend to exclude 'the harder economic analysis' but actually construct their key concept — class — in a manner that systematically marginalises one (economic) aspect of this category, viz. the connection between classes and relations of production in particular modes of production. Thompson's sole and explicit criterion for the existence of class concerns forms of consciousness and collective action or organisation: in the *Making* class is seen as a wholly political and cultural category. The same is true of all his work on the eighteenth century in which terms which denote ethico-political forms ('the crowd' or 'plebians') actually replace (as opposed to merely supplement) terms that denote economic classes or class places (peasants, small producers, proletarians). This is a very common and quite principled culturalist move, not merely a necessary limitation of a piecemeal form of analysis.

The Althusserian criticism of these positions is that they are not Marxist. At one level this is true enough. Abstraction, a key to Marx's method, and relations of production, a key category, are absent from these histories. But the problem is a larger one than faithfulness to Marx's insights. Nor is it an adequate critique of any text to say that it is not Marxist. Such dismissals add nothing to the strength of the tradition which is said to be defended. Besides, as we are learning more and more, there is more than one historical Marx, though there may certainly be better or worse ones. The problem is better stated as follows: culturalist histories belong to that family of sociologies that seek to grasp social phenomena in their own terms, in their forms of appearance in the world. The problem with such sociologies is that they abandon the ground of 'determination' or explanation. The most radical culturalisms refuse questions of structure or process altogether, focusing on small-scale inter-subjective transactions in a circle of 'accounts'. Socialist-humanist histories retain much more of a notion of process than radical ethnomethodology. They retain in particular Marx's 'motor' of class and class struggle. But class is seen wholly as something that sits on the surface of society, available to the ear that 'listens'. It shows up in class consciousness and class organisation, but in these forms alone. Thus the limit cases for culturalism are those periods when ideological processes of containment work most effectively, periods, in other words, of hegemony. The limit case for Thompson might well be the 1850s to 1870s or the period, a century or so later, when the *Making* was planned and written.

In effect culturalist histories are an amalgam of two of Marx's dicta, the first severely truncated: 'Men make history'; 'All history is the history of class struggle'. But how are such classes constituted? How do they come to be in an antagonistic relation? Is anything possible by such human agency? What sets limits to this creativity? What, indeed, constitutes men and women as social (class-ed and sex-ed) beings in the first place? We would want to insist, following the Marx whose insights Althusser has usefully re-stated, that the world cannot be wholly understood in terms of an everyday 'experience'. On the contrary, this 'common sense' may lie at the very centre of inadequate explanations of the social world in which we are placed. It follows that groups or individuals as 'people' cannot be the be-all and end-all of explanation and that we can only understand their consciousness and their praxis via a detour that takes as its object the relations in which they stand.

It is nonetheless important to retain several elements of a culturalist practice. If inadequate as a theoretical principle, 'humanism' should certainly be a constituent in socialist morality and purposes. Similarly the major works in this tradition stand as a permanent reminder that any sociology or concrete history that fails to come to terms with the subjective moment, with 'consciousness', will be fundamentally flawed. Again, the stress on cultural self-making or the auto-genesis of cultural forms, though risking a relapse into Lukacsian categories, reminds us of the importance of appropriation, assent, even affirmation as a moment in more complex ideological processes. It stands as a corrective to all unilateral notions of 'control' or 'ideological domination' or 'tranmission' or 'manipulation'. The centrality of struggle in this problematic has the same anti-functionalist effect. In all these ways, then, we might say that though the culturalist category 'experience' is a confused and heterogeneous one, it designates a space that must be properly theorised in any adequate account of culture/ideology. Finally, the level of specific histories at which culturalist practices normally operate is, in important ways, the privileged level of inquiry. It is the level of the production of really useful knowledge. In the production of such knowledge, however, more abstract discourses must certainly play a part.

Limitations of Structuralism

The purpose of this section is very limited: to show that structuralism does not supply us with an adequate theory of ideology, adequate, that is, for the purpose of concrete analysis. It supplies no full alternative to culturalist practices, however powerful it may be as the basis of a critique of them. Most of the criticisms of structuralism that are made in this section have been made, originally and at great length, by other authors. Most of the arguments are indeed familiar. It is possible, therefore, to be quite brief. (For criticisms of structuralist theories of ideology on which this section draws see esp. Hirst 1976b, 1977; Rancière, 1974; Erben and Gleeson 1977; Coward and Ellis, 1977; *Ideology and Consciousness*, 1977). The difficulties with structuralism are of three main kinds: the problem of the preferred level of abstraction; the tendency, allied to this, to radically simplify the social formation; the slide into a functionalist account of ideological social relations.

Althusser and his co-workers developed a very particular definition of Marx's contribution to knowledge, avowedly one supplied by 'philosophy' (Althusser, 1970, pp. 14-15). But this 'reading' was not limited to the clarification of the underlying intellectual procedures of Marx's work: it pronounced on the manner, method and scientific status of Marx's discoveries *and* on what was seen as basic or essential to the substance of his theories. It attempted to sum up 'Marx's Immense Theoretical Revolution', to encapsulate the scientific originality of the founder of historical materialism. Here we have a philosophy with decidedly un-philosophical ambitions — no mere helpmeet of science, but a fully-fledged theoretical sociology in philosophical disguise.

The philosopher's reading of *Capital* was, in fact, extremely selective. The overall effect of this selectivity, aided by the 'symptomatic reading', was a radical simplification of Marx's results and procedures. This is best seen in Part II of *Reading Capital* in which, despite some discussion of laws of tendency and specific forms of the labour process, Balibar tends to reduce Marx's extended, three-volume analysis of the capitalist mode of production to a few simple formularies: the invariant elements of modes of production in general, their variant modes of combination and an account of transitions in terms of formal non-correspondences (see Ibid., pp. 225ff for a summary of 'the primary theoretical concepts of historical materialism').

All this is allied to a particular view of how Marx's discoveries were made. They are held to have been produced in the course of a critique of political economy. It follows that developments out of Marx can occur through an extended critical commentary on Marx's own work, raising 'practical' concepts to full theoretical status and supplying absences and silences. Without denying the value of this theoretical labour, we must note that in Part I of *Reading Capital* Althusser has very little to say about Marx's method of inquiry, in particular the stages which Marx himself described as 'appropriating the material in detail', and analysing the inner connections and forms of development of the appearances of economic life (Marx, 1976 p. 102). Nor has Althusser much to say about Marx's moment of 'presentation', the process of concentration by which an approximation to the complexity of the real is reached. Although Althusser employs many of the arguments and terms of Marx's *1857 Introduction*, the real problems are literally left in suspension at the end of the first part of *Reading Capital* (see p. 69).

Associated with philosophical competences and the absence of 'history' is the failure to discuss the difficult intellectual movements between levels of abstraction. The founders of structuralism were not writers of histories so that this problem was not centrally theirs. This, however, is the really damaging absence in the Althusserian epistemology. The whole post-Althusserian history of epistemological agonies, ending in the demand for the analysis of current situations but the dis-severance of analysis from theory, might be written in terms of the effects of this absence. In particular, Marx's own concern with making sense of the immediate rush and muddle of observable phenomena is quite lost in the vexed debate about empiricism (e.g. many of the letters in the *Marx-Engels Correspondence* esp. Marx to Danielson, 10 April 1879, p. 296).

In these ways, Althusserianism becomes a mirror image of culturalist and indeed other historiographies. In some ways, Thompson's demonic vision is justified. In practice, Althusserianism does render 'the appropriation of the real in thought' peculiarly difficult. Historians and Althusserians represent aspects of Marx's work whose organic relation in the *Eighteenth Brumaire* or the more 'historical' parts of *Capital* we are only just beginning to understand.

We have already noted that Althusser's general protocols on the nature of social formations have a value, yet this is a good illustration of the distance between the level of abstraction at which structuralism commonly operates and that which might correspond to a properly theoretical history. Althusser's characteristic level is the (abstract) social formation. Just as culturalism grasps social formations in terms of relations of classes (and thereby marginalises, for example, relations of gender) so structuralism simplifies by describing social formations in terms of modes of production and their (ideological and political) 'conditions of existence' (Althusser, 1970, p. 177; Hindess & Hirst 1975). Further complexifications can be reached by recognising that concrete social formations contain more than one mode, or elements from more than one, and that there may be 'variants' of particular modes, forms that are determined by the outcomes of class struggles. One of the most concrete discussions in the whole *oeuvre*, a magical moment indeed, is Althusser's section on the Russian Revolution in 'Contradiction and Overdetermination' in *For Marx*. Here complexity is grasped in terms of co-existing modes each with their own internal contradictions and with external contradictions between them. Yet at the end of this all too brief analysis, Althusser himself signals the failure to embrace the full complexity of the situation. There follows a fascinating meditation on the subject of 'survivals', including '*customs, habits* even *traditions*' (did we hear '*culture*'?) which in practice sketches many of the problems posed by Althusserian abstractness (Althusser, 1969, pp.114-15). If the 'continent of history' is really to be opened up, such 'survivals' will have to be 'thought'.

Finally, it is an old and correct criticism that Althusser's major work on ideology, the essay on ideological state apparatuses, has a marked tendency to functionalism. This is in part the result of attempting to think of ideology or the ideological instance solely as a condition of existence for a given mode of production. The whole sphere of the cultural/ideological, the very processes by which subjectivities are formed, are subsumed within a single function: the reproduction of the conditions of capitalist production. Ideology-in-general (the universal culture-bound condition of human beings) is conflated with the notion of ideology as an instance and the specific conditions, at this level, necessary for capitalist reproduction. Moreover what is correctly understood as a condition or a contingency becomes, in the course of the argument, a continuously achieved outcome. This is further re-inforced by a failure to distinguish between the reproduction of relations in the strict sense and the preparation of agents for these places. Ideology is thus called upon to do a task which, in Marx's analysis, is secured in the only place it can be — in economic production and circulation itself (Marx, 1976 pp. 711-24 and pp. 1060-65). The insistence on the 'materiality' of ideology tends to blur the distinction with economic relations and to endow ideology with something of their necessary force — the sustaining of material life itself. Class struggle is supplied *post hoc*, literally in a later postscript. The neglect of gender relations and specific sexual ideologies accentuates the monolithic character of ideology. The overall effect is to return us to a model of one-dimensional control, in which dominant ideology operates with a totalitarian thoroughness usually ascribed to economic or, more exactly, biological processes. The overriding concern with outcomes — 'reproduction' — suppresses the fact that these conditions have continually to be won — or lost — in particular conflicts and struggles.

It is important, however, to retain elements of a structuralist view of ideology and of other relations. Structuralism's central contribution is to re-assert Marx's own sense of the objective force of social relations and their salience over merely experiential categories. The critique of theoretical humanism and the stress on complex unity is a real re-enrichment of the tradition. Similarly the notion of 'interpellation' and of the construction of subjects provides us with a powerful way of connecting the analysis of particular ideological fields to the 'lived' level of ideology. The work of Ernesto Laclau suggests that a version of interpellation can be employed for more specific historical analysis, without the attendant functionalisms (Laclau, 1977). Problems remain, however, concerning the *ground* of interpellations, the construction of historically-specific, and class and gender-specific forms of individuality in the first place, the prior acculturation of concrete historical subjects. It is possible that psycho-analytic theory, a presence in Althusser's own formulations, may have a part to play here, though it cannot account for the salience of particular ideologies for particular groups and classes in particular historical situations.

Structuralism has also contributed an acute (and sometimes paralysing) state of theoretical and epistemological awareness which is a hall-mark of the tendency, and which we cannot now do without — rather like some original, painful fall from a state of naivety! Finally the general Althusserian protocols, especially 'relative autonomy', may continue to have a value, but have to be subject to a close working through for particular historical conjunctures.

Marx and Gramsci

At this stage in the argument, then, we are left with a number of problems and *lacunae*. Chief among these are the need for a more discriminating set of categories for describing ideological/cultural processes, a more adequate account than that offered by 'experience' to grasp the relation between economic social relations and ideological practices (or between economic classes and ideologies), and above all, a set of terms that permits us to understand ideological struggles in relation to what Gramsci called 'the necessities of production' without relapsing into a functionalism. At the level of polemic and detailed historical work, culturalism certainly opposes the functionalist tendency, but further developments are necessary to permit us to analyse concrete situations of 'relations of force' in something like their experienced complexity. Some of the answers may lie in a brief return to Marx and Gramsci, though what follows can be no more than the briefest indication of a re-reading of these texts.

There are two points, drawn from *Capital*, that are relevant to these dilemmas. The first concerns Marx's distinction between 'phenomenal forms' (the surface forms of everyday life) and 'real relations' (the underlying processes which we must grasp to explain the surface forms). (For classic formulations see Marx, 1976 pp. 279-80 and 1064. But these themes are present in *Capital* all the time.) Some commentators, notably Geras (1972) and Mepham (1974) have seen these formulations as amounting to Marx's mature theory of ideology. Commentators influenced by structuralism have tended to dismiss this claim (Hirst 1976b; cf. Althusser 1970 pp. 187-93).

A third position is possible. Phenomenal forms are the way economic relations intrude upon the occupants of class places, the way they *present* themselves. They do not in themselves produce 'false' knowledge or ideologies. They are, rather, the raw material or object of economic analysis, of conception. The production of ideologies depends, then, on further conditions which operate within thought itself or within a particular (determined) history of the production of ideas. These include the division of mental and material labour, and what Marx calls, in *The German Ideology*, the historical appearance in particular forms of 'active, conceptive ideologists' (Marx, 1970, p. 65). Also relevant here are the particular forms of 'abstraction', on the one side 'thin', 'violent', 'arbitrary', 'feeble' or 'chaotic' and on the other 'historical', which distinguish inadequate from adequate forms of knowledge. Abstraction, a particular operation of the mind, may enable us to penetrate appearances; more commonly abstraction stays at the level of appearances or tends to eternalise relations that have a specific historical scope of reference.[9] This formulation permits us to retain the notion of 'forms' as a *connection* between economic life and thought upon it while retaining the specificity of ideological practices. We shall return

later to this reading of Marx in order to de-construct the culturalist
category 'experience', especially in relation to class experiences and
cultures.

But there is a second way in which ideology/culture is dealt with in
Capital. It is envisaged as the ground of transformations. In this form it
is present, in *Capital* as a kind of sub-text.[10] It belongs to that order of
relations which Marx's main analysis (of accumulation) pre-supposes
but rarely examines in itself. Marx frequently refers to 'the general level
of civilisation' of the labourer, his habits, customs, habitual or conventional standards of life and those skills which are carried in working-
class culture before they are appropriated by capital (e.g. Marx, 1976,
pp. 275, 719-23, 615-17, 620-21). Included too are the 'moral' or
subjective elements in labour and, very importantly, the pre-existing
forms of the family and relations between the sexes. All these elements
lie, strictly, outside the terms of reference of *Capital's* main analysis:
they are not understood as parts or aspects of the capitalist mode of
production. They appear in *Capital's* discourses mainly as frictions,
fetters or inhibitions on the development of the mode, as a basis of
working-class resistance, or as relations that are transformed by the
primary processes that are described. The relation between the proletarian family and machinofacture, for instance, is understood as a transformative action of one set of relations (fully described) on another
(barely sketched) (Marx, 1976 pp. 620-21).

Two interpretative points may now be made linking this element in
Capital to previous arguments. First, we return to the point about
'survivals' and to structuralism's simplification of the social formation.
The sub-text in Marx shows once more how concrete social formations
cannot be grasped simply in terms of the dominant mode of production and its ideological and political conditions of existence. There are
features of the social formation that are articulated to the mode of
production and may be transformed by it, but cannot, without a loss of
complexity and a return to functionalism, be subsumed within it. The
strongest case, here, is the specific forms of patriarchal gender relations that distinguish the family as a site. The family cannot be
assimilated to a mode of production or a class analysis without sup-
pressing what is specific to gender relations and thereby ignoring the
whole weight of the feminist critique, which here, as elsewhere, forces a
reconsideration of Marxist concepts.[11]

More generally, Marx's 'habits and expectations' are analogous to the
expanded notion of culture in the English usage. In *Capital* Marx thinks
the relation between culture and mode of production mainly through

the transformations produced in the labourer's way of life through the force of economic relations themselves, though he also, in the discussion of the Factory Acts, for instance, recognises the part played by the state and legislative regulation. The relation between this set of arguments and those relating to ideology, however, is never fully recouped. It forms, however, a central concern of Gramsci's later writing, especially of the *Prison Notebooks*.

Gramsci employs three key terms of cultural/ideological analysis (where culturalism and structuralism employ only one): 'common sense' which refers, concretely, to the lived culture of a particular class or social group; 'philosophy' (or sometimes 'ideology') which refers to an organised set of conceptions with a more or less transformative relation to lived culture; and 'hegemony' which describes the state of play, as it were, between the whole complex of 'educative' institutions and ideologies on the one hand, and lived culture on the other: the extent to which common sense is made to conform both to 'the necessities of production' and to the construction of consent and a political order.

These terms are in a 'practical state' in Gramsci's writings: they are developed in the course of concrete analysis and strategic assessment. Yet their power and fertility can be immediately seen if we relate them to the concepts already in play in our previous discussion. 'Common sense' might properly be regarded as synonymous with 'culture' and Marx's 'habits and expectations'. It is the more or less spontaneous way of thinking of a particular class (Gramsci often refers to the peasantry). Unlike some simple expressive notions of culture, however, 'common sense' is seen as deeply contradictory, shot through with ideological elements, with elements of 'good sense', but without a knowledge of the historicity and determinate origin of elements in its own folklore (see Gramsci, 1971, pp. 321-43). In a typically nuanced view of 'spontaneity', 'common sense' may either remain deeply ambiguous, 'corporate', limited, contained, but often very combative, or be transformed by capitalist adaptations or by a communist politics: the educative work of the party, of organic intellectuals and 'the philosophy of praxis' (Ibid., 'The Modern Prince'). Much of Gramsci's political analysis is concerned with the conditions under which the popular masses may be hegemonised either through public bourgeois agencies or through a working-class party. 'Ideologies/philosophies' are understood very much in this context and through the particular (class-related) position of the intellectuals who produce them (Ibid., pp. 5-23). Ideologies, if they have the ability to move masses at all, are understood as essentially active and transformative, transformative of common sense views of the world. It is important to add that though Gramsci's 'hegemony' is now very familiar in English cultural theory, it has been appropriated, almost always, in a particular culturalist form. (This applies to the diverse uses of Thompson, Perry Anderson, Raymond Williams, and even to the relatively careful use in Gray, 1976). Hegemony has been appropriated as a concept that refers wholly to super-structural relations or cultural relations of authority. In Gramsci's own usage (Ibid., p. 258) it concerns, rather, the *relation between* structure and superstructure. It incorporates, indeed, a view of base-superstruc-ture relations which is characteristic and perhaps unique. The normal state of this relation is that of massive disjunctions and unevenness; certainly this is, according to Gramsci, the persistent state of the Italian social formation! (see Ibid., 'Americanism and Fordism'). Gramsci describes, in other words, the normality of 'survivals'. Hegemony describes the practices by which some greater uniformity is sought. 'Reproduction', then, is here presented as a hard and constantly-resisted labour, a political and ideological work for capital and for the dominant classes, on very obstinate materials indeed.

Some Conclusions

There is a need to recover the notion of culture as a category of an analysis. By culture we understand the 'way of life' of a particular class or group or, more exactly, its 'lived' ideologies or 'common sense' con-sidered as a complex, located whole. Such a concept is firmly descrip-tive. To employ it, is to insist on the importance, as one moment in the study of ideology, of grasping patterns of belief as they are lived in combination by concrete social individuals. One of the problems with Marxist theories of ideology and consciousness, old and new, is that they have often been un-informed by an actual knowledge of 'common sense'. They have either been highly normative, as in the central tradi-tion around class and class consciousness, or have focused on ideology-in-general and the effects it is supposed to have on its subjects. At best, as for example in the work of Foucault, they have involved the abstrac-tion and examination of complex ideological fields. Such abstractions are necessary but so is a return to a more complex and situated whole.

The indispensability of 'culture' can be seen in different ways. One might note the sheer semantic difficulty of finding a rigorous structura-list equivalent. The culture of a class would have to become 'the sum or ensemble of ideologies lived by . . . ' or even 'the sum of inter-pellated subjects within . . . ' More seriously, it is very difficult to disengage structuralism's 'ideology' from a mode of production analysis in which all ideologies are seen as functionally related to the conditions of production. There is no doubt that there *are* ideological conditions for the existence of a given mode, but this does not, in any concrete society, exhaust all that belongs to the ideological instance. There are cultural elements to which capital is *relatively* indifferent and many which it has great difficulty in changing and which remain massively and residually present. Similarly it is not easy to 'think' the forms of cultural resistance against both capitalism and patriarchy within this frame of reference. But further, the notion of culture is actually a necessary supplement to the useful structuralist concept of interpellation. One notorious difficulty of theories of interpellation concerns the basis or ground of interpellation (understood as the action of ideologies on the individual consciousness). One set of solutions to this problem is to call on psycho-analytic categories and the unconscious. But these categories are altogether too thin and general for adequate historical analysis. A different strategy is to insist that concrete social individuals are always already constructed as class-ed, sex-ed and age-ranked subjects, have already entered into complex cultural forms, already have a complexly formed subjectivity. The 'lonely hour' of the unitary, primary, cultureless interpellation 'never comes'. This points, certainly, to the reconstruction of ideologies and ideological fields and the positioning of the 'subject' within particular discourses, but this will remain very incomplete without a consideration of the salience of ideologies for already constituted (culturally and economically) real subjects. Another way of putting all this is to insist on the need to retain culture-ideology as a couplet, where culture is understood as a ground or result of the work of ideologies. The key problem remains the means by which concrete social individuals, classes and political forces are formed and moved by ideologies, or how an ideology can become a principle of life.

   In the context of the English debate, culture is also important for some of its connotations, especially all the anti-functionalist connotations of self-making or consent. We have already tended to give culture a somewhat more passive connotation than it has in most culturalist texts. But ideological processes as a whole certainly involve the *moment* of self-creation, or active appropriation. Without some such dimension we could not begin to understand why working-class girls do not merely succumb to marriage and motherhood, but actually affirm their femininity and prepare for this destiny; or why working-class boys celebrate the entry into manual labour (MacRobbie, 1977; Willis, 1977).

Yet against the culturalist view of the auto-genesis of culture we would have to insist that what is confirmed or assented to has its own determinate origin, beyond and outside these particular subjectivities.

Finally, we wish to distance ourselves from two positions, the one a tendency of culturalism, the other of its critics. We do not wish to imply that class cultures are all of a piece, or organised around central principles or ideas — collectivity, consciousness of class, individualism etc. The degree of homogeneity and distinctness of class cultures is historically very variable. But it is perhaps the case that all notions of cultures as coherent value systems are liable to be misleading. Gramsci's notion, based upon a familiarity with particular lived forms, of the radical heterogeneity of 'common sense' may be a better broad guide. We should start by looking for contradictions, taboos, displacements rather than unities. This is one way of breaking from the bad, romantic side of 'cultural studies'; another very important way is the recognition of gender-specific elements in popular culture and of the male-dominated cultural forms through which the subordination of girls and women is secured within the class itself.

On the other hand, it is absurd to believe (or still more to theorise) that there is *no* relation between ideological and political forms and economic classes (Cutler, Hindess, Hirst & Husain, 1977, esp. part III). The problem is that most formulations of this relation are not coherent. One common culturalist argument is that classes make their own culture out of the raw material of a class 'experience'. But this is not very helpful: 'experience' conflates the forms that present themselves as the raw material of cognition or which intrude upon material human existence with the (mental) means of their representation. The sense that is made of, say, the salience of the wage form for the physical existence of the labourer is dependent on the categories that are or are not available. Availability of conceptions has its own history, articulated to the history of other relations but not simply identifiable with it. Nonetheless, we would argue that many of the cultural differences in a society can only adequately be explained in relation to economic classes. Marx's 'phenomenal forms' are important here as a way of thinking of the relation of economic life to ideological practices. Salient features of everyday economic life — the various forms of exchange — supply a raw material for the cultural practices of classes. They are one of the principal features of life that has to be explained (or displaced or tabooed) within the culture. They may determine its general direction or mode. It is difficult to see how one could account for the distinctiveness of working-class culture in Britain except in something like these terms: that the culture has been built around the task of making funda-mentally punishing conditions of existence more or less habitable. The problem, perhaps, is not the *fact* of a powerful relation between class position and culture, but what the precise *forms* of the determinations are. Unless we understand this relation to the material we will not be able to understand culture or ideology at all.

Notes

1. This paper began as an attempt to work though the culture-ideology opposition in the wake of helping to edit the journal of the Centre for Contemporary Cultural Studies, *On Ideology*. It later became a working-paper towards sections of a book on working-class culture (J. Clarke, C. Critcher and R. Johnson (eds.), *Working Class Culture: History and Theory*, Hutchinson, Autumn 1979). Several different versions have been discussed in the Centre for Contemporary Cultural Studies over a longish period. I am specially grateful to Greg McLennan, Stuart Hall, Edward Thompson and Philip Corrigan for their comments on earlier drafts, and also, more generally, to the editors of this volume.
2. This is not to say that there are not more technical differences as to sources and so on between historical work on recent or earlier periods.
3. For a more detailed account of the origins of these dilemmas see Johnson, 'Culture and the historians' in *Working Class Culture* (cited above, n. 1).
4. For a more extended treatment of Dobb see R. Johnson, G. McLennan and B. Schwarz (1978).
5. The question of how this outcome arose cannot be treated here. It had to do, however, with the limitations of the chief rivals to a Marxism in Britain, that is literary and high-cultural traditions of the analysis of culture.
6. The potential of Althusserian concepts for historical analysis has rarely been recognised by historians in Britain. One major exception, however, is Gareth Stedman Jones.
7. The question of Marx's major premises cannot be enlarged on here. The CCCS History Group hopes to publish an account of these in relation to historical practice based on work during the year 1977-78. We have learned much from the work of Derek Sayer and Philip Corrigan on these matters.
8. This reading of the formal structure of *Capital* is supported by Marx's general statements about his method, fragmentary though these are, in Marx and Engels, *Selected Letters* and the *1857 Introduction to Grundrisse*.
9. The different forms of abstraction are frequently mentioned, but usually in passing in the *Marx-Engels Correspondence*.
10. I am very grateful to Andrew Tolson for first drawing my attention to the 'cultural' sub-text in *Capital*.
11. For elaborations of several relevant aspects of Marxist-feminist theory see CCCS Women's Studies Group (1978). The formulations here and elsewhere in this essay have been heavily influenced by discussions with members of this group.

4 SEXUALITY AND REPRODUCTION: THREE 'OFFICIAL' INSTANCES

Lucy Bland, Trisha McCabe and Frank Mort

This paper addresses itself to the problem of analysing the relations of procreation and of fertility control and their connection with the reproduction of labour power under capitalism.[1] We examine the ways in which specific forms of sexual ideology, in articulation with those processes, are structured in terms of patriarchal relations. We would define patriarchal relations as encompassing: fertility control, control over sexuality, over procreation, over a woman's labour power, and over the labour power of children. We attempt this work through an initial process of theoretical clarification, followed by particular empirical analyses. We believe that theoretical work is necessary and complementary to historical/empirical investigation, in that the construction of general theoretical concepts is a pre-condition for thinking through *structurally* the specificities of concrete analyses.

Our empirical work is centred on two government reports and one piece of 'official ideology': the *Beveridge Report on Social Insurance and Allied Services* (1942), the *Wolfenden Report on Homosexual Offences and Female Prostitution* (1957), and Newsom's book *The Education of Girls* (1948). Historically, the period of our investigation covers over fifteen years, and we would hesitate to say that the three instances occupy a 'conjuncture'. Rather, their coherence lies in their specific concerns. All three instances touch upon the same matrix of practices: marriage, the family, sexuality and procreation, understood through a particular set of ideologies. *Beveridge* explicitly forges a link between the question of procreation and the reproduction of labour power by the use of particular ideologies for women, *Newsom* is concerned with the reproduction of a sex-specific form of labour power through the state education system (in the training of girls for a particular place in the circuit of reproduction), while *Wolfenden* attempts to classify and regulate (legally and ideologically) 'perverse' sexualities, by awarding primacy to reproductive sexuality. However, we would also stress that these three instances must be located historically, in the economic and politico-ideological shifts of the post-War period of reconstruction.

Politically we see our work here as important. The 'conditions of

78

existence' of patriarchal structures are reproduced in the present, but an analysis of *Beveridge, Newsom* and *Wolfenden* offers some understanding of the way in which those patriarchal structures have been formed and crystallised, and are still 'present in their effects'. Furthermore, an understanding of the conditions of procreation, and of fertility control are a crucial concern for feminist politics; questions of abortion and contraception are deeply embedded in the history and struggle around definitions of femininity and of a woman's 'place'. The demands for free abortion and contraception should not be simply material demands, but must challenge the underlying *ideologies* on which the debate is predicated.

We should continue to acknowledge Engels' formulation in the 1884 Preface to *The Origin of the Family, Private Property and the State* as a point of departure for the understanding of procreation:

> According to the materialistic conception, the determining factor in history is, in the last resort, the production and reproduction of immediate life. But this is itself of a twofold character. On the one hand, the production of the means of subsistence, of food, clothing and shelter and the tools requisite therefore; on the other the production of human beings themselves, the propagation of the species [Engels, 1973, p. 449].

But in a sense, Engels' recognition of the centrality of procreation, as a process *paralleling* social production, seems ultimately less helpful than Marx's own cryptic remarks on the subject in *Capital*, Volume One; for the relationship between production and procreation is never theorised by Engels in the subsequent text of *The Origins of the Family*. Marx's own brief comments are structurally of a different order, in that procreation is thought through *from the point of view of the capitalist mode of production and its reproduction*. The production and reproduction of 'that means of production so indispensable to the capitalist: the labourer himself' (Marx, 1974, pp. 536-7) though necessarily taking place outside the sphere of the labour process (outside the sphere of 'productive consumption' where labour power is consumed) is equally necessarily seen as a factor in the production and reproduction of capital. Procreation is clearly centrally placed in the process of 'individual consumption' taking place historically in the family, where 'muscles, nerves, bones and brains of existing labourers are reproduced, and new labourers are begotten' (Ibid., p. 537).

But this is still analytically distinct from insisting that procreation (together with domestic labour (Bland *et al.*, 1978)) is not merely an essential factor in the reproduction of the capitalist mode of production, but rather forms an integral part of it. In a sense, the whole of *Capital* is an extended analysis of the capitalist mode of production and its expanded reproduction. 'Reproduction' is used in an utterly non-metaphorical sense by Marx: it is quite literally *re*-production, including the reproduction of the forces of production (both the means of production and the reproduction of labour power and the labourer her/himself) and the reproduction of the relations of production. What is crucial to note here, both theoretically and politically, is that the *site* of the reproduction of those elements, except the reproduction of labour power and the reproduction of fresh generations of labourers, is contained within the sphere of production, circulation and exchange itself. The site of the replacement and replenishment of the capital/labour relation, the sphere of procreation and domestic labour, is not contained within *Capital's* analysis of the capitalist mode of production.

We would insist that debates around the nature of the relationship between the family and the capitalist mode of production are not merely academic arguments: they are intimately related to the way in which sexual politics is conceptualised *as a political practice.* Differing analyses of the position of the family and the nature of the power relations contained within it produce widely varying understandings of the terrain on which struggles against sexual oppression should be conducted. A too 'comfortable' and functionalist fit between the family and the mode of production can lead to the collapse of the specificity of feminist demands into class politics, while an insistence on the total autonomy of sexual relations and practices can often lead to a form of political separatism. It is within the space between those two polarities that we attempt to construct our theoretical work here.

The capitalist mode of production obviously requires a constant supply of fresh labourers (and fresh capitalists!) as a pre-condition of its reproduction, but that process takes place within the sphere of 'individual' as opposed to 'productive' consumption. Now clearly, at one level, Marx is insistent that the sphere of individual private consumption remains a factor 'in the production and reproduction of capital' (Marx, 1974, p. 537). Certainly the post-1945 period sees a new phase in the penetration of capital into the sphere of domestic consumption, and a new growth of consumer demand (see Bogdanor and Skidelsky, 1970). That 'individual, private sphere' is *presupposed* by Marx in his specific analysis of social production, in the sense that the historical transformations and the particular forms of sexual division and subordination in the family are not explored. Further, the analytic distinction made by Marx between the spheres of individual consumption and productive consumption – the distinction between social production and 'private life' – presupposes a particular stage of development of the capitalist mode of production itself, at which the *site* of socially productive labour is no longer simultaneously the site of the reproduction and replenishment of that labour (see Zaretsky, 1976). Furthermore, Marx's analysis takes as given (as a historical feature of capital accumulation) the consolidation and strengthening of the sexual division of labour within social production and within the family. However, at another level of analysis, i.e. logically and theoretically as opposed to historically, Marx argues that the sexual division of labour will break down with the shift into machinofacture. The reproduction and maintenance of the labour force have historically been performed by *women* in relations of dependence to male supervision and control, within the family, as it is removed from the sphere of productive consumption.

We are suggesting that these presuppositions[2] are not part of the capitalist mode of production, rather they are articulated with it, and over-determined and transformed by it. The family, as a site of economic, political, legal and ideological relations, has a longer history and dynamic from that of the capitalist mode of production; a history of the shifts and transformations in patriarchal relations. Significantly, Althusser's conception of the family as an ideological apparatus of the State cannot account for that independent history: in the essay on *Ideology and Ideological State Apparatuses* (Althusser, 1971) the family exists solely to contribute to the maintenance of capitalist relations of production – it has no other history or dynamic. In any analysis of the material processes and political, legal and ideological effects located within the family, we should, we believe, cease to regard the effectivity of the capitalist mode of production as what Laclau in another context has called the: 'Deus ex Machina whose omnipresence frees us from all explanatory problems' (Laclau, 1977, pp. 34-5).

What, then, are the implications of the conclusions drawn in general concerning the family in its articulation with the mode of production for the particular analysis of procreation, and for the ideological definitions around reproductive sexuality? Clearly, as Maureen Mackintosh insists (1977) an account of human reproduction and its particular structure of sexual relations is, and should be, complementary to any analysis of the mode of production. Yet given that Mackintosh admits to the 'mode of human reproduction some autonomy of content', its centrality for her lies in what she sees as a direct relationship between procreation and the demand for labour power, and ultimately between procreation and the reproduction of classes: 'The relations of human reproduction — the subordination of women, the control of her sexuality and fertility and her children — are the means by which the reproduction of labour power and the insertion of individuals into the class structure are controlled under Capitalism' (Mackintosh, 1977, p.124). Mackintosh makes a clear and direct connection between control over procreation and the demand for a certain quantitative and qualitative level of the labour force.

Empirical analysis does go some way towards verifying Mackintosh's thesis that there is indeed a connection between historically specific quantitative and qualitative demands for labour power and the regulation and control of women's fertility and procreative capacity. (Yet, as Edholm, Harris and Young argue, the *site* of procreation remains removed from production and is not as yet subject to 'the wholesale penetration of the law of value' (1977, p. 111.)). *The Beveridge Report*, for example, condenses a concern over the regulation of procreation and the demand for a particular quantity and quality of labour power. The state, in its supervision and control of the reproduction of labour power, has never wholly left the sphere of procreation to the 'workers' instincts of self-preservation'. However, we would maintain (in distinction to Mackintosh) that the two processes — the demand for and control over a certain level of labour power, and control over procreation — are in no sense synonymous; and certainly that the insertion of individuals into the class structure involves quite other processes at the ideological and political levels. The *demand* for a particular quantity and quality of labour power is exercised primarily through the capitalist labour market, and through the industrial reserve army of labour, while *regulation and control* over labour power are achieved largely through the state education system and other forms of state intervention, as is clear in *Newsom* and *Beveridge*. Furthermore, as a process the intervention of the state has also been fundamentally determined by class struggle and represents real gains made by the working class, though not necessarily for *women*, given that the state acts patriarchally through its utilisation and transformation of existing patriarchal relations.

At a general level we would maintain that determinations of fertility control and on the processes of procreation must be seen as distinct from control over the reproduction of labour power under capitalist relations. For example, a woman's control of her fertility may be affected by her position in social production (see Gittins, 1977) or by such questions as the demand for child labour (see McLaren, 1978, p.220) and by changes and developments in the technical means of production (such as abortion and the Pill) and their accessibility. Also, it is important to stress that the history of the control of fertility and the processes of procreation must be seen in terms of struggles around sexuality (see for example Davies, 1978 and Mitchell, 1977).

Any examination of the way in which sexuality, fertility and procreation have been controlled under capitalism must include a recognition of the articulation of that set of practices with certain configurations at the ideological level. The ideologies of motherhood and maternal deprivation, ideologies of domesticity, ideologies of romance and of female sexuality (centrally its structuring through procreation) together with the ideological primacy awarded to heterosexual genital sexuality as organised around procreation and the political, legal and ideological restrictions surrounding other 'perverse' or 'deviant' sexualities, all occupy a particular positionality in articulation with the process of procreation and with sexuality and fertility control. Moreover, sexual ideologies are organised patriarchally, in that they are structured through power relations involving the subordination of women and sexual 'minorities'.

Our work on the post-War period has brought us to examine proposed legislation that touches on the regulation of procreation, sexuality and fertility through the construction and use of particular forms of sexual ideology. *Beveridge*, for example, shows a concern with the control of the position of women in the reproductive sphere articulated through the use of particular forms of sexual ideology (principally the ideologies of motherhood and domesticity). It is the problems posed by attempting to examine 'the work' of sexual ideologies in relation to the processes of procreation, sexuality and fertility that present themselves most immediately in our empirical work.

At a general level, we should be self-conscious and explicit about the state of underdevelopment of Marxist concepts relating to ideology, and to the theorisation of *sexual* ideologies in particular. Our work in this area occupies a space within Marxist-feminist theory — as yet little more. Broadly speaking, work on the area of sexual ideology has been given either through sociological categories, particularly those of the functionalist and interactionist schools (Gagnon and Simon, 1973; Plummer, 1975), or through those concepts developed politically by the Women's Movement and the Gay Movement. These latter concepts were originally in no sense 'orthodoxly' Marxist, and for good reason. Work on the ideologies of sexuality and sex-oppression were often

developed in contra-distinction and even antagonism to analyses of the
economic level. It is the terrain of what is, at worst, a real dualism that
we now inhabit. Work, for example, on the political economy of
women — whether in terms of female wage labour or domestic labour —
has consistently focused exclusively on the economic level. It has
rarely combined that type of analysis with an examination of the *ideological* determinants on the economic position of women (Beechey,
1977 and Political Economy of Women Group, 1975). Certainly there
are historical reasons for this type of separation: the relative state of
under-development of those economic concepts themselves, and the
struggle for the acknowledgement of the 'material' base of women's
oppression.

It is in considering the work of ideology that the problems begin to
be felt most acutely. To transpose Althusser's functionalist model of
ideology as existing to reproduce the social relations of production (for
a critique see Hirst, 1976b) to the patriarchal relations which structure
sexual ideology (i.e. sexual ideologies existing merely to reproduce the
relations of procreation) is to perpetuate the functionalist error.
Ideologies of heterosexual sexuality, of motherhood, of maternal
deprivation, of domesticity (and ideological restriction on 'other' sexualities) do not necessarily exist to reproduce the relations of procreation. Particular forms of sexual ideology also have some relationship
to the existing state of the whole 'ideological field', to the specific
relations between ideological discourses. Sexual ideologies may be
combined with other ideologies, often with one ideology acting as the
dominant motif, in a process of 'condensation' and convergence (see
Laclau, 1977, p. 102). *Beveridge*, *Newsom* and *Wolfenden* are not only
constructed through particular ideological configurations relating to
reproductive sexuality, but are also crossed with nationalist and imperialist ideologies, which themselves 'work over' sexual ideologies.
Motherhood (in *Beveridge*) or 'true' and 'natural' femininity in *Newsom*,
are articulated with nationalist and imperialist discourses; while in
Wolfenden debates over national decline and the loss of Empire are
linked to the proliferation of 'perverse' and 'degenerate' sexual practices.

Further, government reports and ensuing state legislation present
particular problems for the analysis of ideology. They represent a highly
'worked up' form of ideology, which, though having obvious connections with the existing state of ideological and political forces, also has a
partial autonomy from them. Government reports and state legislation
should be seen as constructed according to the rules of a particular
discourse or practice, which will possess its own specificity. A crucial

question here concerns the articulation between dominant *ideologies* and the particular structures of juridical practice, and the mutual determinations of the one level on the other. Marxist theory has, to date, tended to elide the specificity of the *legal* with broader politico-juridical relations. It is for these reasons that we feel it necessary to problematise the status and effectivity of the juridical level, and its position in the functioning of the state, in our particular work here.

However, there remains a real tension between what we have developed conceptually and the empirical moment of our analysis. But we do hold to both the theoretical and the empirical criteria. Theoretical abstractions should be internally consistent, rigorous and self-consciously formulated, but they are not the end-point in the production of 'useful knowledge': 'they are tools to think with, with a definite historical scope of reference . . . derived in relation to particular historical conditions, for the purpose of the analysis of concrete situations' (Johnson, 1978; cf. his chapter in this volume). In that respect we would stress the need for an epistemology which moves from high abstraction to an appropriation of the complexity of the real in thought (see Marx, 1973, p. 101).

Procreation, Labour Power and Sexual Ideologies: The Beveridge Report 1942

The *Beveridge Report*, as a body of proposed legislation, condenses both debates and concern about the rate of procreation with the desirability for a specific kind of labour-power. We wish here to examine the report in terms of these condensations, their articulation with and through particular ideologies and their relations to wider economic, political and ideological forces. First, however, it seems important briefly to situate *Beveridge* historically.

The Committee on Social Insurance and Allied Services, headed by William Beveridge, was set up in June 1941 to make a survey of the existing national scheme of social security. At a general level, demand for such a report and the subsequent enthusiastic response to its proposals must be seen primarily in terms of the economic and political mobilisations of the War, the War's 'popular radicalism' (see Miliband, 1972), recent memories of inter-war conditions, and the middle-class exposure to the still existing poverty and inadequacy of many social services through the experience of evacuation which 'revealed to the whole people the black spots of its social life', (*Economist*, 1 May 1943; cf. *Our Towns*, 1943). Thus *Beveridge* can be seen as articulating a view that already had widespread political support, 'interpreting the spirit of the times' (Harris, 1977, p. 414), though from a government viewpoint there were pragmatic reasons for encouraging consideration of social reforms during the war, and presenting a vision of Reconstruction — primarily the need to foster morale and 'solidarity'.

The report's purported main concern is with tackling Want: one of the five giants on the road to reconstruction — the other four giants being Disease, Ignorance, Squalor and Idleness, to be remedied by a National Health Service, Education, Housing and Full Employment. This concern is crucially and quite explicitly interconnected with a desire to improve the quality and increase the quantity of Britain's labour power. *Beveridge*'s very definition of 'want' as a lack of the means of healty subsistence is hinged to a concept of fitness to *serve* as citizen or worker:

> the aim of the Plan for Social Security is to abolish want by ensuring that every citizen willing to serve according to his powers has at all times an income sufficient to meet his responsibilities . . . The Plan is one to secure income for subsistence in order to make and keep men fit for service [Beveridge, 1943, pp. 165 and 170].

Beveridge takes the existence of want as due primarily to interruption or loss of earning power and secondarily to the failure to relate income during earning to family size:

> Better distribution of purchasing power is required among wage-earners themselves, as between times of earning and not earning, and between times of heavy family responsibilities and of light or no family responsibilities. Such better distribution . . . can increase wealth by maintaining physical vigour (p. 167).

This notion of physical vigour is similar to Rowntree's notion of 'maintenance of physical efficiency', the 'other side' to the idea of physical degeneration central to the Liberal Reforms 1906-11.

Beveridge thus proposed two main elements to its overall assault on want, namely the introduction of National Insurance and of Family Allowances. (*Beveridge* also proposed a supplementary benefits scheme, but it was seen as a residual diminishing safety net). Through an examination of the National Insurance proposals in relation to women, we are able to see how the report's use and reinforcement of the patriarchal ideologies of domesticity and motherhood and its ideological 'placing' of women centrally within the home are crucially related to its concern with the falling birth rate. In a consideration of Children's (or Family) Allowances we can observe how the condensing of the concern with the falling birth rate and the desire for a particular *kind* of labour force are articulated through and to these ideologies and their 'placing' of women.

The report proposes that married women should be defined as a distinct insurance class. This is rationalised through presenting marriage as in itself conveying a new economic status to the married woman, a new status insufficiently recognised under existing insurance schemes. To mark the 'rite de passage' into marriage, *Beveridge* proposes a marriage grant, (although this is not a central part of the Scheme, seen as desirable rather than essential). But *Beveridge*'s Plan does not merely recognise a married woman's new status: 'every woman on marriage will become a *new person*, acquiring new rights and not carrying on into marriage claims to unemployment or disability benefit in respect of contributions made before marriage' (p. 131, our emphasis).

Beveridge is concerned to reinforce and encourage marriage, apparent in the proposed material inducement of the marriage grant, the proposals in relation to childbirth within marriage, and in its ideological construction of marriage as a crucially *vital* occupation and career. However, before considering this ideological construction of marriage, it is important to recognise that *Beveridge*'s proposals have real effects for the materiality of marriage, acting to reinforce the institutionalisation of the married woman's economic dependence on her husband. This reinforcement of dependency is legitimated through the *a priori* assumption that the vast majority of married women are not waged workers. (As we shall discuss later, this assumption has proved erroneous in relation to post-War Britain). However, those married women who are waged workers are to receive lower benefits than single women 'on practical grounds and grounds of equity', namely that a married woman has a husband's earnings on which to depend, (which also means, claims *Beveridge*, that she has a different *attitude* to her work than a single woman), her earnings are more likely to be interrupted by sickness than a single woman, (although, as Land points out, this goes against the Report's notion of 'pooling of risks'), and her earnings are also more likely to be interrupted through childbirth, (thereby, as Wilson (1977, p. 151) remarks, tacitly defining procreation as a disability). For the married woman who does not waged work, her husband's contributions and benefits are paid and received for them both as a team, as a single economic unit.

But despite this proposed reinforcement of economic dependency,

Beveridge explicitly denies that married women are treated as dependents of their husbands: 'the position of housewives . . . is recognized by treating them, not as dependents of their husbands, but as *partners* sharing benefit and pension when there are no earnings to share' (p.52, our emphasis). This forms one aspect of his ideological construction of marriage: the claim that his proposals treat 'man and wife as a team . . . each of whose partners is *equally* essential' (p. 49, our emphasis).

Yet this claim of equality, partnership and teamwork within marriage acts to displace the report's central presentation of marriage in terms of the ideologies of domesticity of motherhood. Throughout, the report defines married women of working age as housewives, irrespective of whether or not they are waged workers. By this label alone married women have already been constructed ideologically as located within the home. This ideology of domesticity[3] is extended and reinforced by *Beveridge*'s insistence that housewives are occupied persons (prior to *Beveridge* the census included unwaged married women among the unoccupied), carrying out work 'which is vital though unpaid, without which their husbands could not do their paid work and without which the nation could not continue' (p.49). The ideology is further extended by *Beveridge*'s assertion (which we have already mentioned), that the vast majority of women would cease to be waged workers on marriage.

In the report's construction of marriage it is however the ideology of motherhood which is at the core. Motherhood, presented as the 'natural' focus of marriage, as a *duty* of married women, is directly encouraged, materially and ideologically. *Beveridge*, explicitly addressing the popular concern with the falling birth rate (see Scott James, 1943), asserts that maternity, as 'the principal object of marriage' (p. 50), is not adequately provided for. It proposes child allowances, and a maternity grant for all married women on the birth of each child, along with medical attention and midwifery and nursing services as part of the comprehensive health service (p. 132). Further, a maternity benefit is to be given to married women 'gainfully occupied', on condition that they give up their waged work for the time being.

> In the national interest it is important that the interruption by childbirth should be as complete as possible; the expectant mother should be under no economic pressure to continue work as long as she can and to return to it as soon as she can [p. 49].

Beveridge proposes the maternity benefit to be for thirteen weeks at a rate more than 50 per cent above the normal unemployment rate for men and single women. Hence *Beveridge* displays a very explicit concern with the qualitative conditions under which a child is born. This concern is highlighted in the debate in the report as to whether unmarried mothers, whom *Beveridge* wrongly supposed would remain insignificant in numbers, should be eligible for maternity grants and benefits. Although it is felt that, given the interest of the *child*, unmarried mothers probably should be so entitled, we are reminded that 'the interest of the state is not in getting children born, but in getting them born in conditions which secure to them the *proper* domestic environment and care' (p. 135, our emphasis). By implication, childbirth outside marriage is deemed not to secure the necessary proper domestic environment. This reveals the report's concern with the yoking of sexuality to the family, couched within a definite position on 'immorality'. For example, a separate allowance for deserted, separated and divorced wives is recommended only on condition that they are not responsible for the breakdown of the marriage. Concern as to the welfare of the child is also apparent in the proposals for widowhood. While permanent pensions will no longer be granted to a widow of working age without children (marking a definite shift in attitudes towards the widow), a widow with care of dependent children will be granted a guardian benefit and children's allowance.

In the assault on Want, *Beveridge* sees Family Allowances as a crucial part of the securing of a national minimum for families of every size; that is to say, family allowances are meant as a form of income redistribution in addition to the social insurance system (but an income redistribution within the working class, rather than between classes). Yet Beveridge himself admits, both in the report and elsewhere, that his proposal for Family Allowances has further objectives:

> With its present rate of reproduction, the British race cannot continue; means of reversing the recent course of the birth rate must be found . . . children's allowances can help to restore the birth rate, both by making it possible for parents who desire more children to bring them into the world without damaging the chances of those already born, and as a signal of the national interest in children, setting the tone of public opinion . . . The foundations of a healthy life must be laid in childhood [Beveridge, 1942, p. 154].[4]

and

If the sole objective of Family Allowances were the abolition of want, then such a saving [reducing Family Allowances from 8 shillings to 4 shillings] might be worth consideration. But in my view it would be wrong for two other reasons: as narrowing the gap between earning and benefit and . . . in order to improve both the quality and quantity of the population [Beveridge, 1943, p.125].

During World War II, Family Allowances won support from the government for reasons which John MacNicol (1978) convincingly argues had less to do with family poverty (despite impressions given in the *Beveridge Report*), and far more to do with management of the economy. By the late 1930's both the Government bodies dealing with the able-bodied unemployed, the Unemployed Assistance Board and the Unemployment Insurance Statutory Committee (chaired by Beveridge), had virtually come round to a recommendation of family allowances, as the solution to the problem of benefit/wages overlap. And for the government it was the cheapest and most desirable solution to the problem. The other alternative would have been inconceivable: government intervention into large areas of industry in order to guarantee a nutritionally defensible minimum wage (MacNicol, 1978, pp. 191-2, 197). In the short term family allowances were seen as a means of controlling wages and thereby reducing the risk of runaway wartime inflation; in the long term it was thought that in any post-war re-organised system of social security, rates of unemployment benefit and assistance should be appreciably lower than low wage levels in order to produce labour mobility and work incentives essential to an economy geared to full employment. (Full employment was the most important of the three assumptions on which *Beveridge*'s plan rested).

The Report is of course not explicit as to the view, based on Keynesian economics (see Harris, 1977, pp. 408-12), that family allowances would reduce the need and demand for overall wage increases. (In fact many trade unionists accepted the introduction of allowances only on condition that they were financed out of general taxation, and not by the employers, fearing that this would result in the depression of wages). But *Beveridge* is more explicit as to the concern with encouraging the work ethic and labour mobility — both elements in a desire for a particular *quality* of labour power. In the inter-war years, dependants' allowances were added to unemployment pay but not to wages, thereby supposedly threatening the work incentive of men with large families: 'it is dangerous to allow benefit during unemployment or disability to equal or exceed earnings during work. But, without allowances for children during earning and not earning alike, this danger cannot be avoided' (Beveridge, 1942, p. 154). 'Idleness which destroys wealth and corrupts men, whether they are well-fed or not . . .' (Ibid, p. 170).

It is in part the concern with the maintenance of a man's work incentive that encourages *Beveridge*'s proviso that children's allowances should not be paid to the first child. Also involved here, quite explicitly, is the desire that financial responsibility should not be totally removed from the parents (pp. 155-7). In relation to labour mobility, *Beveridge* notes that 'the maintenance of employment . . . will be impossible without greater fluidity of labour and other resources in the aftermath of war than has been achieved in the past' (Beveridge, 1942 p.154; also see p. 19).

It is clear therefore that the question of Family Allowances for *Beveridge* includes a concern with the reproduction of labour power both quantitatively (responding to the falling birth rate), and qualitatively (a labour force both mobile and imbued with the work ethic). We would argue that the ideologies of motherhood and domesticity are in articulation with both these aspects of reproduction: not only have they an obvious relation to a drive to increase family size, but they can also be seen as related to questions of mobility and work incentive. Women's location within the home as a non-waged worker makes for a mobile family unit: it is the husband's labour which is required to be mobile; if the woman/wife was to work outside the home as well, this might act as a brake on his mobility. Further, as Penny Summerfield (1977) illustrates in relation to the demand for *married women*'s labour in the war, women's role in the family runs counter to demands for their geographic mobility. Also, for the family unit to remain 'stable' in the face of increased labour mobility, its stability needs to be reinforced. Stress on ideologies of motherhood and domesticity address this need for reinforcement; the family is seen as a 'still point in a turning world'. In relation to the work ethic, an ideology locating the woman within the home as an economic dependant of her husband acts to reinforce such an ethic in that a man has his wife as well as his children to maintain.

It is important to recognise the ways in which the proposals in *Beveridge* in relation to women, particularly married women, are presented as both desirable and obvious. Firstly, they are backed up by certain assumptions and ideologies, such as the ideologies of motherhood and domesticity, which are couched in terms of common sense and public opinion, with frequence reference to certain principles being 'in accord with the sentiments of British people' or with 'the

general stream of public opinion'. Secondly these ideologies are
presented to us as empirical, common-sensical facts and thereby
naturalised: 'Naturalisation', as Bromley (1977, p. 33) points out,
following Gramsci, is 'a key mechanism of common-sense thought' in
that 'it closes knowledge, ends debate and *dissolves contradiction*' (our
emphasis). Yet reference to the British people is further extended;
speaking the language of representative democracy, *Beveridge* constructs
a notion of the people as united around the nation, the national family.
Marriage and motherhood, as previously (Davin, 1978), receive their
ultimate legitimisation through being presented as a vital service and
duty of British women for the interest of the nation, paralleling the
service and duty of the British nation to defend its country and Empire
at times of war. The 'people' are addressed gender-specifically, with
gender-specific duties and responsibilities as British citizens. For women,
responsibility lies centrally in motherhood. Marriage, constituted with
its twin ideologies of domesticity and above all motherhood, is
located within the nation and thereby subordinated to it. A few of the
quotes already given have indicated the appeal to the national interest:
'the great majority of married women must be regarded as occupied
on work which is vital though unpaid . . . without which the *nation*
could not continue' (p. 49, our emphasis). 'In the *national* interest it is
important that the interruption of childbirth should be as complete as
possible' (p. 49, our emphasis), 'children's allowances act . . . as a
signal to the *national* interest in children, setting the tone of public
opinion' (p. 154, our emphasis).

    Yet it is perhaps in his view that: 'in the next thirty years housewives
as mothers have vital work to do in ensuring the adequate continuance
of the British race and of British ideals in the world' (p. 53), that we
find the ideological welding of marriage, domesticity, motherhood,
Nation, Empire and eugenics at its most succinct in *Beveridge*. We
should also note that any concern with over- or under-population is in
part a political and ideological concern. Anxiety about Britain's falling
birthrate is directly related to Britain's diminishing economic, political
and ideological imperialist power, as well as fears of labour shortage.

    As we have already mentioned, *Beveridge* did not predict that the post-
War period would see an expansion of married women's participation in
the labour market. Yet even during the war there was already awareness
in some quarters that there would be a demand for women's labour
after the war. For example, an inquiry made in 1944 (Thomas, 1944)
for the Ministry of Reconstruction, directly addresses itself to the

question of working women's attitudes towards post-War employment, and recognises that there would probably be labour shortages requiring female employment. Further, given that *Beveridge* is centrally committed to the establishment of *male* full employment, it perhaps seems strange that the fact that women might constitute a reserve army was overlooked. However, it could be argued that stress on ideologies of motherhood and domesticity fits in with women's role as a reserve army of labour — work being seen as secondary (cheap), dispensable and ideologically not part of a woman's 'natural' role, given also that the post-War labour shortage was not expected to last. Yet ideological and material inducements to remain within the home can actually work against a role for women as an industrial reserve army in so far as women may not find waged work sufficiently appealing to enter the labour market at all.

In this context it is relevant briefly to consider the way in which the contradiction between woman's role as reproducer and her role as waged worker is addressed in another and later government report. In the Report of the Royal Commission on Population (1949) a population policy is formulated, combining on the one hand a desire to encourage larger families, with, on the other, a perception of women's participation in the work force as desirable given the post-War labour shortage. Immigration is explicitly seen as undesirable (*Population Report*, pp. 225). In addition it is recognised that fertility control is now an accepted part of married life: 'Public policy should assume, and seek to encourage, the spread of voluntary parenthood . . . ' (Ibid, p. 227). Thus its body of proposals includes both greater financial assistance to families (in the form, for example, of high Family Allowances), in part to encourage larger families, and provision of such social services for mothers and children as home helps and more nurseries, both of which would of course facilitate women's entry into the labour force. These proposals are combined with a recommendation that 'advice on contraception to married persons wanting it should be accepted as a duty of the National Health Service' (p. 229). It is accepted first that voluntary fertility control should not necessarily imply smaller families, if there is adequate provision for mothers and children, and secondly that having larger families does not necessarily restrict women from entering the labour market if there is both sufficient provision of child-care facilities and access to contraception in order to space births rationally. By the 1950s however, with the rise of Bowlbyism, and the notion of maternal deprivation, and a general reinforcement of the ideology of motherhood, disapproval of the 'working mother' again came to the fore.

Beveridge, on the other hand, has a problematic other than the management of this 'contradiction' for women. *Beveridge* can perhaps be seen as facing two ways at once: back to notions of dependency and deserving/undeserving poor inherent in the Poor Law traditions; forward to an era demanding a more mobile 'modern' labour force, operating under a hegemony of a consensual 'equality of opportunity', in which women's work is conceived of as 'equal' and complementary to men's, but constructed as 'equal but different'. We would maintain that above all, it is the ideologies around women's role that are brought in to 'negotiate' these two sides to *Beveridge*'s vision of a particular kind of reconstruction.

The Education of Girls or the Reproduction of Sexed Labour Power

Newsom's *Education of Girls* (1948) has a status rather different from either the *Beveridge* or *Wolfenden Reports* since it represents Newsom's personal views and is written in a more conversational, idiosyncratic and sometimes sensationalist style; written with the 'intention to attract attention and if necessary to shock'.

At the time of writing Newsom was a Schools' Inspector, and was later to be the chairman (*sic*) of the committee which produced the Report of the Minister of Education's Central Advisory Council: *Half Our Future* (1963); a fairly clear, if not direct trajectory can be traced from the recommendations made to the institution or intensification of specific courses for girls. Newsom's *Education of Girls* came at a point in the debates around education when the concern to provide education suited to inherited (sex specific) ability was shifting towards concerns with the individual child in relation to her/his future occupation as the *Norwood Report* (1943) made explicit: the function of education was seen as being 'to help each individual realise the powers of his [*sic*] personality, body, mind and spirit in a thorough active membership of society'. This, together with the developing concepts of 'child-centredness' and 'relevance', encouraged the placing of the child at the centre of education, as, for example, in the *Crowther Report* (1959) but primarily in *Half Our Future* (1963) which in many ways systematised 'progressive' teaching methods. This shift can be located within the general social democratic move towards 'equality of opportunity'. Many of the concerns expressed in the *Newsom Report – Half Our Future –* can be seen in *The Education of Girls*, though the latter's overt concern with biological determination locates it at an early stage within this shift; and in some senses it can be said to mark one of its privileged moments. The book is important both for the ideological shifts it makes in the debates around the sexuality of girls and the implications it has for their education, and for the ways in which this shift is made. To quote from the 'Preface' by R.A. Butler, '(Newsom's) work contains a marked degree of erudition and much common sense' (Newsom, 1948, p. 9) and it is on this 'commonsensical' approach to the subject of girls' education that we want to concentrate here. Our concern is with the ways in which ideologies of motherhood and domesticity — of femininity — are articulated through common sense, by means of the assumption of a shared understanding with the (male) reader in order to make them seem obvious. Thus the 'Preface' promises, in a 'wise and humorous way', simply common sense.

An immediate example is provided in the first paragraph of the book, in which Newsom 'lays down' 'the *assumptions* on which the arguments have been based' (our emphasis).

> The first assumption . . . is that men and women have marked physiological and psychological differences as individuals even though they have a great deal in common. To *the ordinary reader* this may seem *a blinding glimpse of the obvious*, but I assure *him* that many learned writers, mainly female, have argued that, apart from certain minor differences in the organs of human reproduction, men and women are identical in their physical needs and mental processes [p. 12; our emphasis].

This appeal to the common reader, together with the reference to *certain* minor differences in human reproductive organs is an important mechanism for getting across ideas which Newsom is fully aware are controversial. Newsom is attempting here to shift the ideological ground upon which female sexuality is thought through in education, and by making connections with popularly held assumption and beliefs to gain consent for the sex specific education to which he is giving support. We do not want to imply a conspiratorial motivation for these suggestions: they represent a way of making sense of certain real relations between the sexes, such as the production and reproduction of sexed labour power that exist through patriarchal structures. Given the debate around the school's function in social reproduction (Bourdieu and Passeron, or the work of the CCCS Education Group) and the qualitative reproduction of labour power, Newsom's book offers clear examples of the ways in which certain, often contradictory, ideologies are negotiated — made sense of — and become part of popular knowledge. For example, the notion of a child's individual development and the view of girls as a single homogeneous group, defined according to sex are contradictory; as are conceptualisations of the individual needs and interests of pupils as against the 'needs of industry' or the 'national interest'. Newsom articulates these ideologies around one main function of the school: the production and reproduction of sexed labour power, seen ideologically in terms of social reproduction — the reproduction of a community with sexed subjects.

Such tensions around different ideologies are negotiated mainly through the ideology of domesticity and motherhood, always linked to marriage (and to the national interest) and hinged on biological differences but *understood* in terms of complementarity: women or girls are 'equal but different'. The argument is premised on a supposed achieved feminist victory for equality of the sexes and Newsom uses this assertion of 'equality' as the basis for proposing further superficially non-discriminatory, differentiation between the sexes in education, though nonetheless later condemning 'this mad passion for equality, this modern perversion, [whose] corrupting influence dates from the end of the last century' (p. 11).

Newsom hails the 1944 Education Act as a 'moment of triumph' for those working for equal opportunity in education (he cites Frances Buss, Emily Davies and Dorothea Beale) and as embodying the unconditional surrender of male privilege. This is despite the fact that the *Norwood Report* (1943), which led to the setting up of the tri-partite system under the 1944 Act had by its innovative concern with the individual child and her/his 'special interests and aptitudes' demarcated areas of 'natural interest' according to gender. It split the school population into three 'levels of ability' but it was the third level, that of the Secondary Modern school, that the *Norwood Report* had seen as providing the most suitable education for girls; Ann-Marie Wolpe points out that 'only when they spoke in terms of domestic subjects did they make specific reference to girls and clearly they tied this up with their future marital roles' (1974, p. 145). Newsom's insistence that 'for half a century women's education has been interpreted as the ability to perform the same functions as men' is clearly incorrect; the effect of his work is to shift the nature of the education of girls more firmly in the direction of their functions as future home-makers and mothers, not simply to initiate it as he suggests. The *Hadow Report* on 'Differentiation of the Curriculum for Boys and Girls respectively in Secondary Schools' (1923) to which Newsom refers, did recommend on physical grounds that girls should take the School Certificate and Higher Certifi-

cate a year later than boys . . . ' (Newsom, 1948, pp. 19-20), and the
Hadow Report also comments (Newsom does not quote this) that

> . . . the boys subsequently overtake the girls in power of
> reasoning. On the emotional side, however, (their) interests are
> moving further and further apart . . . This difference is doubtless
> largely due to differences in the degree to which common instincts
> are inherited by boys and girls respectively . . . For instance, the
> maternal, affectionate and submissive instincts are stronger in girls,
> the hunting, fighting and assertive instincts are more marked in boys
> (pp. 52-3).

The development in the tone and style in *The Education of Girls* is a
clear indication of the way in which Newsom gradually shifts his
emphasis from 'how things are' to 'how they ought to be'. Woman's
main role is as Mother, he says, and goes on: 'I am not arguing that this
is a desirable state of affairs or forgetting that it may be radically
altered in the future. I affirm that at present, *and for the past two
thousand years* it is a true generalisation' (p. 12; our emphasis). His
assertion about 'how things are' is undercut by the reference to the past
two thousand years i.e. since the existence of Christianity and Christian
morality — what we know as civilisation — constructing woman's 'role'
as 'natural' in a civilised community.

The stress in the book on keeping together the family and on home-
making is presented as woman's *biological* destiny, rather than as her *social*
function. Skills and domesticity are given a biological basis; women who
do not conform to this are assumed to have a biological malfunction —
femininity is the fulfilment of woman's natural, biological function of
motherhood; a position which parallels *Beveridge*'s notion of the duty
and sacrifice of woman as mother.

> To work through others is not derogatory to human dignity . . . this
> mission of women is a far greater one than can be fulfilled by
> attaining the minor political or professional successes, which in the
> past generation they have imitatively adopted from men, a tendency
> fostered by those who have failed to perform — not necessarily
> through any fault of their own — *the essentially feminine function in
> society* . . . almost all intelligent women agree with this assumption
> and . . . those who do not . . . however able and intelligent they
> may be are *normally deficient* in the quality of womanliness and the
> particular physical and mental attributes of their sex [p. 109; our

emphasis].

These 'deficient' women are clearly defined as a minority group by the appeal to the (normal) reader, and to 'normal' intelligent women's opinions, and Newsom's view of femininity, and the conceptualisation of domesticity and motherhood supported by his argument can clearly be seen as the reference point — that of reproductive heterosexuality — for understanding such 'deviations'. He points out how women in the professions of teaching and nursing can 'sublimate' or 'transfer' their maternal instinct; these occupations have a 'natural affinity with woman's *biological function* in society.' However, the non-fulfilment of the maternal instincts and therefore the repression of 'normal sexuality' can produce 'unfeminine' women, 'involuntary virgins . . . who feel they've missed their way in life', who may direct the girls they teach towards ' a communal, woman-ridden world' (p. 146). This warning is extended to cover other 'bitter' women:

> The woman who is unhappily married should be kept out of the schools, for she is apt to be bitter and resentful . . . such tragedies are often due to major *failings in adjustment and development*, and they produce states of mind which are both *infectious* and undesirable (p. 146; our emphasis).

A woman's failure in marriage is seen to be biologically based, often related to her attractiveness or feminine qualities. Teachers 'should be for the most part attractive women who, even if unmarried, look as though they could have been married if they had liked . . . ' (p. 149). If female sexuality is constructed as the fulfilment or the potential fulfilment of maternal instinct, then logically for Newsom lesbians need to be kept out of the schools:

> if children take for their models adults who have not progressed beyond the stage [of admiring one's own sex], *they may themselves become incapable of healthy growth* . . . When the emotions *should* be taking a heterosexual direction *the companionship of the abnormal is stultifying*. This danger . . . is greater in girls' schools because, contrary to general belief, the effects of homosexuality are even more serious in women than in men [p. 149; our emphasis].

In the classroom, therefore, the emphasis on domesticity needs to be increased.

In grammar schools, it is argued, girls tend to be concerned overmuch with their careers, 'forgetful of Samuel Johnson's dictum that "a man is better pleased when he has a good dinner upon the table than when his wife talks Greek." . . . to produce an 'Honard a l'Americaine' [a what?] to perfection needs as much wit as to construe one of the more obscure passages of Bérénice' [p. 82].

Part of the argument for an education that involves the teaching of domestic skills is Newsom's (admittedly progressive) recognition of work in the home as work; and his perception of it as something to be learned. But this is also designated as *women*'s work by the stress on 'how things are' and the contradictory reference points of instinct and biological function. This contradiction is mediated in part, as in *Beveridge*, by the notion of marriage as a career and of housewives as occupied persons. Being a housewife is

an *occupation* of peculiar importance, requiring many skills, which is practiced by 85 per cent of the women in this country for the major part of their adult lives . . . the part played by education in this *career* [is] helping her to be more *effectively engaged* upon it [p. 28; our emphasis].

Newsom criticises 'the tendency to underestimate the skill and intelligence needed to run an efficient home' but returns to arguing for a biological base for these skills. He recognises the truth (in part) of the arguments that housework is drudgery, but mobilises the notion of free will premises on woman's 'equality' to justify it:

No woman in this age of equality of opportunity, of careers open to all, of equal education and political rights . . . is compelled to get married and accept the degradation involved. Yet she chooses it deliberately as her main occupation . . . [p. 25]

The emphasis on the 'proper development' and re-learning of skills (which Newsom applies specifically to working class girls in *Half Our Future*) together with the emphasis on essentially middle-class standards and taste, is aimed primarily at making the girl a better wife and mother. This is understood through Newsom's view of the mother as a consumer, and therefore as essential to the economic as well as the moral wellbeing of the nation, and of the declining Empire:

our standards of design, and therefore our very continuance as a

great commercial nation, will depend on our education of the
consumer to the point where *she* rejects the functionally futile and
aesthetically inept and demands what is fitting and beautiful . . . It
is not an exaggeration to say that woman as purchaser holds the
future standards of living in this country in her hands . . . If she
buys in ignorance then our national standards will degenerate . . .
[Our] good designs must be bought, both to encourage the manu-
facturers and to extinguish the producers of inferior commodities
which desecrate our homes and destroy our reputation abroad
[p. 102; our emphasis] .

Within the family, *Newsom* clearly links women's servicing role with
the 'national interest', both economically and morally: girls as *'the
mother(s) of future generations of our race'* are educated for that
function. The family (microcosm) becomes the *national* family. So
Butler can take up and extend Newsom's ideas in the light of the post-
War labour shortage:

Even though our girls may be taught to be good cooks and mothers,
we cannot, with our present limited manpower resources, risk
leaving undeveloped the mind of any girl who can *serve* her homeland
as well as Mr. Newsom would wish her to *serve* her home [p. 10;
our emphasis] .

Sexual 'Deviancy' and Sexual Ideology — The Wolfenden Report of the Committee on Homosexual Offences and Prostitution, 1957

We have already attempted to abstract the political, legal and ideological restrictions surrounding 'deviant' or 'perverse' sexualities in their
relation to the centrality awarded to heterosexual genital sexuality
organised around procreation. Further, we have attempted to define
those restrictions and controls as a particular variant of patriarchal
relations. State legislation, sociology and the political writings which
have emerged from the Gay Movement and the Women's Movement
have consistently located the definition of sexual 'deviancy' or
'perversion' in its relation to the norm of heterosexual relations
legitimised within the family. Specifically, it has been in relation to
the organisation of reproductive sexuality within the family that other
sexualities have been classified, defined and controlled. Reproductive
sexuality as an ideological construct represents the process whereby
procreation (under determinate conditions of heterosexual monogamy
within the family) is awarded a privileged place in the definitions of

other forms of sexuality and sexual practice.

However, we have also insisted that there remains a tension between what we have attempted theoretically in our approach to the questions of procreation and the control of sexuality and our understanding of the empirical instances we examine. The *Wolfenden Report*, in both its sections on homosexuality and prostitution, does touch on the same matrix of practices: the key issues of sexuality, the family, marriage and procreation. Yet *Wolfenden* cannot be understood in any simple sense as a set of recommendations for legislation to control forms of sexual practice which pose a threat to reproductive sexuality, and ultimately to the reproduction of labour power. As with *Beveridge* and *Newsom*, *Wolfenden* must be located historically and understood as acted on by a multiplicity of determinations (economic, political, legal and ideological) not all of which are in any sense concerned with the reproduction of labour power. Further, *Wolfenden* is crossed by nationalist and imperialist ideologies, and has a political and ideological relation to the part played by 'reformism' in the post-War construction of hegemony (Hall, 1978b), while in a sense the central unifying principle of the report is the conception of the relation of morality and the law — the distinction between *public* decency and *private* moral conduct. None of these wider articulations can be reduced to any 'essential' concern of the Report with control over procreation — though they may stand in some relation to the reproductive sphere.

The ideological centrality of heterosexual, monogamous familial relations do, however, surface in a quite particular way in the Report. *Male* homosexuality (and the investigations of the Committee are almost exclusively gender specific, ostensibly for the reason that lesbianism is not defined as an offence under criminal law), is structured in relation to 'a general loosening of former moral standards' (Wolfenden, p. 20). The structured absence of any discussion of lesbianism relates crucially to the overall position of women — and to the absence of the comparable growth of a sub-structure for lesbians (Weeks, 1977, pp. 87-111). The Wolfenden Committee are emphatic in deploring 'this damage to what we regard as the basic unit of society', and explicitly define 'deviant' sexual practices as all being 'reprehensible from the point of view of harm to the family' (*Report*, p. 22). In that context it is not surprising that 'preventive measures and research to diminish the incidence of homosexual offences' should include the continuing stress on 'the desirability of a healthy home background' (Ibid., p. 77). More particularly though, the ideological primacy awarded to heterosexual genital sexuality is seen as a quite specific point of reference for the moral censure and condemnation of homosexual acts themselves. The Report contains a highly detailed discussion and classification of the particular groups of homosexual offences: buggery, attempted buggery, indecent assault, acts of gross indecency, to soliciting and importuning. Much of the debate in this section centres on the question of retaining buggery as a separate offence, in that: 'it is particularly objectionable because it involves coitus and this simulates more nearly than any other homosexual act the normal act of sexual intercourse' (Ibid., p. 33). Thus ideological and legal restrictions are concerned not only with the general social and moral questions of public order and decency, they are in *Wolfenden* extended to include discussion and intimate control of the physical sexual act itself.

Wolfenden presents prostitution as a social fact deplorable to the great majority of ordinary people, an 'evil, which any society which claims to be civilised should seek to rid itself of', but admits that prostitution can be ended 'only through measures directed to a better understanding of the nature and obligation of sexual relationships and to raising of the social and moral outlook of society as a whole' (p. 80). It perceives this to be the work not of criminal law but of church, mental health organisations and the institution of moral welfare, family welfare and child and marriage guidance. Yet the aetiology of prostitution also has a more psychologistic aspect, with a notion of the 'human weaknesses which cause the customer to seek the prostitute and the prostitute to meet the demand' (p. 100). Certainly in relation to an understanding of the *prostitute*, *Wolfenden* does resort to psychology. 'In these days economic factors can not account for it [prostitution] to any large or decisive extent' (p. 79). This is of course the 'age of affluence', the 1950's, when poverty was widely thought to have disappeared. The Report therefore argues that there is 'some additional psychological element in the personality of the individual woman who becomes a prostitute' (p. 79). There is no interest as to what the psychology of the prostitute's client might be. Yet this absence, in addition to the notion put forward of prostitution as due in part to human weakness, can be taken as implying a tacit acceptance of what was undoubtedly (and still is) a 'commonsensical' view of the sexuality of the man as 'naturally' involving a greater sex drive than that of the woman. As Mary McIntosh (1978a) notes: 'A common view, that of the "double standard" of sexual morality, is that frequenting prostitutes, perhaps more than any other forms of promiscuity, is forgivable in the male, while being a prostitute, again perhaps more than any other forms of promiscuity, is totally reprehensible in the female' (p. 53).

Further, their stress on the visibility of prostitution acts to legitimate the curbing of the actions of the *prostitute* rather than those of her male client. Prostitutes 'parade themselves more habitually and openly than their prospective customers, and do by their continual presence affront the sense of decency of the ordinary citizen' (p. 87). As if to excuse the double standard they attempt to cover themselves with the aside that although 'from a moral point of view there may be little or nothing to choose between the prostitute and her customer' (p. 87), it is not the duty of the law to concern itself with immorality as such, but with questions of public decency. The operation of double standards is in fact most apparent in relation to their brief discussion of kerb-crawling. They feel that although it 'is undoubtedly a nuisance to many *well-behaved* women . . . , the difficulties of proof would be consider-able, and the possibility of a very damaging charge being levelled at an innocent motorist must also be borne in mind' (p. 87; our emphasis). They thus feel unable to make any recommendations.

The prostitute is defined by implication as 'badly behaved' in contra-distinction to the 'well-behaved' woman. The possibility of a woman being wrongly accused of being a prostitute is not taken as problematic, presumably because the committee feel that there is little danger in mistaking a 'well-behaved' woman for the badly behaved, the prostitute. This dualism between the virgin and the whore is of course centrally located within common sense. The idea that they can in no way be confused is contained in the very fact of their ideological polarity. It is by means of the dichotomy posed between the well-behaved woman and the prostitute that we are able to consider the way in which prosti-tution is situated *vis-à-vis* the family. The contrast of 'well-behaved' woman/prostitute contains the implication that the former is located within the private sphere (namely the family), with her sexuality sanctioned ultimately only within the family, while the latter is located in the public sphere, out on the streets, openly selling her sexuality.

The Report attempts to place debates around homosexuality in the broader context of the aftermath of the 'conditions of wartime' and 'the emotional insecurity, community instability and weakening of family inherent in the social changes of our civilisation' (p. 20). The references may be oblique in the Report itself, but we should be alert to the shifts and changes in the matrix of sexual and 'moral' practices touched on by *Wolfenden*. For 'emotional insecurity' read problem families and deprived children (Bowlby, 1953), for 'community instability' read the breakdown of the old pre-War patterns of community (Young and Wilmott, 1957), for the 'weakening of the family' read the contradictions thrown up by the increase in waged work among married women, the concern over the growth of antagonistic youth cultures, (Cohen, 1972) and the faint beginnings of sexual permissiveness and 'libertyville' (Gamble, 1974).

In relation to prostitution, we suggest that its greater 'visibility' in this period, the mid-1950s, is in part related to the fact that the 1950s saw the ascendance of the ideologies of motherhood, and to a lesser extent domesticity, as expounded in the *Beveridge Report* and taken up and expanded in a particular way by Bowlby and others, specifically in terms of the irresponsibility of the working mother and the risks of maternal deprivation. It is in this context that the prostitute can be seen as a woman not merely selling her sexuality, but also as visibly flouting the ideologies around the centrality of woman as wife, home-maker and mother, with her sexuality tied to her role as reproducer. Yet there is another way in which prostitution can perhaps be seen as acting as a challenge and a threat. In the 1950s 'there was a new stress on the duty of the married couple to provide each other with sexual pleasure as a cement of the relationship' (Weeks, 1977 p. 158). The idea of a good sex life as cementing family life was reinforced by attitudes towards contraception, which was seen primarily as a means of raising one's standard of living within the family rather than for use outside marriage (Family Planning Association, 1957). Unlike the discussion of prostitution in the 1950s, the debates around the Contagious Diseases Acts of the 1860s, true to Victorian morality, viewed the middle-class wife as basically asexual, thus legitimising the 'sexually frustrated' husband's resort to prostitution. The 1950s however, could in no way hold to such a legitimisation. We might speculate that prostitution in the 1950s was seen as a direct threat to the family and the sanctioning of pleasurable sex within this sphere.

Yet it would be fundamentally misguided to regard the relation between sexual ideologies and the family and procreation as constituting the determinate organising principle of *Wolfenden.* A cursory glance at the set of ideologies contained in the Report should reveal that it is not concerned solely with the classification of homosexual practices and prostitution from the point of legitimised procreation and sexuality. It is these other ideological configurations that should direct us outwards, in a movement away from the specific concern with sexuality and pro-creation, to the wider political, economic and ideological shifts of the post-War period. *Wolfenden* is located within those overall shifts of the post-War years; it contributes to the movements and 'social changes in our civilisation' in its re-definition of the mode and limits of control of sexual practice. It is in fact a highly significant moment in the restructuring of the field of morality and sexual conduct, and as such it does 'prepare the ground' (though not unproblematically, and certainly not in any evolutionary sense) for the vast increase in 'permissive' legislation which post-dates it. The emotionally-charged parliamentary debates which immediately followed the publication of the Report serve as a useful indicator of the wider set of ideologies which are condensed in *Wolfenden*. Opponents of the Committee's recommendations on homosexuality (that henceforward homosexual acts between consenting adult males should no longer be punishable under criminal law), continually orchestrate sexual 'deviancy' with the themes of nationalism and imperialism. *Wolfenden*'s recommendations on homosexuality are not enacted in legislation until The Sexual Offences Act of 1967, while the 'tighter' recommendations on prostitution are incorporated into The Street Offences Act in 1959. Homosexual law reform is opposed not only on the grounds of its affront to the family and heterosexuality, but also in view of its threat to the 'moral fibre', the 'physique of the nation' (see Lord Winterton to the House of Lords, in *Hansard*, 19 May 1954, and statements by Lord Montgomery, quoted in Montgomery-Hyde, 1970, p. 262).

If we do attempt to define a chief organising principle in *Wolfenden* — a factor which focuses and condenses the multiple concerns around a common nucleus of meaning — then it should be located in its concern with the law-morality couplet. It is the point of reference for both sections of the Report, and further, it is the principal theme which orchestrates the concern with the sphere of the family, sexuality and reproduction with the wider concerns of criminality, the State, and ultimately, with the social and political shifts of the period.

The Committee was originally set up in response to the growing visibility of homosexuality and prostitution; as the Report itself states: it was 'a response to the demand of public opinion that the streets must be cleaned up' (p. 81). Yet its wider articulations reach out beyond the immediate historical particularities. Stuart Hall, in his judicious use of Foucault's study of criminality *Discipline and Punish* (Foucault, 1977) has located the Report's primary significance in its construction of 'a new regulatory dispensation of the power to punish or not to punish, to regulate by law or leave to the self-regulation of contracting parties' (Hall, 1978b). Certainly it is clear that an attempted re-working or re-statement of the law's relation to sexual and moral conduct is an explicit part of the Report's concern. The second chapter

entitled 'Approaches to the Problem' contains what Wolfenden himself has referred to as the Report's 'underlying philosophy' (Wolfenden,
1976, p. 138). This section defines quite particularly the terms and
limits of its investigation – the Committee is appointed to consider:
'the *law* and practice relating to homosexual *offences*' and 'the *law* and
practice relating to *offences against the criminal law* in connection
with prostitution and solicitation for immoral purposes' (Report, p. 7;
our emphases). In accordance with that principle, the function of the
law in the field of sexuality and morality is, for *Wolfenden*, essentially
public: 'to preserve public order and decency, to protect the citizen
from what is offensive and injurious, and to provide safeguards against
exploitation and corruption of others' (Ibid., pp. 9-10). But the
Committee is also explicit on that area of conduct which, in its view, is
not law's concern:

> It is not . . . the function of the law to interfere in *the private lives*
> *of citizens*, or to seek to enforce any particular pattern of
> behaviour, further than is necessary to carry out the purposes we
> have outlined [Ibid., p. 10; our emphasis].

It is in this explicit statement on the role and effectiveness of the
law in relation to the public/private dimension that *Wolfenden* on
homosexuality redefines and reworks the nature of legal intervention in
the field. In marking that differentiation the Report initiates for homosexuality a new relation between what in sexual and moral terms is
public and what is private – between what is punishable by the State
as sexual irregularity, and the space given over to the personal responsibility and consent of 'mature agents'. Further, in initiating that shift
for homosexuality it also redefines the terms on which power is
exercised in the two spheres, between what is legally punishable as a
criminal offence, and what is privately 'permitted', though still subject
to 'extra-juridical' forms of control.

Certainly the history of state intervention in the sphere of sexual
relations and practices does not reveal, prior to *Wolfenden*, the opening
of that 'permissive space'. In the nineteenth century the 'workers'
instincts of self-preservation' were an explicit concern of the legal arm
of the state. Control may often have been monolithic and undifferentiated (as indicated by continual references to a catch-all term like
'vice' to cover a multiplicity of sexual practices), but the latter part of
the nineteenth century saw increasing state intervention in this sphere,
either directly (through legislation concerned with the regulation of

prostitution in the Contagious Diseases Acts, the raising of the age of consent, control of male homosexuality, and legislation on marriage and divorce)[5] or as the concern surfaces as a recurrent moral theme in other reports and parliamentary Acts (e.g. bastardy and illegitimacy in the 1834 Poor Law Report, the moral concern with female sexuality in the Factory Acts, and concern over the control of working-class sexual practices in legislation on Public Health, Housing and Sanitation). This latter 'tradition' of legislation is carried through into *Beveridge*, where the construction of particular ideologies of motherhood and femininity also contains explicit censure of those who stand outside the ideological definitions.

Wolfenden in its section on homosexuality does quite clearly mark a shift in the form and effectiveness of the legal intervention of the State in the field. It is 'permissive' in that it opens up an area of private, individual 'consent' while maintaining if not tightening its control of the *public* manifestation of 'irregular' sexual conduct. In that sense it prepares and restructures the field for subsequent 'permissive' reforms, to which it can be related — the whole thrust of 1960s legislation grouped around the family, sexuality, reproduction matrix, and other related 'moral' issues. Here we would include: The Homicide Act (1957), The Obscene Publications Act (1959), The Suicide Act (1961), The Murder (Abolition) Act (1965), The Family Planning Act (1967), The Abortion Act (1967), The Legislation on Divorce (1969) on Theatre Censorship (1968), and on the law governing Sunday Entertainments (see Hall, 1978b).

Yet if that much can be said at the level of general proscriptions in relation to the innovatory quality of *Wolfenden*, and its relation to other later moments of 'permissive' legislation, then we should be aware of the dangers of attempting to construct that 'tradition' monolithically. That is to say, if we can re-construct something of a general pattern, then it is a pattern that is differentiated, interrupted and crossed by a multiplicity of other determinations. Similarly, we should insist that the restructuring of the legality/illegality division acts on and transforms *differently* each particular sexual or moral practice. That differentiation is clear in *Wolfenden* itself; prostitution has a different history from that of homosexuality, and as a sexual practice it is shaped differently by the new recommendations.

In fact, prostitution stands rather differently in relation to this public/private distinction; the sanctioning of such a distinction in relation to prostitution has a long history and is directly related to the 'double standard' of sexual morality. The Committee's view that the function of criminal law includes the concern with offence against public order and decency and the exposure of the ordinary citizen to the offensive; these are taken to define the *visibility* of prostitution as falling within the concern of criminal law and requiring regulation. The Committee feel that the right of the normal decent citizen to go about the streets without an affront to his/her sense of decency should be the prime consideration and in their view 'both loitering and importuning for the purpose of prostitution are self-evidently public nuisances' (p. 87). To remove prostitutes from public notice, to take them off the streets, the Committee recommends the strengthening of police powers of arrest, removal of the necessary evidence of 'annoyance' to passers-by and an increase in penalties for persistent soliciting, with an ultimate maximum of three months imprisonment (increased from 14 days).

But it is evident that *Wolfenden* is not only unconcerned with prostitution in the private sphere but tacitly sanctions its existence. For example, the Committee asserts that:

> It is right that the law should guard against the congregation in any one place of undesirables of any type [but] too rigorous enforcement of the law in this respect might well have the effect, in some places, of driving prostitutes whose conduct at the present time is *inoffensive*, on to the streets, where their very presence would offend [Wolfenden Report, p. 113; our emphasis].

Thus it is explicitly admitted that if prostitution is 'contained' out of sight from the public eye, it remains inoffensive. It is not unexpected therefore that the implementation of the report's recommendations in the Street Offences Act (1959) has not led (nor was perhaps intended to lead) to any noticeable decrease in the rate of prostitution. Prostitutes are now of course far less visible on the streets, but the 1959 Act effectively institutionalised a class-specific split between the street walker, subject to greater penalties and restrictions than before, and the call girl who, located within the private sphere, has increased in number. It is interesting to note in fact that Wolfenden is aware of the possibilities of this increase: 'we think it is possible, indeed probable, that there will be an extension of the call girl system and perhaps, a growth in the activities of touts' (p. 96). The Report explicitly states that it regards this as less injurious than the presence of prostitutes on the streets. That the recommendations of *Wolfenden* have resulted in directing many prostitutes into the private sphere cannot necessarily be seen as progressive for the women concerned. As Wilson (1977, p. 67)

rightly remarks 'the Committee's recommendations in practice facilitated the organisation of call-girl services and the rationalisation and
greater organisation of prostitution — by men naturally — so that these
women had even less control over their lives than before'. And as
Stuart Hall (1978b) points out, the 'liberation' of private prostitution
for an increased rate of commercial exploitation stimulated its re-
organisation along more 'modern' lines, complementing the 'commercial
ethic' of the period.

Wolfenden's recommendations on homosexuality, while they opened
up a privatised space in which adult male homosexuals could now
operate without the threat of criminal sanction, in no sense advocated
the abandonment of 'control' from that space. Power is no longer to be
exercised through the operation of the law, but what the Report
recommends for homosexuality is the *diversification* of forms of control in the proliferation of new discourses for the regulation of male
homosexuals. It explicitly marked out a 'course of treatment' for the
homosexual which is distinct from that of the criminal model — henceforward, medicine, therapy, psychology and sociological research are to
form alternative strategies for the exercise of power (pp. 62-72,
pp. 77-8). The State abandons legal control of the homosexual, only to
call into play a set of discourses which constitute a new form of
intimate regulation of male homosexual practice in the private sphere.
The increased attention given to sexual deviancy in *Wolfenden* by the
State (the proliferation of 'official' discourses around sexual 'deviancy')
constitutes a new strategy for the operation of power — power is exercised by the very act of 'putting into discourse itself.'[6]

Conclusion

The central focus of our analysis has been the attempt to understand
the articulation of the relations of procreation, fertility control and the
regulation of sexuality with concerns over the reproduction of labour
power. Feminist work in this area stresses the need to examine the
specificity of this articulation, and, further, insists that in any account
of the capitalist mode of production the reproduction of labour power
cannot be assumed as automatic. However, our particular historical
analyses have alerted us to the dangers of examining the sexuality-
family-procreation matrix solely from the position of the reproduction
of labour power. Functionalism has a significant history here, whether
in its development through orthodox sociological accounts of the
family, or in particular Marxist debates which exclusively stress the
'logic' and 'demands' of capital. Functional questions should be asked

in any examination of the relation between the regulation of procreation and sexuality and the reproduction of labour power, but they can
only serve as a point of departure.

Beveridge and *Newsom* are both illustrative of how the question of
reproduction of labour power is in articulation with specific sexual
ideologies, but our analysis of *Beveridge*, in particular, also demonstrates
how that articulation must be historically located within political and
ideological movements of the day. More problematically still, our
analysis of *Wolfenden* leads us to insist that the report's central concerns (debates around the form of legal intervention in the sphere of
sexual conduct, and over the status of public morality and private
consent) cannot be collapsed into any underlying preoccupation with
the reproduction of labour power through the regulation of 'perverse'
sexual practices.

Sexual ideologies may be in articulation with particular political
ideologies — ideologies constructed through various political practices —
or themselves fused with such ideologies. The construction of these
political ideologies must be seen as taking place in the context of
struggles around hegemony in the political arena. Thus we would argue
that in any subsequent analyses of sexual ideologies their relation to
political ideologies and the struggle over hegemony must be taken into
consideration.

Notes

1. We wish to particularly thank Rachel Harrison, Janice Winship and
Richard Johnson who have all helped in the writing of this paper.
2. The whole question of Marx's presuppositions on the family and the nature
of sexual relations is crucially related to his whole method of working in *Capital*,
i.e. what is held constant for the sake of the specific analysis of the capitalist mode
of production. Statements such as 'all other circumstances remaining the same'
(*Capital*, I, p. 531) consistently preface particular areas of analysis in the text.
The whole history of the family is 'assumed' as one of the 'historical and moral
elements in the determination of labour power', and is left at the level of simple
abstraction and trans-historical description.
3. The movement for scientific home management and child care had already
started in the 1930s. See C. Hall, 1977 and D. Gittins, 1977.
4. A survey by Slater and Woodside (1951) found public resentment to such
inducement: 'they showed indignation that the production of large numbers of
children should be expected of them as a duty'.
5. Examples of nineteenth century legislation in the field include: The Infants
Custody Act (1839), The Matrimonial Causes Act (1857 and 1878), The Contagious Diseases Acts (1864, 1866, 1868) and the Labouchère Amendment Act
(1885).
6. Foucault's speculation in *La Volonté de savoir* (Foucault, 1976, p. 21) on

the way in which power is exercised by the very construction of discourses around sexuality seems highly relevant in the context of *Wolfenden*'s treatment of homosexuality.

5 IDEOLOGY, ECONOMY AND THE BRITISH CINEMA

John Hill

Analysis of the cinema's place within capitalism can broadly be seen to have entailed a double focus for Marxists, both generated and legitimated by a sense of what constitutes a proper and recognisable Marxist concern. In general terms this might be characterised as a concern both with determination and with effectivity. On the one hand, a 'materialist' concern to place cinema via its social and economic determinants whether grasped in terms of technology, economy (cinema's subservience to the logic of capital accumulation), class base or conjunctural complex. On the other, a 'critical' concern to place the cinema via its role within the social formation, to account for cinema in its ideological clothes, its complicity with a continuing structure of domination. Yet the articulation of these twin foci has remained problematic. The emphasis here is on articulation, with its demand for a structured combination which is more than mere addition or a setting of the two beside each other as equal but alternative choices (precisely the language of 'on the one hand' and 'on the other'). Such difficulty is not merely the product of bad analysis or conceptual confusion (though this may of course be the case) but is symptomatic of a more generalised problem of emphasis within Marxist analysis with its polar temptations of economism and idealism. In both cases the problem of articulation is effectively displaced through a dissolution of one of the terms into the other: the effect of ideology becomes directly 'readable' in the sum of its determinations (the ownership of the cinematic means of production, the logic of the market, and so on) or alternatively the determinative complex becomes evacuated from the ideological scene, 'unreadable' either directly or indirectly. And in occupation of the hinterland is the compromise whereby ideology and economy are seen to coalesce, but in some unexplicated liaison whose specific parameters and modalities remain occluded (take, for example, the Comolli/ Narboni (1971) formulation: 'every film . . . is determined by the ideology which produces it . . . but is all the more thoroughly and completely determined because . . . its very manufacture mobilises powerful economic forces' (p. 30). Indeed, the necessity to resort to such ultimately evasive formulations such as 'all the more' seems almost

112

to be the condition upon which such work can begin: how 'relative', for example, is the 'relative' in 'relative autonomy' and what precisely is 'relative' to what; and just what is 'mediating' what in the notion of 'mediation'? And it may be precisely because of this that, when attempts are inaugurated to combine the twin modes of analysis, the 'balance' so often tends to be lost and one is emphasised at the expense of the other. This would seem to be the case in the two examples discussed here: both set out with the broad ambition of examining textual ideology through an analysis of its conditions of production, but both end up by giving one privilege over the other. Thus in the case of Murdock and Golding (1977a; but see also 1974a and 1974b and their contribution to this volume) media (and ideological) specificity is largely collapsed into economy while for *Cahiers du Cinéma* (1972) the reverse is true — film (and ideological) specificity is largely evacuated of its determinations.

In 'Capitalism, Communication and Class Relations', Graham Murdock and Peter Golding explicitly attack those brands of Marxist theory which have placed cultural criticism above economic analysis, beginning with cultural artefacts and then working backwards to the economic base rather than vice versa. Although for them this proclivity can be accounted for in terms of a reaction against economic determinism and the popularity of 'critical philosophy', Murdock and Golding nonetheless argue that by abandoning any sustained analysis of the economic base we are 'thereby jettisoning the very elements that give Marxist sociology its distinctiveness and explanatory power' (1977a, p. 17) and that while not wishing to return to economic determinism would nevertheless claim 'that control over material resources and their changing distribution are ultimately the most powerful of the many levers in cultural production' (p. 20). The thesis is fleshed out with material on media integration and diversification and concludes with two general consequences for cultural production of the economic processes outlined: '1) the range of material available will tend to decline as market forces exclude all but the commercially successful and 2) this evolutionary process is not random, but systematically excludes those voices lacking economic power and resources' (p. 37).

It is of course possible to quibble with Murdock and Golding at the level of empirical observation — their under-emphasis on the need for originality in the drive for media expansion and similar under-emphasis on the possibility of oppositional viewpoints within the commercial media, consequent upon their problematic conflation of the long-term interest of capital in general and short-term interest of the individual entrepreneur[1] — but the concern here is rather with the way the general problem of ideology and economy is established and resolved by them. The concern here circulates around the 'gap' which remains for Murdock and Golding between economic production on the one hand and media forms on the other, which is only overcome for them through the dissolution of media specificity (the particular organisations of matters of expression) and consequent reduction of the media to transcriptions of socio-political ideologies originated elsewhere. Thus, for example, Murdock and Golding criticise a large proportion of media studies for concentrating almost entirely on news and failing to address themselves to 'the main dramatic, fictional and entertainment forms which make up the bulk of most people's media fare' (p. 36) — yet it is precisely these forms which Murdock and Golding themselves would seem unable to account for in the absence of any provision of the means for their conceptualisation. At most their concluding theses would allow them to account for the repetition and exclusion of particular forms once constituted but not for their dominance within the media nor for their particular operations. Or they can only do so through an attribution of unproblematic transparency to these forms whereby the difference between the various media in terms of matters of expression and conventions can be elided and the way formal conventions actually work in meaning-production be ignored. Thus when Murdock and Golding discuss the 'readings' of media imagery presented by others such as Poulantzas, Berger and Barthes, judging it a 'bald beginning', it is in turn difficult to see how Murdock and Golding can even reach such a bare starting point purely from their perspective. For 'imagery' is not only the end product of an economic process, but the product of a work of signification as well with its own internal dynamics and operations (and internal history), which is precisely the domain then that Murdock and Golding ignore.

It is this field which Stephen Heath has tried to capture in his use of the term 'machine': 'cinema itself seized exactly between industry and product as the stock of constraints and definitions from which film can be distinguished as a specific signifying practice' (1976, p. 256), where 'specificity' implies not only a sense of media peculiarity but also a semiotic particularity (signification through both codes unique to the cinema and broader socio-cultural ones) and 'practice' stresses process: 'film as a work of production of meanings'. That is to say, film does not merely 'express' or 'represent' but is itself an active process of signification through which meaning is produced. Two consequences for a consideration of ideology seem to follow. First, that the media are not merely 'empty' forms which neutrally transcribe socio-political ideo-logies, but enjoy their own level of effectivity which is the property of the cinematic 'machine' and not the cinematic institution. One attempt to theorise this, for example, at a general level can be seen in the work of Jean-Paul Fargier (1971) where cinema is considered not merely as a vector of ideologies already in circulation, but as producing its own specific ideology: 'the impression of reality'. Now whether or not we accept fully this formulation (for example, it is not at all clear that the 'impression' is fundamental to 'bourgeois cinema' or that its appear-ance is irreducibly ideological), it does nonetheless help clarify the point that the 'ideological effect' of the cinema cannot be understood outside of the operations of its particular conventions and constraints which then, because they carry their own specific effectivities, cannot be seen necessarily to correspond to a maker's personality or 'inten-tions' nor likewise his or her social and political beliefs. As Francis Mulhern has argued for literature, so with reservations (considered below) it would here be accepted for film: 'the formal characteristics of a literary text cannot be considered as the aesthetic expression of its author's pre-existing ideological positions . . . Moreover, the ideological positions affirmed by a literary text need not even coincide with the positions formally adopted by its author. They are the determinate effects of the form of the text, and may in fact be deeply inconsistent with the latter' (1975, p. 85). Second, it follows that if the media do not merely express ideologies, they must then be considered as actively constitutive of ideologies. That is to say, ideologies are not merely ingredients to be detected in the media, but also its products. And again, as active productions, ideologies are not merely to be seen as sets of positivities but also as processes of exclusion — with these 'exclu-sions' potentially being able to feed back to disturb or deform their progenitive system (and thereby furnishing our analysis with a notion of 'contradiction' retrieved from both a reductionism which would merely place it as a reflection of contradictions determined at the level of the economic and the homeostasis of a reproduction-orientated Marxist functionalism — though as we shall see later not then without difficulties). For Murdock and Golding, however, it is the former relationship (ideologies as ingredients): 'The first task is to spell out the nature of the ruling ideology, and to specify the propositions and assumptions of which it is composed. Secondly, the appearance and entrenchment of such propositions and assumptions in media output needs to be clearly demonstrated' (1977a, p. 35). But the ruling ideology is not just 'entrenched' in the media: it is actually produced.

For there is no general or abstract system which is the ruling ideology: rather the ruling ideology is only constituted in and through the concrete: '[Ideology] is there and yet it is not there. It appears indeed if the general structure of a dominant ideology is almost impossible to grasp, reflexively and analytically as a whole. The dominant ideology always appears, precisely, in and through the particular' (Hall 1972b, p. 82). Indeed, as Hall and his colleagues at the Centre for Contemporary Cultural Studies at Birmingham University have gone on to show, the task of the media as part of the State may indeed be to create an ideological unity where none before existed (Hall *et al*., 1976; Chambers *et al*., 1977): 'Far from expressing or reflecting an already given class interest, television is one of the sites where ideological elements and positions are articulated into a specific type of political class discourse' (Chambers *et al*., 1977, p. 114). And this may be part of the problem. For Murdock and Golding classes are by and large seen as already constituted, with their own social and economic identities which can then be reflected or not reflected within the media, rather than as complex and contradictory unities without any necessary homogeneity at the cultural level but rather 'represented' through a variety of forms.

However, given the impossibility of grasping ideology purely in terms of class origins we must then avoid evacuating class from our analysis altogether. Thus, from beginning with similar premises, one tendency has been to define ideology neither by its class base nor its reproduction of the social formation but merely as that part of the social formation that exists when we subtract the political and economic levels. Raymond Williams (1973) has argued that if the concept of 'social totality' is to be retrieved from a mere sociology of interconnections, then it must include a notion of 'domination'. Likewise I would wish to argue that if ideology is to be rescued from a significatory egalitarianism (and conjunctural analysis from a new form of empiricism) it must also include a notion of ideologies not just as discursive systems but as ultimately maintaining a structure of dominance. Not of course directly or crudely, but in complex and contradictory ways whose specific potencies and inflections have to be analysed in particular and concrete ways. This is not then to imply a subscription to the thesis of cultural transparency. It is quite possible to concede that human beings may always be subjects insofar as they are constituted in and through discursive practices of whose grounds they are not conscious, but this does not then imply that they will always be subjected (in the sense of subjection) to the particular discursive practices of capitalism. For here cultural opacity is not necessarily allied to relations of domination, just as ideology is not then coterminous with discourse.

Likewise I would not wish these conclusions to lead to an abandonment of the problem of determination (and here I would part company with Hindess (1977) and Hirst (1976b) whose either/or choice of total autonomy or total determination can find no theoretical coherence for this in-between). Just as we cannot read off cinema's signifying practices from its material conditions of existence, so we cannot provide a coherent account of cinema which evacuates such material agencies and apparatuses. Because they don't tell it all, it does not follow that they then tell us nothing (likewise 'creators'' intentions and socio-political ideologies). But just as class is not a monolith, so determination must not be conceived as single-layered and uni-directional, but rather multi-layered and complex and operant within 'ideology' (the constraints of the 'machine') as well as between 'ideology' and 'economy'.

Returning to Golding and Murdock via their more recent paper as represented in this volume it can be seen that they address themselves to a number of the problems posed here largely to re-assert their initial position of the privileging of the economic but with the novel input of a specific polemic against 'textural [sic] analysis'. As this can be read as both a 'defence' of their own position and an 'attack' on some of the positions posed here, their three main arguments may well merit further investigation. Golding and Murdock firstly maintain that textual analysis cannot provide an adequate account of the relations of production governing a text's construction. This is undoubtedly correct, but nonetheless turns the pertinent issue on its head: for while indeed production relations may not be able to be read back from textual analysis this does not then imply the converse — that textual processes can then be read forward from those same relations of production.[2] Golding and Murdock's second argument refers to inference. Textual analysis is a form of 'content analysis' (a label hardly doing justice to the significant advances of much textual analysis over content analysis as classically understood) and is thus necessarily 'circumstantial' and 'qualitative'. Again the argument is carried on by means of a reversal. A thesis on methodological capabilities is made to do service instead of the required conceptual analysis. Rather than the problems of theory generating demands of methodological procedure, technical possibilities adjudicate the value of theory instead. Furthermore it is an argument that can really only make sense if we are to assume that inference is something peculiar to content analysis rather than a condition general to sociology. It would indeed be a barren and denuded sociology (at best an operationism whereby concepts become fully defined by their procedures of measurement) that could lay claim to have resolved the problems of inference. The third argument of Golding and Murdock is that exclusive concentration on textual analysis would necessarily be truncated and partial in its explanation of ideological production. This is, of course, true — but in establishing the opposite case Golding and Murdock are in danger of an equal partialness and truncation. They themselves recognise that economic analysis cannot be sufficient in itself, but then fail to theorise that very 'insufficiency' thereby themselves 'bracketing off' the very issues which are at stake.

If then it can be argued that Golding and Murdock devalue the significatory level of the media and that this has effects for how they can formulate a theory of ideology, let us now look at the reverse tendency in the work of the *Cahiers du Cinéma* editorial group (1972) and its implications. An increasingly common response to this analysis of 'Young Mr. Lincoln' is to note the inadequacy of *Cahiers*' attempt to define the historical determinations of the film but nonetheless to applaud the actual textual analysis as if the two were quite happily separable (Campbell, 1977, p. 30; Caughie, 1977-8, p. 93) despite the defined object of the piece:

> . . . to distinguish the historicity of [a number of 'classic' films including 'Young Mr. Lincoln's'] inscription: the relation of these films to the codes (social, cultural . . .) for which they are a site of intersection, and to other films themselves held in an intertextual space: therefore, the relation of these films to the ideology which they convey, a particular 'phase' which they represent, and to the events (present, past, historical, mythical, fictional) which they aimed to represent' [*Cahiers du Cinéma*, 1972, p. 6].

While agreeing with such writers in their diagnosis of a certain failure, I would nonetheless not want to gloss this over in terms of 'the intrinsic difficulty of the task' or an 'unhappy contingency' but rather I would see the imbalance as consequent on the premises founding the analysis and thus necessarily undermining the original 'object'.

Unlike Golding and Murdock, whose object was to account for fairly general features of the media in terms of the structural principles of the economy, *Cahiers* selected a specific media artefact — one film — which they sought to account for in fairly specific ways. This they then did through a rather 'unmaterialist' mode of operation – accounting for the movie's appearance in terms of the intention of one man: the Republican Zanuck wanted to make a film about the Republican Lincoln in order to promote a Republican victory in the Presidential election of 1940. Brewster (1973) suggests that, faced with the difficulty of substantiating such a thesis, this specific ideological purpose is ignored in favour of the more general one of 'the reformulation of the historical figure of Lincoln on the level of the myth and the eternal' (*Cahiers du Cinéma*, 1972, p. 13). However, it seems that this division is more than a symptom of intellectual difficulty, but rather of theoretical choice. Thus a division can be seen being made between the ideological determinations of the film (Zanuck's purpose) and the ideological undertaking actualised in the film, the latter not in fact being a property of the former, and hence clarifying *Cahiers'* distinction between their own analysis and that which they call 'demystification' whereby 'an artistic product' is 'linked to its socio-historical context according to a linear, expressive, direct causality' (p. 7).

The consequence of this then is that political and economic analysis can only have a limited function and can only loosely, if at all, place the film's ideological role (which is not to question the essential 'correctness' of *Cahiers'* refusal to 'read off' ideology from its social determinants, but rather to examine its theoretical effects). And this conjoins with the other object that *Cahiers* set themselves. For in differentiating themselves from other types of reading (commentary, interpretation, mechanistic structuralism and demystification) *Cahiers* specify their project as that of an 'active reading'. At one level this can be seen as according recognition to the 'work' of the text, its process of signification. *Cahiers* are not content merely to abstract broad 'ideological statements' in one simultaneous operation, but rather wish to follow 'the film's process of becoming-a-text', its 'dynamic inscription'. This might be seen as an operation which traces the audience's diachronic experience of watching a film, but for *Cahiers* it involves more: 'A process of active reading is to make them say what they have to say within what they leave unsaid, to reveal their constituent lacks' (p. 8). In such terms, then, the initial concern with a socio-historical situating can be seen to be misplaced, for there is no textual meaning to be discovered independent of consumption anyway, which becomes in fact of more decisive importance than the moment of production: 'We do not hesitate to force the text, even to re-write it insofar as the film only constitutes itself as a text by integration of the reader's knowledge' (p. 37). But the dilemmas are in the very formulation. For if the text only exists through 'integration of the reader's knowledge' in what sense can they be said to be 'forcing' or 're-writing'? Does the object-text have an existence independent of the knowing subject after all, or is there at least some recognition of 'correctness' in the process of 'meaning-extraction'? The problem can be posed in terms of validity — does the by and large correct observation that the text only exists through the 'integration of the reader's knowledge' allow *carte blanche* in analysis, or do there remain 'controls' or 'limit-positions' which continue to govern the analysing discourse?

Clearly *Cahiers* are concerned that their reading should not be viewed as a purely personal or idiosyncratic one (they make recurring references to readings being 'authorised', of occurrences in the film bringing out its 'true meaning', and so on); but they are equally clearly, through their use of the language of psychoanalysis, not attempting to reproduce a 'lay' reading or any actual historical reading. Indeed, they pose their critical activity as exactly opposite to the norms of conventional consumption: 'a kind of non-reading' (p. 6) governed by the 'transparence' and 'presence' of 'classic' representation and narrative. The problem is then not only of what guarantees their reading (can the methodological licence apparently legitimated by their founding premises be overcome without theoretical circularity?[3]) but perhaps more importantly for our purposes, what this might mean in relation to our understanding of ideology. What are we told about the ideological project of the film, whether successful or failed, if the reading which *Cahiers* locates was never in fact accessible to a general audience? (A claim referring us back to the privileged warrant of psychoanalysis to explicate the unconscious workings of ideology would, apart from problems of validity, still have to cope with the problems of the dehistoricised and decontextualised versions of the unconscious and ideology it sought to work with). A division could perhaps be made between the film's general ideological undertaking — the reformulation of the historical figure of Lincoln — which could then be viewed as fairly accessible to an audience ('transparent' and 'present') — and *Cahiers'* analysis of the costs of producing that ideological formulation, the repressions involved. But what then is the significance of *Cahiers'* formulation to the effect that 'a distortion of the ideological project by the writing of the film' is manifested within the film (1972, p. 37)? For whom is the ideological project distorted if it takes a skilled reading based on psychoanalysis to reveal it, and in just what way is our understanding of the film's ideological effectivity altered?

Subsequent work (Willemen, 1971 and 1972-3; Johnston, 1975)

which has built upon *Cahiers'* protocols has then evaded such issues by necessarily abandoning historical analysis altogether and deriving its legitimacy either from its use-value for contemporary criticism (the institution of a more 'progressive' mode of reading texts) or for contemporary film-making (the strategies it might suggest). Readings are then quite self-consciously constructed in opposition to actual historical readings (whether skilled or lay), the evidence of which then becomes irrelevant (though Willemen (1972-3) at once conjoins an acceptance of the audience's non-awareness of textual contradictions with the demand for a historical sensitivity if contemporary critics are not to 'misread' Sirk's films just as the claims of relevance for aesthetic strategies, unnoticed in their own day, rests on an unexplicated assumption as to their pertinence for a contemporary audience). As such then it is clear that the attempt to combine economic and ideological analysis has been effectively removed from the agenda (Kuhn, 1975). Accompanying such 'revisions' has been a 'stronger' repudiation of the possibility at all of the enterprise here called for, made in terms of current work on the theory of history, whereby film analysis can only be carried on in and for the present with validity being guaranteed by political knowledge of the current conjuncture (Hindess and Hirst, 1975; Tribe, 1977-8; McCabe, 1977; Ellis, 1977). As yet however it is difficult to see whether such work has been adequately able to resolve its own problems of relativism and political opportunism (the ritual invocation of the 'current conjuncture' remaining as yet peculiarly empty of foundational concepts).

It is in this way then that the *Cahiers* analysis reveals a complementary set of problems to those considered in relation to Murdock and Golding. Whereas Murdock and Golding fail to pay adequate attention to significatory processes, *Cahiers* conversely emphasise these to the point of accrediting them an almost total autonomy. This is in turn allied to the problem of consumption. For Murdock and Golding the problem did not arise — for them the audience can by and large be 'read out' from the media texts themselves. *Cahiers*, on the other hand, correctly refuse to see the audience as locked into some pre-ordained textual meaning, but in doing so tend to dissolve the text altogether and ignore the socio-historical context in which it is received. The importance here is to suggest that just as the text cannot be read off directly from production, so audience response cannot be read back from properties of the text only. The emphasis on signification breaks with notions of the passive consumer — audiences are rather seen as actively productive of meaning through a knowledge and activation of codes (but not then as self-conscious 'decoders') — but this must then be understood in actual conditions of social and historical readership. Neale (1977) has argued in the case of propaganda that 'it can't simply be a matter of reading off a set of textual characteristics. What has to be identified is the use to which a particular text is put, to its function within a particular situation, to its place within cinema conceived as a social practice' (p. 39). This is the case for Neale because he wants to see propaganda as a form of address which 'produces a position of social struggle' (p. 32) and, for him, such a position cannot be purely the product of textual address. However, while Neale himself would not want to do this, it does seem possible to generalise this to notions of textual 'effectivity' (including ideological effectivity) beyond those which imply forms of social action. And thus an analysis of media ideology could not rest with an analysis of production and text alone but must in turn include a theory of readership and analysis of consumption (indeed outside of which there is no text at all). So just as production and text are articulated through the 'machine' of social and historical cinematic conventions and constraints, so the 'machine' of socially and historically placed readership cuts across the text and its audience.

The 'meaning' then of a film is not something to be discovered purely in the text itself (into which the spectator may or may not be bound) but is constituted in the interaction between the text and its users. The early claim of semiotics to be in some way able to account for a text's functioning through an immanent analysis was essentially misfounded in its failure to perceive that any textual system could only have meaning in relation to codes not purely textual, and that the recognition, distribution and activation of these would vary socially and historically. On the other hand the fact that we are concerned with codes, that is systems of regularity, should indicate that this does not then imply textual meaning to be dispersed altogether whereby all readings become equal and novelty becomes a virtue in itself. Likewise it does not abandon us to uses and gratifications theory with its collapse of the text into an individualistic and psychologistic problematic. Rather we would want to argue that readership must be understood in terms of broader patterns of socio-cultural consumption whereby texts are read both 'aesthetically', in terms of codes specifically 'artistic', and 'socially', in relation to the broader contours of life-experience engendered via class, race, sex and nation, where again these are not conceived as homogeneous but variegated (and thereby resisting the associated assumptions often governing analyses of the passive consumer of the development of society itself towards a 'mass' homogeneity; as Swingewood argues, 'capitalist economy and technology and capitalist culture — have achieved new principles of economic and cultural richness and diversity . . . the development of the capitalist mode of production has served to augment, not destroy, civil society' (1977, p.x.). If a notion such as 'preferred reading' then is to have a value, it is not as a means of fixing one interpretation over and above others, but rather a means of accounting for how, under certain conditions, a text will tend to be read in particular ways because of the way meaning is placed through the articulation of particular aesthetic, social and historical codes.

In this we can see that the task of ideological analysis is not the production of new meanings but rather of accounting for how old meanings are generated for and through particular audiences (which is not then to posit the unified sign-community of much early semiotics), the novelty lying in this analysis and the new problematic in which it is placed. Following from this it is clear that the readings which such analysis predicates should not be so fashioned as to contradict the evidence of actual socio-historical readings. Indeed, there is a real danger that as film analysis develops an ever more complex and sophisticated battery of methodological tools it loses sight of social analyses in favour of the institution of its own skilled community of readers with its own particular credentials (the codes of academia and advanced interdisciplinary discourses such as semiotics and psychoanalysis). This is not to deny the importance of such disciplines, but to argue that their value lies not in the discovery of some new signified (a new way of capturing the text's 'true meaning'), or the liberation of the signifier in the interests of subversion, but in accounting for the processes of signification through which particular meanings are produced in specific contexts. As Barthes puts it in his influential *S/Z*: 're-reading is an operation contrary to the commercial and ideological habits of our society' (1975, p. 15). But then whether his own multiple re-reading is an analysis of how the form of realism is textually produced with all its concomitant difficulties, or merely the introduction of a new (more 'writerly') mode of consumption, would be open to dispute. Likewise this is not then to argue that each and every meaning is to be found raised to the level of consciousness. Obviously within our culture certain very central types of meaning surround us without being explicitly recognised — but the identification of such 'non-consciousness' is not then arbitrary and unless some 'control' at the level of experience (which does not thereby become privileged in analysis) is exercised a licence is spawned which in all likelihood may only have the remotest of links with an understanding of the production and reproduction of ideologies. Put another way, because our methodology is anti-phenomenological, it does not then make phenomenology irrelevant: a confusion which seems to vitiate the critiques of phenomenology in Metz and Culler respectively by Henderson (1975) and Tribe (1976).

In translating these concerns to the British cinema, it can at once be seen that work has hardly begun. In part symptomatic of a contempt for the 'entropy' and 'wretched cultural provincialism' (Anderson 1964, p. 50) of British culture in general, in part symptomatic of a hostility to the nullity of British cinema in particular, the effect has been for attention to be turned further afield, often to Hollywood with its more immediate appeals of life-force and dynamism. To quote once more Wollen's often repeated remark: 'The English cinema . . . is still utterly amorphous, unclassified, unperceived' (1972, p. 115).

And within the work that has been done, the tendency has been towards compartmentalisation and a refusal of theory. On the one hand, documentation of the structure of the industry with little attempt to theorise the relation of this to films actually produced (except perhaps numerically), on the other critical exegeses outside of any reference to either conditions of production or reception. And, in between, the 'histories' with their juxtapositions of 'social background', incidental economic details and film commentary, but with little attempt to specify relationships beyond the most general. A few attempts have been made in the direction of a more sophisticated historiography but these have usually been handicapped through being controlled by an ill-theorised conception of 'reflection'. Thus, Durgnat (1970; but see also 1976) calls his work 'A Mirror for England' while Barr (1977; but see also 1974) sees his task as accounting for the particular ramifications of Ealing's claim (inscribed upon a plaque erected at the studios in 1955) to be 'projecting Britain and the British character': and in doing so, not only attempting an 'inner history' of the nation, but of the rise and fall of Ealing studios themselves The double problem (both significatory and social) of whether film can be said to reflect at all and if so just what or whom and in what way (issues to which it must be admitted Barr is the more sensitive) is resolved through an assumption of a national 'consensus' whereby film does not strictly speaking 'reflect' at all but merely becomes part of the 'mood' or 'spirit of the times'. In both cases the writers are thereby absolved from any responsibility to disentangle the particular levels and interrelations of the social formation in favour of an idealist notion of culture, removed from its material bases, evacuated of its divisions and run together into an undifferentiated mesh of experience, privileged and unquestioned. Thus, for Barr, it can make sense to substitute the 'old-fashioned impressionistic' term 'national character' with presumably the modern but for Barr equally impressionistic term 'ideology' (1977, p. 108).

However, it is not altogether coincidental that hostility to the British cinema and analysis of it predominantly in terms of reflection should have been prominent in the literature. For although I have argued against a notion of the media as mere 'transcriptions' and 'reflections', the British cinema has nonetheless been frequently identified as possessing a peculiar quality which has rendered its forms invisible and largely subservient to 'contents' (and hence the hostility towards film-makers for their failure to utilise fully 'the resources of the medium'). As Elsaesser has put it, in the British cinema 'the level of coherence is constituted by an extra-cinematic system (the hypothetical "consensus" or "middle class") brought into the films from outside in order to make them "legible" and not by a cinematic specificity and a formal coherence controlling the aesthetic means by which ideological contents are reflected, transformed or critically expressed within a film' (1972, p. 10) and thus for him rendering a socio-ideological critique of the British cinema all the more appropriate because of its otherwise signifying paucity. And although Elsaesser elides a particular critical preference for a mode of ciné-signification with cinematic specificity itself and hence under-emphasises the significatory 'work' required to produce formal invisibility (and extra-cinematic coherence which is not just then reflected), his reading of the British cinema clearly accords with not only the aesthetic but also the political dismissal of that cinema for its adoption of an unproblematic realist form, whose ideological effects are precisely seen as properties of the form and only in a limited way its supposed structuring contents.

Putting this another way, if the British cinema can be seen to be largely 'form-less', recent debate about 'realism' has been peculiarly 'content-less'. Thus for McCabe (1974, but see also 1975-6, 1976a and 1976b) the 'classic realist text' is to be defined formally in terms of its hierarchy of discourses, and can be seen to subsume not only the nineteenth-century novel but the standard fictional forms of film and television; while for Burch 'the edifice of illusionism' may be seen as housing 'all the representational practices which rise to dominance along

with the bourgeoisie during the eighteenth and nineteenth centuries'
and continuing 'to dominate massively the cultural life of all capitalist
and most socialist countries today' and this has organic links with 'the
illusion of parliamentary representation' upon which political class
domination is maintained (1976, pp. 54-5). And thus for Burch the
analysis of a film's ideological effectivity requires no 'specific attention
to the film's diegesis' but rather to the less 'geographically and historically localised' relation of signifier and signified which is the *modus
operandi* of representation (1974, pp. 49-50). Now it is clear that both
authors are correct to abandon the endless tail-chasing exercise of
attempting to define realism by reference to some 'known' eternal
reality. Realism has no absolutist kernel but constitutes a set of constructed conventions whereby particular identifications of the 'real' are
accorded plausibility. But on the other hand it is likewise by no means
apparent that all realisms can then be subsumed under one great
Realism (or one Realism with a few sub-variants) and that evaluations
of effectivity (in terms of subject-positionality and so on) can be made
independently of specific social and historical contexts and specific
'contents' (with which the 'forms' of realism are inextricably in articulation). That is to say, evaluation of the effectivity of realism (including
its conservative or progressive qualities) is like evaluation of ideologies
– dependent on context, its conditions of production and of consumption and its relations to other discourses (both specifically aesthetic and
socio-political), dominant and subordinate in a particular period.

Indeed, examination of the history of 'realisms' would suggest that
the claim generally made for a 'new realism' in the arts is rarely made
in terms of technique alone, but is usually embodied within a complex
repository of social values and attitudes. Because realism is generally
bound up with a social extension (the inclusion of hitherto neglected
sections of the population) it is usually part of a broader claim to
legitimacy by a social group or at least a social syntax not specifically
aesthetic. And thus the 'real' in the process of being constructed will
discover its groundings less in relation to some supposed external
referent and more in the symbolic universe from which it emerges.
Thus to take an example of the documentary movement of the 1930s,
its particular demand for observation and fidelity in the arts was not
merely a technical project but an active social response to the crises of
the inter-war period. As Hall has put it: 'The documentary style, though
at one level a form of writing, photographing, filming, recording, was at
another level, an emergent form of social consciousness: it registered, in
the formation of a social rhetoric, the emergent structure of feeling, in

the immediate pre-war and the war periods' (1972a, p. 100). Likewise the 'realist' movement which began to infiltrate the British commercial cinema at the end of the 1950s constituted part of a particular response to the development of post-war British capitalism and in particular its trajectory in the 1950s — and as such can be seen to have a different ideological significance despite its 'technical' similarities with the documentary movement.

It can be seen then that something of a double prescription is being offered here with potentially opposite pulls on the analysis. That is to say, if purchase is to be secured on the specific socio-historical effectivity of realist forms, analysis must be inter-discursive (as opposed to immanent) for the grounds of their 'sense' to be apprehended (extra-textual 'contents' carrying their own pre-stressed significance) but without then assuming an unproblematic expressiveness or reflection (the sense of the real is specifically a textual constitution). Thus constructing the cultural field in which certain films might be seen to operate is not to look for the absent origin or cause of the films' effects nor to attempt in some way to go behind the back of the text and pull out its authentic meaning. Rather it is part of an attempt to specify some of the particular conditions upon which realist forms necessarily exist and in terms of which their claims to legitimacy can only have sense (the logic of realism precisely claiming its validity through that which it represents).

Thus what we are designating as a particular realist movement — referring to a cluster of films circa 1959-63 including such films as *Room at the Top* (1959), *Saturday Night and Sunday Morning* (1960), *A Taste of Honey* (1961), *The Loneliness of the Long Distance Runner* (1962), *A Kind of Loving* (1962) and the like — can be seen to draw upon a particular field of ideas which focuses issues for it and provides its 'sense' of reality. What it draws upon is a particular 'handling' of the data of social development by particular social groups and their construction into an account of changes within British capitalism. This constellation then, loosely translatable as a sort of 'ethical revisionism', can be seen to take shape pre-eminently within groupings on the left but drawing also on academic social science and the commonplaces of party political rhetoric. Thus the data of full employment, increasing productivity and post-war stability (with its mix of Keynesianism, mixed economy, and welfare state) was first accorded an undue achievement (in the absence of attention being drawn to the persistence of inequalities despite absolute increases in living standards or the 'temporary palliatives' (Pinto-Duschinsky, 1970, p. 59) — particularly in the case of sterling — and the 'fortuitous circumstances' (Bogdanor and Skidelsky, 1970, p. 8) — such as the rapid growth in world trade and fall in commodity prices in the 1952-55 period — upon which such 'affluence' had been built) and then correspondingly read as under-mining fundamental supports of a socialist economic strategy, the response to which was to effect a displacement away from a programme of economic advance towards an emphasis on socialism as an ethical system. Thus the editorial of the first *Universities and Left Review* (Spring 1957) complains that 'It was inevitable that the post-war gener-ation should identify socialism at worst with the barbarities of Stalinist Russia, at best with the low pressure society of Welfare Britain' (p. 1) and presses its case as follows: 'The pressing need now is that socialist intellectuals should face the damage which Stalinism and Welfare Capitalism have done to socialist values — a sustained socialist move-ment must be informed by the belief that the moral imagination can now intervene creatively in human history' (p. 11). In doing so the classic armoury of cultural criticism was revamped to do service to the moral nullity of a consumer-durables society.

Hoggart's influential book, *The Uses of Literacy*, accordingly agrees upon the new economic emancipation of the working class, but con-tinues to argue that 'commerce' rules the working class culturally and that 'this subjection promises to be stronger than the old because the chains of cultural subordination are both easier to wear and harder to strike away than those of economic subordination' (1957, p. 201). Thus in such analyses economic progress far from advancing the cause of socialism, could be read as undermining the very qualities required to sustain it. Crucial here was the opposition of a traditional working class grounded in a network of community and moral integrity now being eroded by the advance of mass society (just as a 'popular art' organic to such a tradition, expressing and confirming its values, was being eroded by a new synthetic and inauthentic mass art). Within such a complex then the call for 'reality' became less an epistemological one and more a moral one — a contradiction in part touched upon by Pauline Kael in her earlier lampoon against a similar set of critics: 'Surely Mr. Corbluth has let the cat out of the social realist bag: manual workers are more real than other people' (1966, p. 343). At one level this is of course absurd, but yet Kael's point fails to perceive the texture of feeling from which such a claim might be made. For in a sense for the 'sociolect' the manual working class were 'more real' precisely because their tradition represented an authenticity and vitality absent from mass, and indeed probably middle-class culture. But this claim was not made in the name of a class in ascendance, but rather in decline and because that class was considered to be happy in such decline ('easily wearing its subordination') had largely to be represented by 'outsiders' ('socialist intellectuals') who had the cultural capital and 'moral imagination' to understand the costs of society's development and whose role of dissent was seen to increase in proportion to the working class's decline (Angry Young Men, CND, and so on). And this, in the absence of any particular social base, could easily slide into reactionary nostalgia (the Leavis legacy) or a generalised anti-materialism (thus for Hoggart the real villain of the piece is 'commerce' considered in abstraction from any particular production relations). Thus it is not strictly true that class was not represented as an issue in the culture (Dyer, 1977b, p. 16), but rather that class was accorded a recognition precisely at the time that its continuation as a substantial social force was no longer credited; and likewise the demand for 'class representation' was not so much a progressive affirmation of class and the unbridgeable gap between capital and labour in the face of an apparent victory of consent as a final moral farewell to the working class as they made their exit from the social stage (making way for 'youth' and other compartmentalised groupings trapped alike under the umbrella of the 'social problem').

But if the realist movement within the cinema can be seen as part of a broader social syntax it did not then merely express such attitudes at the level appropriate to it but was itself constitutive of that response which was likewise refracted through the particular context and struggles of the British film industry and its cinematic conventions. Thus the critique of commerce was particularised in terms of the specific commercial practices of the cinema with its stifling of creativity and corresponding restrictiveness of representation. 'Commerce' in the cinema had likewise created nullity and stereotyped uniformity against which, it was argued, must stand 'artists' (outsiders) of passion and imagination who could restore vitality and freshness to the cinema. This would be achieved through re-connecting with 'a sense of life' and 'reality' (the potential contradiction between art and reality being overcome through a notion of 'commitment' whereby authentic art could only be created in a context of social responsibility). This meant not only a re-connection with the traditional working-class but a genuinely popular art in which audiences could share and recognise themselves rather than escape from themselves in the fantasies of mass art. As Tony Richardson, director of *A Taste of Honey, The Loneliness of The Long-distance Runner*, etc., said in an interview: 'I would like to go on doing the sort of subjects I am doing now. Subjects related to the world we are living in, the roles and the issues that are facing people in the society we are living in. I think films should be an immensely dynamic and potent force within society . . . '.

As the quote suggests, the novelty of the movement was largely conceived in terms of 'contents' (subjects) — of the presentation of the working class on the screen no longer as the stock types or comic butts of 'commercial' British cinema, but as 'real', 'fully-rounded' characters in 'real' settings (the regions, cities, factories etc.) with 'real' problems (both everyday and of the culture — freedom/restraint, purity/corruption, tradition/modernity, affluence/authenticity). And the ramifications of the notions of 'reality' dominated both promotion and critical reception: the 'reality' either being accepted and welcomed, denied as in fact 'false', or accepted but criticised in the interests of art (which requires more than a reproduction of reality) or entertainment (people already get enough of reality). However, this appropriation at the level of the 'represented' (whereby validity and authenticity are seen to reside primarily in proportion to the authenticity and validity of the pro-filmic event) away from its mode of representation was not accidental but also the product of the cinematic 'machine' which consisted not just of an ingrained notion of technique (the 180-degree rule, shot matching, editing for spatio-temporal continuity, diegetic and configurational continuity, concentration on particular scales of shots and angles, etc.) but the 'naturalisation' of these in terms of preconceptions of cinema and other available cinematic discourses. This might be characterised as not only an ingrained tradition of craftsmanship and film making (well discussed by Dyer (1977b) in terms of the 'organic film') but a subservience of this craft to the importance of 'themes and 'ideas' (characterised by MacArthur (1977) as the 'Anglo-American critical tradition' but finding a particular enshrinement in two influential British film movements; thus Tudor's verdict on the documentarists: 'Aesthetics is reduced to morally prescribed social theory' (1974, p. 75) and Alan Lovell's on Free Cinema: 'Free Cinema didn't show any great interest in aesthetic problems' (Lovell and Hillier 1972, p. 143)). These in turn intertwine with a fundamentalism and hostility towards stylisation which is not then just a 'fallacy of Realism' dependent on the bad faith or just plain idiocy of critics and film makers but an implantation with historical and material roots, such as the importance of documentary for both non-commercial and commercial film-making (the inheritance of British war movies and Ealing), the insulation of British culture from European modernism in the 1920s and 1930s at the very time that the 'documentary spirit' was achieving its hegemony across the arts and the selective appropriation of modernist ideas in the 1950s (the reception of Brecht, for example), the general denigration of cinema and consequent critical neglect, with its concomitant annexation by the moral entrepreneurs whose problematic (the media as producing direct social effects) is merely inverted in the liberal-humanist project for a 'socially conscious' film (just as film for the British left has been predominantly functional to direct political and economic struggles), the lack of entry into the industry from those social groups traditionally filling 'creative' roles (and hence very often the evidence of a substantial émigré input at times of apparent vitality), the lack of serious state interest in film and so on. Originality is thus bounded by conventions of the privileged signified and the good/intelligible film, but is yet able to be seen as introducing an 'increased reality' by extending the logic of the basic terms. Thus, the 'new' represented is also legitimated by its representation being in negative relation to 'false' or clichéd cinematic conventions which it then replaces through minimised melodrama, location shooting, unknown regional actors etc. – with the push towards *cinéma vérité* then being held in check by expectations of what would constitute a 'proper' film.

But these senses of limits are not merely the constitutive expectations of audiences and film-makers (which may yet be all the more powerful because of their 'unconscious' internalisation) but are also embedded in the practical routines of institutionalised producers which, as we have argued, are not necessarily determinative but which nonetheless exert both pressures and restraints. Ellis (1977) has drawn a distinction between the space of cinema within the social formation, which he defines in terms of its conditions of existence and relations to other institutions of representation, and cinema's internal organisation, the actual active form cinema takes. And in these terms it is clear that in the period under consideration the space of cinema was in the process of being re-defined, a process which was consequently expressed through its internal organisation. Thus the appearance of televison not only re-located cinema's place within the relations of representation (increasing the importance, for example, of the X-film with its possibilities for representation denied to TV) but began to force the well known 'decline of the cinema', while the internal organisation of the industry was re-shaped in acknowledgement of its new conditions of existence. Withdrawal from direct production by the major combines was intensified, studios were disposed of or leased, and capitalisation of projects became almost exclusively dependent on the individual entrepreneur, now perhaps backed by the state in the form of 'end money' provided by the NFFC. With a replacement of direct combine control of production by an indirect one through maintained control of distribution and exhibition and a new 'openness' to ideas which might turn the tide of decline, a possibility of innovation was allowed though subject to the demands of financial success. Thus despite the difficulties of capitalisation faced by earlier projects — *Look Back in Anger* only got Warners' finance and hence ABC handling because Burton was owed a picture which they would have had to pay him for anyway; *Saturday Night and Sunday Morning* failed to find a backer when Joseph Janni owned the rights and later when made by Woodfall only hit lucky due to a Warners' West End cinema falling vacant, and the film was only able to fill the vacancy through producer Harry Saltzman's previous ties with Warners — by the time of *This Sporting Life* the commercial viability of the 'realists' had been established to such an extent that Karel Reisz's suggestion of Lindsay Anderson as director was accepted without demur despite Anderson's lack of previous feature experience. However, with the film's financial failure, full circle was turned with Rank's chairman, John Davis, being quick to inform us that the public didn't want 'dreary kitchen-sink dramas' and that 'independent producers . . . should make films of entertainment value' (Husra, 1964). That this signalled to a large extent the end of the movement tells us something of the limits of the challenge that had been made to the industry. Control had been conceived in terms of an overcoming of the fragmentation of skills concomitant upon cinema's 'factory system' through a unification of control under the director, and this was to some extent 'won' in the leeway given to independents, but it was a control dependent on a system founded upon monopoly in distribution and exhibition which through its 'distribution guarantees' accorded the duopoly a right of appraisal and definitional status over the category of 'entertainment'. This could dominate over competing versions of others and in this case ultimately did so (though it might also be argued that the movement destroyed itself anyway through becoming seen to be 'conventional' and hence de-legitimising its claims to 'reality').

The purpose here then, in an albeit abbreviated fashion, has been to suggest the need to avoid a-priorism and over-abstraction in the theorisation of both ideology and realism (the two being here brought together through the dominance of realism within British cinema, whose characterisation has been necessarily selective, and the attempts of current work to define realism as intrinsically ideological). An emphasis on effectivity has suggested the necessity of analysis neither in terms of origins nor textual characteristics alone, but in relation to the particular complex of circumstances in which film texts are materialised. For the case discussed here, then, I have argued for a recognition of first, the socio-historical specificity of media ideologies (without which a grasp of certain of their sense would be impossible) but one which, secondly, maintains an awareness of cinematic specificity (the determinations of the 'machine') and its particular level of effectivity which is not then, thirdly, understood in terms of autonomy but rather in terms of the positions and spaces constructed at the level of the economic. Hence as a consequence of all three I hold that progressive or reactionary qualities cannot be assessed independently of the conditions of production of film-making, available modes of consumption as well as other available cinematic and socio-political discourses within the culture. And thus the ideological performance of the films is not a unitary one read off from a class base or a production process but a complex, un-unified one articulated in relation both to specific cinematic discourses and to socio-political ones which in part they support (constitute) but from which they also in part dissent.

Notes

1. Cf. Murdock and Golding's position that oppositional views 'are easily swamped by the volume of mainstream output' (p. 38) with Alvin Gouldner's claim for the 'contradictions' internal to a system of producing accounts of social reality that is grounded in private ownership: 'The hegemonic class's profit imperative therefore ends by undermining the very culture on which its own legitimacy rests' (1976, p. 157). The obverse of this can also be formulated – commercial imperatives will not necessarily lead to an investment in that which would appear conducive to capital's long-term interests. Take, for example, the case of *The Angry Silence*. In *Film World* Ivor Montagu (1964) argues 'Seeing the income level of those who control the controlling circuits in this country, such a film, had it been ten times cruder than it was, must inevitably have been certain of distribution and exhibition before ever it was begun' (p. 271). Yet this was precisely what it was not. Only one company could be found with any interest at all in the film and only then after £40,000 had been lopped off the bill through a sacrifice of fees by many of the leading participants in favour of a share of the profits, such as they might be.

2. Indeed, the whole issue is something of a red herring relying on a peculiar selection of a representative for semiotics (Terry Eagleton) and an assumed unproblematic reading of a rather confused claim. Far from being a 'very reasonable' assertion it is unclear what a text's 'internalisation' of its production relations might mean (if to be more than a mere axiom of the sort that every text is produced within a particular set of production relations). Eagleton himself reveals a hesitancy, and through his unsure employment of the notion of 'literary mode of production' tends to effect an unhappy elision of two distinct types of relations under the category of 'literary relations of production' – relations largely understood as those of the mode of production proper and those operant

between text and audience. And thus while probably attempting a 'stronger' and thus more tenuous claim he is likely to be more correctly seen as constructing an argument about relations of consumption and not relations of production at all and hence to be reading forward from text to audience (interestingly one of the relations submerged in Murdock and Golding's analysis) rather than back from text to production relations, as full quotation of the relevant passage reveals: 'One might add, too, that every literary text in some sense internalises its social relations of production – that every text intimates by its very conventions the way it is to be consumed, encodes within itself its own ideology of how, by whom and for whom it was produced. Every text obliquely posits a putative reader, defining its productability in terms of a certain capacity for consumption' (Eagleton, 1976, p. 48).

3. Brewster (1973) attempts this by establishing rules of pertinence in accordance with motivations generated within the textual system itself (though insofar as the 'implicit reader' which this is supposed to predicate is never empirically found not altogether without contradiction). Henderson (1973/74) rightly criticises Brewster for his attempt to impose Metzian terms within a foreign problematic, but in re-stating *Cahiers*' own rules of pertinence he hardly resolves the issue which Brewster was at least attempting to face: 'The *Cahiers* reading goes beyond the text relating what is present to what is absent, thereby defining its own principles of pertinence' (Henderson, 1973/74, p. 43). The rules of pertinence then may be the properties of the studying discourse (*Cahiers*' reading) rather than of the text itself (*Young Mr Lincoln*), but then that hardly exempts that discourse from the demands of validity and coherence.

6 RETHINKING STEREOTYPES

T.E. Perkins

Two major interests inform this paper.[1] Firstly, as Richard Dyer has argued, it is politically important to understand 'just what stereotypes are, how they function, ideologically and aesthetically, and why they are so resilient in the face of our rejection of them' (Dyer, 1977a). This paper attempts to indicate where we should look for answers to these problems, and to propose some tentative hypotheses about stereotypes which might provide ideas for future research and may have some relevance for political action. It should be regarded strictly as a working paper many of whose ideas are insufficiently worked out.

The second interest which informs the paper is the theory of ideology and the concept of values as used in sociological theory. While I believe that a Marxist approach provides the most convincing and full account of ideology, I nevertheless find myself confused by current attempts to theorise ideology. Not the least of my problems arises from the unwillingness of theorists to give some empirical content to their theories. Consequently the usefulness of these theories in the analysis of actual ideological processes or in understanding a phenomenon like stereotypes is as yet hard to assess. At least part of my interest derives from this: stereotypes seem to be ideological phenomena and should therefore be capable of being accounted for by any theory of ideology; conversely as ideological phenomena of a peculiarly 'public' and easily identifiable kind they may provide a useful means of studying the practice of ideology. However, such an undertaking requires a broader perspective on stereotypes than that typically provided by psychological studies of particular groups. We need a perspective that can account for their findings, but also one which allows us at least to test hypotheses about stereotypes as ideological concepts. At the moment the generally accepted definitions of, and assumptions about, stereotypes may actually prevent one from making many theoretical statements about how stereotypes work ideologically. To say this is, of course, to draw attention to some explicit theoretical presuppositions about ideology on which my discussion of stereotypes is based. Let me outline these briefly, in terms of broad problem areas.

Ideology must be understood as being both a 'worked out' system of ideas and as being inconsistent, incoherent and unsystematic. The two levels are not totally separate or independent of each other — on the contrary, 'Every philosophical current leaves behind a sedimentation of "common sense" . . . Common sense . . . is continually transforming itself, enriching itself with scientific ideas . . . ' (Gramsci, 1971 p. 326, n. 5). The linkages implied here are not clearly worked out, and part of our task must now be to clarify them. We cannot understand ideology as operating merely in one of these modes, at one level only. It is the coexistence of both levels and their articulation with each other as well as with other practices that is crucial to any theorisation of how ideology functions, or of how any particular component functions. Although these problems are not explicitly broached in this paper, it will I think be clear that they inform many of the ideas put forward about stereotypes. Potentially stereotypes provide a means of studying a cross-section of ideology rather than a single stratum.

Secondly, any theory which purports to explain ideology must be able to explain the emergence of counter-ideologies and related pheno- mena (for example, temporary declines in 'legitimacy' of a ruling ideology). How can we explain protest of groups such as of women and gays, if the only way they can understand the world is through ideology? The problem is surely that while we must recognise (and theorise) the extent to which ideology does determine thought (and activity), we must allow that this determination is not, and can not be, total. It may be that we must posit the capacity for 'creative', non-ideologically- determined thought (I call it 'creative' for want of a better word), as a human capacity, rather than merely as an ideological effect which is therefore by implication false. The understandable reluctance to posit any quality as a 'human' capacity/potential, for fear of seeming to posit an essential of human nature (a mistaken fear in my view) seems to have led even anti-historicists such as Althusser to an ultimately his- toricist position where an unacknowledged invisible force is the only possible source of change and protest. The explanation of counter- ideologies is made even more difficult by a conception of ideology in general as unilaterally and uniformly imposed on identical, and identically situated, individuals. To explain protest we must admit the possibility of evaluating ideology, or an element of an ideology. Since not everyone protests at the same time, we must also account for this differential evaluation. It is after all unlikely that a structural change that is sufficient to generate a counter-ideology will not also be gener- ally significant and 'visible'. We have to explain why only particular groups are moved to protest (gays for example), and we cannot do that with a uniform, unilateral model of ideological imposition. The only explanation which I find convincing is one which presupposes a capacity of individuals, as members of a group, to evaluate an 'ideology' as mis-representing 'reality', as being illegitimate. That this process will be influenced by the ruling ideology is admitted. But to be influenced by something is not to be totally determined and 'caused' by it.

Behind Gramsci's notion of hegemony lies a recognition that the effectiveness of ideology cannot be relied on, but is constantly vulner-able, constantly a source of, and a 'site' of conflict. The definition of ideology cannot, in this view, presuppose that it is unilaterally and unproblematically effective. An additional point I would wish to emphasise is that the problem is not merely to bring the recalcitrant back into line. It is the ideology itself which has to be constantly re-created and redefined. While the broad outlines of the ruling ideology are firm and *relatively* stable, the solutions to specific problems are not pre-given, they do not emerge 'logically' or automatically. They are negotiated within a framework. And this negotiation is itself a source of ideology's effectiveness, of particular contradictions and the location of future problems.

Thirdly, it will be evident in the discussion that follows that notions of truth and falsity, reality and appearance, must lie behind any dis-cussion of stereotypes. One feature of ideology which I think remark-able is its capacity to make what is false become true. It can do this only because it is structurally reinforced. Or to put it the other way round, the structural determinants of ideology, the relations to which ideology refers, the activities which are the source of ideas and modes of thinking, are dominant. Women and blacks may be legislatively defined as equal, but the major determinant of their ideological position remains their structural position — their conditions of existence. When I say that ideology makes what is false become true I may overstate the case. But in dealing with stereotypes one has to come to terms with actual (concrete) differences between social groups. These differences, (which stereotypes often identify) are in a very important sense 'real' and therefore 'valid'. They are a mark of ideology's effectivity. This is not the whole story — the 'real' differences are also 'false', partly because of the constitution of the categories men/women as categories with different qualities when really they cannot be so differentiated. But to say that may be to posit an individual 'true self' or 'potential' which, if left to his/her own devices, would have developed differently. If we do not posit at least an 'individual potential' it is difficult to see on what grounds we can make any claims about truth and falsity in connection with stereotypes, let alone argue that they are repressive:

what do they repress?

Let me conclude this section with three comments on the relevance of the preceding remarks to my work on stereotypes. Firstly, to have said that it is 'politically' important to understand how stereotypes work implies the possibility of conscious and effective political activity. Secondly, to insist on the complexity and problematic nature of ideology is to presuppose that ideology is never totally effective and indeed cannot be. If protest movements can (sometimes) 'open up' contradictions then an understanding of stereotypes is crucial, since stereotypes are so often a focal point of activity. Thirdly, if we are to understand how stereotypes function ideologically, we must understand the articulation of both systematic and commonsense levels with relations of production. We cannot do this by looking merely at stereotypes of women or gays in advertisements, books, films or plays, because that will not tell us why and how much stereotypes are effective. We must analyse the other locations of stereotypes as well, and discover how they are constituted.

I should like first to focus on what seem to me to be dominant and often misleading assumptions about the nature of stereotypes, and which, as I said earlier, often prevent us from making theoretical statements about how stereotypes function ideologically.

According to these assumptions stereotypes are: (1) always erroneous in content; (2) pejorative concepts; (3) about groups with whom we have little/no social contact; by implication therefore, are not held about one's own group; (4) about minority groups (or about oppressed groups); (5) simple; (6) rigid and do not change; (7) not structurally reinforced. It is also assumed that (8) the existence of contradictory stereotypes is evidence that they are erroneous, but of nothing else; (9) people either 'hold' stereotypes of a group (believe them to be true) or do not; (10) because someone holds a stereotype of a group, his/her behaviour towards a member of that group can be predicted.

Although there is no discussion here of the last assumption, it is included because it refers to an area of considerable importance and complexity which has had to remain outside the scope of this paper. The ways in which we 'use' stereotypes of our own group to control relationships, and even to manipulate our oppressors, is one example of the importance of 'behaviour' and stereotypes.

The concept of 'stereotype' was first introduced into the social sciences by Lippmann in 1922 (see Harding, 1968), and his version remains the most widely accepted by social scientists and laymen alike. It includes most of the above assumptions. If a concept is referred to as a stereotype, then the implication is that it is simple rather than complex or differentiated; erroneous rather than accurate; secondhand, rather than from direct experience; and resistant to modification by new experience (Harding, 1968). I wish to argue that while stereotypes do take this form on occasion, it is only the first of these characteristics that can be considered a part of the definition of 'stereotype', and even here I have reservations.

In so far as all typifications are simplifications since they select common features and exclude differences, then all typifications are undifferentiated (and in that sense they are also erroneous). Is it then simply a matter of degree? Should we conceptualise stereotypes as being at one end of a continuum, such that they select fewer characteristics (thereby excluding more)? This seems to be the case if we think of such stereotypes as 'dumb blonde' or 'happy-go-lucky negro'. Furthermore, this is the criterion used in empirical research to decide whether or not a stereotype exists. However, this 'simplicity' is in two senses deceptive: firstly, it may in *some* cases be better described as abstractness. That is to say that some stereotypes operate on a higher level of generalisation than other typifications; to refer 'correctly' to someone as a 'dumb blonde', and to understand what is meant by that implies a great deal more than hair colour and intelligence. It refers immediately to *her* sex, which refers to her status in society, her relationship to men, her inability to behave or think rationally, and so on. In short, it implies knowledge of a complex social structure (in this way stereotypes are like symbols). So it is misleading to say stereotypes are simple *rather than* complex. They are simple and complex. Secondly, the description of stereotypes as simple rather than *differentiated* is similarly deceptive. The fact that there is a higher consensus (uniformity) about the adjectives which describe the characteristics of some groups, than there is about those which describe other groups, may tell us a lot about the social situation of the group being described, and does not necessarily imply prejudice or distortion. It may be the case that members of this group can 'legitimately' be characterised by three or four attributes. We cannot assume that there is an ideal number of adjectives by which to describe a group.

This is not to say that simplicity, complexity and differentiation are entirely irrelevant to the definition of stereotypes, but that they can be, and have been, misleading. Nevertheless these terms do identify the area in which we must look for differences between stereotypes and

other typifications. For example it seems that differentiation of stereotypes is often accommodated by alternative stereotypes — 'dumb
blonde'/'cunning minx' — rather than by an expansion of the stereotype.
I will return to these questions later.

The implication that stereotypes are 'erroneous rather than accurate'
is widely accepted as part of the definition of stereotypes; inaccuracy in
this context implying a false account of objective reality — blondes are
not dumb, negroes are not happy-go-lucky. There are two main objec-
tions to this. Firstly, a lot of empirical research into, for example racial
stereotypes, has led some theorists to oppose 'inaccuracy' with a
'kernel of truth' hypothesis. Secondly, if we claim that stereotypes are
erroneous, then their potential ideological role is considerably reduced.
If there were really no positive correlation between the content (per-
ceived attributes) of a stereotype and the characteristics (actual
attributes) of the group concerned, it would be tantamount to arguing
either that the social (that is, commonly accepted) definitions of you
have no effect on you, in which case it would be very difficult to see
how ideology or socialisation works at all; or, that stereotypes do not
represent social definitions and are sociologically insignificant since
they are manifestations of pathological behaviour and thus mainly the
concern of psychologists; or that they affect only your behaviour but
not your 'true self', thus implying a divorce between behaviour and
self. This argument is, as I have already suggested, relevant, although
not in this form. The question of accuracy appears to be the central
problem in the discussion of stereotypes, and I will return to it towards
the end of the paper. At the moment I will mention in passing the
possibility that stereotypes very often have the same structure as
ideology in so far as they are both true and false. To presuppose that
the content of stereotypes is always inaccurate, in the sense normally
used, will prevent us from understanding stereotypes as ideological
concepts.

The claim that stereotypes are 'secondhand rather than from direct
experience' is similar to Klapp's distinction between stereotypes (as
referring to things outside one's social world) and social types (referring
to things with which one is familiar). Intuitively this seems valid.
However, the consequences of accepting this distinction are unacceptable. This would rule out stereotypes of men and women, at the very
least, since we all have direct experience of the opposite sex. Also it
rules out stereotypes of one's own group, and hence the argument that
stereotypes about one's group influence one's definition of oneself, and
conversely, it ignores the influence of stereotypes on people's behaviour

towards members of other groups. For example a teacher's stereotype of working-class children may affect the teacher's expectations of the child (and thus the child itself). So the potential role of stereotypes in socialisation, and thus in ideology, is once again reduced to a very secondary one. Secondhandness is anyway characteristic of the vast majority of our concepts and cannot therefore be used to distinguish between stereotypes and other concepts.

Is it then 'resistance to modification by new experience' that is the key factor? The assumption here is that, normally, contact with the group in question would change the concept to bring it into line with reality, but that new experience will not modify a stereotype. Disregarding the fact that the assumption of inaccuracy is built into the notion of resistance, the main implication is that in contrast to other concepts, stereotypes are especially resistant (or rigid). This receives support from research into 'erroneous' and highly pejorative stereotypes which serve important psychological functions (for those holding the stereotypes) and which cannot be given up without traumatic consequences. But such stereotypes are a special case. Most concepts are resistant in the sense that they require more than one deviant case to change the concept. In order to assess whether stereotypes are particularly rigid, we need to study the conditions under which concepts change, how much information is necessary, how important the continued existence of confirmatory information is, and how important the stereotype's conceptual status is (how much else would have to change). This must surely be essential to our understanding of ideology. We cannot simply assert that stereotypes are rigid. We must look at the social relationships to which they refer, and at their conceptual status, and ask under what conditions are stereotypes more or less resistant to modification. This is not to deny that stereotypes are very 'strong' concepts, and this may be a distinguishing feature. The strength of a stereotype results from a combination of three factors: its 'simplicity'; its immediate recognisability (which makes its communicative role very important), and its implicit reference to an assumed consensus about some attribute or complex social relationships. Stereotypes are in this respect prototypes of 'shared cultural meanings'. They are nothing if not social. It is because of these characteristics that they are so useful in socialisation − which in turn adds to their relative strength.

In trying to broaden the definition of stereotype to make it applicable to the analysis of ideology, there is a risk that it will simply become indistinguishable from 'role'. According to sociological tradition, a role is a 'set of expectations and obligations to act in certain ways in certain settings'. The child, in being taught the behaviour appropriate to his/her (or others') status (role expectations) is also taught something more, a more general lesson: that is, that group membership is important and extremely significant; in a sense it 'determines' behaviour — different groups behave differently and have different characteristics, different rights and duties and consequently groups are related to each other in different, structured, ways — some deserve more respect than others and so on. (Schools may now be particularly important in reinforcing and elaborating on this learning of group identity and significance. Universal, compulsory education may have played an important part in diminishing the influence of the trend to personalised socialisation in the family).

To learn how to behave, then, involves learning to recognise (and then evaluate) people as members of groups — that is to apply group concepts to social as well as to physical phenomena. The definition of oneself, and others, as a member of a group is absolutely essential to the ideological effectiveness of stereotypes. To learn about groups is to learn about status. Roles describe the dynamic aspect of status.

What then is the relationship between role, status and stereotype? *Status* refers to a position in society which entails a certain set of rights and duties. *Role* refers to the performance of those rights and duties, it is relational. *Stereotype* refers to both role and status at the same time, and the reference is perhaps always predominantly evaluative. (Adjectives are most important, and are often combined with or reduced to value-laden nouns — dumb blonde, bum, nigger. But stereotypes are not always so succinct.) Stereotypes do not necessarily exist about all statuses. There is not a stereotype of a typist or a cardboard-box maker. There may be an 'image' of the sort of person that is likely to be a typist, but it is very much more fluid, generalised and descriptive than a stereotype is and may be entirely personal. I should acknowledge here that I am still not sure about how to identify the boundaries of stereotypes. I will make two points to clarify the matter. Firstly, it may be that there is not a 'national' stereotype of a typist, but that there is a localised one — that is to say that those who come into close or frequent contact with a group of typists do hold a stereotype of typists. It is possible that to this extent all statuses do give rise to local stereotypes. I should add to this that of course there are at least two stereotypes which include typists — namely the stereotype of women in general, which, combined with a class stereotype, defines the parameters of a general definition of a typist. But this is of a different order to, say, the prostitute or 'career woman' stereotype. Secondly, the boundaries of stereotypes are ultimately, I think, indefinable. What one can say, however, is that some stereotypes are much more 'highly defined' than others. The degree of definition reflects the degree of consensus that a stereotype exists, which does not mean to say that the stereotype is 'accurate'. I can illustrate this best by an example – I was discussing with a few people the 'mother's boy' stereotype, and we all agreed about its content. I then asked about 'father's girl'; this produced three different interpretations – all of which were semi-convincing, but none of which seemed definitive. Similarly with 'happy-go-lucky negro' as against 'teacher'. I would say then that the first one in each pair is a much more highly defined stereotype, and that the latter is relatively weak. But in both cases, the latter still constitutes a stereotype in a way that cardboard-box maker does not. We can introduce an arbitrary cut-off point – 50 per cent agreement and more is a stereotype; and indeed to do so is valid. But that fails to include the evaluative dimension which seems to distinguish stereotypes most clearly from roles.

Roles and statuses are also of course, intrinsically evaluative concepts. But the nature of, and the presentness of, the evaluation is different. A stereotype brings to the surface and makes explicit and central what is concealed in the concept of status or role. With a status or role we are commonly enjoined (by sociology textbooks) to look beneath them to discover the norms and values they supposedly 'rest on'; with a stereotype we must look beneath the evaluation to see the complex social relationships that are being referred to. This does not mean that stereotypes are simple *reflections* of social values; to suggest so would be to oversimplify the case. Stereotypes are selections and arrangements of particular values and their relevance to specific roles.

Because stereotypes tend to be evaluative descriptions rather than 'factual' ones, much of the learning of stereotypes can take place independently, that is to say, without specific reference to the group concerned. Children learn the meanings of such concepts as 'dumb', 'happy-go-lucky', 'uppity', 'dirty', 'lazy' and so on, regardless of whether or not they know that they attach to the nouns 'blonde', 'negro' or 'wog'; these adjectives all have specific, and often very subtle, evaluations attached to them, evaluations which form part of a socially defined structure of evaluation. 'Happy-go-lucky' means more than a 'cheerful', since it has negative as well as positive overtones, and implies a specific sort of 'irresponsibility' which has a particular significance in our society. Similarly 'uppity' means something significantly different from 'self-respect' or 'sticking up for your rights'. To know how to use these adjectives correctly implies understanding of the different criteria that must be applied in evaluating (similar) behaviour. If the adjective is then used to describe a group rather than (as previously in the child's experience) an individual or an isolated action, the group's status is automatically defined. If the child learns the stereotype (for example, the term 'dirty wog') early in life then his/her subsequent learning of the full range of meanings of the adjective will (automatically) change the meaning of the stereotype for the child, and it will gradually lose its 'innocence' and become integrated into a complex system of evaluations that the child is learning. The superficially simple form of stereotypes combined with the specific evaluations makes their acquisition easy, and makes them particularly powerful means of conveying ideological information.

There is such a strong — if understandable — tendency to define stereotypes as pejorative that pejorativeness has become almost built into the meaning of the word 'stereotype'. 'Pejorative' implies a point of view, and there is a danger that if we build into the word 'stereotype' the assumption that they are pejorative concepts, we will unthinkingly be involved in adopting the point of view from which certain characteristics are seen to be 'bad', rather than asking (when appropriate) *why* are these characteristics 'bad.' (This happened of course in the early days of the women's movement.) I would argue anyway that there are stereotypes of all structurally central groups — class, race, gender, age. There is a male (he-man) stereotype, a WASP stereotype, a heterosexual stereotype, an upper class (leader) stereotype. These stereotypes are important because other stereotypes are partially defined in terms of, or in opposition to, them. The happy-go-lucky negro attains at least some of its meaning and force from its opposition to the 'puritan' characteristics (sombre and responsible) of the WASP. Positive stereotypes are an important part of the ideology and are important in the socialisation of both dominant and oppressed groups. In order to focus attention on the ideological nature of stereotypes it might be much more useful to talk of pejorative stereotypes and laudatory stereotypes, rather than to conceal the 'pejorativeness' in the meaning of the term.

It should now be clear that it is necessary to find a definition of stereotypes which neither includes nor excludes the assumptions just discussed — erroneousness, rigidity and so on. What is evident is that the various disputes have in fact identified the various forms taken by stereotypes. Lippmann's four characteristics describe one form of stereotype. What I want to suggest is that the nature and form of stereotypes vary, that this variation may not be arbitrary but may be related to the ideological or aesthetic functions of the stereotypes and/or to the structural position of the stereotyped group. We need to define 'stereotype' in a sufficiently open way so as to allow for the various forms it takes and yet try to isolate its distinctive characteristics. I would suggest that the following characteristics are essential parts of stereotypes:

A stereotype is:

(a) *A group concept*: It describes a group. Personality traits (broadly defined) predominate.

(b) *It is held by a group*: There is a very considerable uniformity about its content. Cannot have a 'private' stereotype.

(c) *Reflects an 'inferior judgemental process'*: (But not therefore leading necessarily to an inaccurate conclusion.) Stereotypes short-circuit or block capacity for objective and analytic judgements in favour of well-worn catch-all reactions (Fishman, 1956). To some extent all concepts do this — stereotypes do it to a much greater extent.

(d) (b) and (c) give rise to *simple structure* (mentioned earlier) which frequently conceals complexity (see (e)).

(e) High probability that social stereotypes will be *predominantly evaluative*.

(f) *A concept* — and like other concepts it is a selective, cognitive organising system, and a feature of human thought (Vinacke, 1957).

Two other points need to be made about stereotypes. Firstly, stereotypes can be 'held' in two ways. They can be 'held' in the sense that they are 'believed in'. And they can be 'held' in the sense that we know that a stereotype exists about a particular group and what its content is, even though we don't necessarily believe it. However, the division between these two is not always clear. It is not merely a question of either believing or not believing, but also of the strength and consistency of the belief. The nature of stereotypes is such that most people do hold them in the sense of knowing about them, just as they know the basic tenets of Christian belief; that is they are widely *distributed*. This wide distribution makes them readily available for use in interpreting the world, if the occasion demands, just as God may be invoked by semi-believers/semi-agnostics. The political (and ideological) importance of the wide distribution of stereotypes is that they can be, and are, appealed to at certain times. The current racist revival relies on people's knowledge of stereotypes, in the same way as a religious revival appeals to people's background of Christian knowledge with its explanatory potential and emotional content.

Secondly, stereotypes have what I refer to as a 'flexible range'. Essentially the same stereotype ('irrational woman') can be presented very starkly and blatantly or relatively complexly and 'realistically'. Cartoonists or comedians often appeal to the most stark (and exaggerated) version of a stereotype. Aesthetic disputes about whether or not a certain character in a film is a 'stereotype' may concern a relatively complex and 'realistic' version of a stereotype. This flexibility is undoubtedly important in maintaining credibility and communicability.

The form taken by stereotypes varies and some of this variation can be explained in terms of the group's structural position. Not all stereotypes perform identical ideological functions, nor are they related to 'objective reality' in the same way. Indeed they could not be. As will be seen later, stereotypes develop in various situations and cope with different sorts of problems. All I can do here is to outline one way of categorising stereotypes, and suggest reasons for, and consequences of, a couple of variations.

There are stereotypes about:

1. *Major Structural Groups*: colour (black/white); gender (male/female); class (upper/middle/working); age (child/young/adult/old). (Can make jokes about MS groups to mass audience.) *Everybody* is a member of *each* group.
2. *Structurally Significant and Salient Groups*: ethnic groups (Jews/ Scots); artists and scientists; mothers-in-law; adolescents in the 1950s. (Comedians' topical jokes mainly from this group.)
3. *Isolated Groups*: social and/or geographic isolation. Gays; American Indians; students in the past; gypsies. (Can't make jokes about this group to mass audience unless it also belongs to another category — probably to *pariah*.)
4. *Pariah Groups*: gays; blacks; Communists in USA?; junkies? (Can make jokes to mass audience — but *may* be 'bad taste' to do so.) Groups here will also belong to another group (1-3).
5. *Opponent Groups*: upper-class twit; male chauvinist pig; reds; fascists. (Can *sometimes* make jokes to mass audience.) These contrast to others in so far as they are often developed by protesting,

deviant or oppressed groups, about their opponents. They can be subdivided into: *counter stereotypes* — e.g. male chauvinist pig — which form part of a counter-ideology and are sufficiently developed to be about a particular group (status and role); and *blanket stereotypes* — which refer to all non-believers — all non-Marxists are fascists; all non-fascists are reds. *Counters* originate from a critical attempt at reinterpretation or re-evaluation (pejorative rather than laudatory) of a dominant group. *Blankets* reinforce group solidarity by claiming a monopoly on knowledge of the 'truth' and grouping all rival claims to 'truth' as equally irrelevant and invalid.

6. *Socially/Ideologically Insignificant Groups:* milkmen; redheads.

Stereotypes of major structural groups tend to be thoroughly integrated into a number of practices. They are structurally supported — for example by laws, traditions, institutions, and so on. They are consequently relatively stable and definitively central in socialisation. They are also widely and consistently believed in and are highly effective in providing people with explanations and definitions of themselves and of others. A consequence of these characteristics is that they are most likely to be 'valid'. That is to say that we are most likely to find these attributes described by the stereotype in members of these groups (aggressive men, submissive women). Stereotypes of pariah groups are also strongly reinforced structurally and widely distributed. However, belief in them is inconsistent, but very subject to manipulation at particular times. They are, by definition, highly pejorative. Their effectiveness may be considerable, but precisely because of their almost totally negative character and lack of subtlety they are more likely to be counter-productive and at times to produce completely opposite tendencies (for example the 'puritanism' of the Black Muslims). It is important to emphasise that it would be impossible for all stereotypes of oppressed groups in our society to take this particular form. It works only because it applies to relatively few groups. The psychological and social consequences of such pariah stereotypes if applied to all oppressed groups would imply a population completely untypical of (and indeed unsuited to) Western capitalism — let alone liberal democracy. The total exclusion from society implied by pariah stereotypes is inappropriate to a working class or female stereotype.

Stereotypes — About Which Groups?

As I said earlier stereotypes refer to statuses, but not all statuses give rise to a stereotype. A stereotype will probably develop about a group because it has, or is presenting, a problem (for example, changing status, difficult but central relationships, and so on). Consequently most stereotypes do concern oppressed groups (because a dominant group's position is relatively stable and unproblematic).

First, a group which is presenting a problem also has a problem. If its changing structural position is presenting other groups with problems of redefinition or re-evaluation then the group itself faces these problems (of self definition and self evaluation). Stereotypes help everyone define the group.

Secondly, it may be the group itself which initially defines the situation as problematic, for example by protesting. Whether or not this is the result of structural change is an empirical question, but one of great importance to discussions about ideology. As we know, stereotypes will be a focal point of protest about a group's position.

These two points imply the following hypotheses:

A. (i) If a group's structural position or saliency changes, a stereotype will develop about that group.
  (ii) This is most likely to happen if the change is relatively quick and/ or significant.
B. If a group protests about its position and the challenge is sufficiently threatening to the ideology a stereotype will develop about the group. (Bra-burning women's libbers.)

In addition to these I would add:

C. If, in the above cases, a stereotype already exists then an alternative stereotype will develop. In some cases this alternative stereotype may eventually take over; in other cases it may remain as an alternative (additional) stereotype.

Examples:
  of structural change, A + C: housewife — career woman.
  of protest change, B + C: happy-go-lucky negro — uppity negro.

Gays do not yet seem to have presented a challenge which is sufficiently threatening to generate an alternative stereotype. It is of course particularly difficult for gays to do this since they have no 'legitimate' role in society.

Empirical support for these hypotheses could come from stereotypes in Group 2, or from research into changes of stereotypes. For example,

have stereotypes of the working class and women become more
numerous? Have student stereotypes changed over the last forty years?
Alternative stereotypes also develop for groups whose socialisation
poses particular problems. The socialisation of all oppressed groups is
problematic but there are differences in detail. These differences seem
to account for some of the variation in number and strength of
oppressed stereotypes.

Who Defines Stereotypes, and How is Definition Reached?

This immensely complex question has to be asked even if the answer is
beyond our grasp. To ask the question is to attempt to get away from
the mechanistic, pre-determined and unproblematic notion of ideology
I mentioned at the beginning of this paper — it is *not* to imply a con-
spiracy theory. The re-definition of stereotypes caused by the
'problems' mentioned occurs at various levels and is determined by a
number of factors, including old stereotypes, new conditions of existence, the nature of the group's protest, and so on. One of the ways in
which the mass media operate to support the ruling ideology is in this
re-defining process and in the circulation of new definitions or a range
of new definitions. I am not suggesting that this is calculated. The media
respond to what they think the audience want, which includes 'new' or
topical series as well as old favourites. The circulation of new definitions is important both to the group concerned and to other members
of society. Group members or potential members (depending on the
nature of the group) are offered the new definitions and interpretations.
They can potentially influence (but not totally determine) its content,
and they may in turn be influenced by the media. ('This is what
sympathy with blacks/women/gays/adolescents/students/strikers involves'). Re-definition through the mass media takes place in all types
of programme. Some series, (*Rock Follies, Bring on the Girls, Miss
Jones and Son*, to name a few), may be seen as part of a process of
redefining (female) stereotypes (as are 'topical' characters in old series).
Miss Jones and Son reflects a change in saliency namely the social
stigma attached to unmarried mothers has declined: we now have
'single parents', but this is still ultimately an unacceptable arrangement.
The media are rethinking (re-negotiating?) the unmarried mother
stereotype. This is not to use 'stereotype' in the way, for example,
critics of the media do — as a negative evaluation of, say, a fictional
character. Such a usage anyway implies an already existing stereotype. I
am talking about social stereotypes in general, and the way in which the
'shared cultural meanings' are constituted by the media, among others.

Stereotypes and Socialisation 'Problems'

Stereotypes form an important part of the socialisation of major structural groups. Stereotypes of these groups are legitimations of their positions. But there are significant differences. For example, there are relatively few stereotypes about men — and a vast number about women. There are strong 'negro' stereotypes, but not very many. Why? It may be helpful first to think of the following categorisation:

	Visibility	
Class	+ve	−ve
+ve	Blacks (colour)	Working class (class)
−ve	Women (Gender)	Gay (Gender/Sexuality?)

In functionalist sociology, socialisation is conceived as essentially unproblematic, although it may at times be 'unsuccessful'. This conception is I think invalid, but is frequently found in Marxism as well. The conception of ideology as unilaterally imposed on identically situated individuals presents similar problems.

In opposition to this, I would argue that the socialisation of any oppressed group is essentially problematic in so far as contradictory value orientations must be learnt. On the one hand they must (like all members of society) adopt a value structure which defines particular attributes as more valuable than others. Those attributes, they learn, characterise the dominant group. In so far as socialisation is to a large extent concerned with learning to aspire towards social values and to recognise the desirability of those values, there is a contradiction in the socialisation of groups who 'may' not, in fact, aspire to those values. Girls, blacks and to a lesser extent, the working class, must also be taught that they themselves 'do not have' these desirable attributes and that they *should not* aspire to them. They must aim for values which have a relatively low status. The fact that it is acceptable for girls to be 'tomboys' but not for boys to be 'sissy' reflects the fact that girls *have to* adopt a double standard, and that boys *must not*. This contradiction is of course aggravated by an 'egalitarian' ideology.

The situation of American blacks is illustrative of the essentially problematic, because contradictory, nature of socialisation. On the one

hand they must adopt the 'American Creed', the sex roles of white
society (dominant, employed, responsible, male/submissive, unemployed, home-making, female) and the materialistic values of capitalist
society. The centrality (sanctity) of the family is crucial — notwithstanding the divorce rate. However the structure of the negro family[2]
has been subjected to completely different influences from the white
family. Slavery prevented (in some cases forbade) the development of a
nuclear, patriarchal family and rather encouraged the development of a
matriarchal family; females were breeding machines, and males had no
conjugal rights and could be separated from their children and 'wife' at
the owner's will. This matriarchal pattern was continued when negroes
migrated to the cities where men were generally less able to find
employment than women who were able to work as domestics. The
negro woman in the city, therefore, often became the breadwinner. The
man was characteristically unemployed. His consciousness was
sufficiently determined by the values of dominant white society to
recognise that the man 'ought' to be the breadwinner and consequently
to feel that he didn't 'deserve' to adopt the traditional American
father's role in the family. The 'irresponsibility' which is part of the
'happy-go-lucky' stereotype derives its contemporary meaning from this
situation. To be unemployed is of course always presented,
ideologically, as a result of individual 'laziness' and so on, rather than in
terms of the system. (This is true for male unemployed whites as well,
just as — interestingly enough — the *necessity* of female employment is
concealed). The negro stereotype is then closely related to the negro's
structural position and is constantly reinforced by that situation. But it
is not a straightforward 'reflection' of that position, but rather an interpretation of it. At the same time it defines for the negro the acceptable
definition of himself — that is, the definition and explanation which
will be accepted by others, a definition which excludes him from
competition for social rewards. By contrast the 'uppity' negro defines
an unacceptable attitude — it represents a 'failure' in socialisation in so
far as the contradiction between the tenets of the American Creed on
the one hand and the exclusion of negroes from its compass on the
other has not been resolved — the Creed's claims about equality have
been taken at face value. Because the socialisation of blacks is problematic they give rise to strong stereotypes. But because of their cohesiveness in the sense of visibility, socio-economic status, and probable
ghetto situation, they do not give rise to very many stereotypes.

By contrast, women's socialisation is equally problematic (strong
stereotypes) but much more complex because of relative lack of

cohesiveness and of their institutionalised intimacy with men – hence it gives rise to a greater number of stereotypes. In so far as socio-economic class is generally ascribed in terms of the husband's or father's position, women can be characterised as being in a transclass situation. Gays are too. (This does not mean that it is impossible to conceive of them as a class. What is recognised is the overwhelming importance in socialisation of the socially defined status.) What is particular about women's position?

They have *very strong affective and instrumental social relationships with men, their oppressors*. These relationships are, in marriage at least, increasingly supposed to be 'equal'. At the same time however, they are acknowledged to be 'inferior'. Their transclass situation makes it particularly difficult to generate a group identity of their own. In this respect they are similar to gays, but it is even more difficult for women because of their isolation and their intimate relationship to men. The 'ghetto' situation of some (more fortunate?) gays provides some potential. The visibility of women also makes it particularly difficult to resist stereotypes, since the stereotype can be, and is, applied before any interaction takes place. In this respect, of course they are like other visible groups, particularly blacks and men (and of course whites in certain situations). These particular characteristics of women are likely to make their socialisation particularly problematic, especially in a society which makes claims to being an egalitarian democracy.

The situation of gays is different in at least two important respects. Whereas women, blacks and the working class are all exposed to stereo-types of *themselves* from birth onwards, this is not the case with gays. Gays may well be exposed to the gay stereotype for a long time before they have defined themselves as gay. It is arguable that for some/many gays the stereotypes may influence their 'decision' that they are gay. It seems that there are very few, if any, stereotypes that allow women to be aggressive or men to be caring and gentle except those relating to homosexuality (aggressive, predatory lesbian, motherly queer). Interest-ingly there is not (I think) a submissive lesbian stereotype, although there is an aggressive, in the sense of sadistic, queer stereotype. In terms of the effectiveness of stereotypes, the non-ascribed, non-visible, non-class, late, definition of gays must be considered. The possibility of 'choice' for gays is important – not merely in whether the stereotype is effective; it should also be considered that gay stereotypes may serve to prevent some 'gays' from defining themselves as such. And in this respect the gay stereotype will be more like other non-ascribed stereo-types – for example occupational ones. One probability is that gays will be more conscious of stereotypes as stereotypes — whether or not they accept them as accurate. (In fact, the non-visibility of gays combined with their 'illegitimacy' means that very often the only way they can communicate their gayness is by using the stereotype, for example the physical mannerisms or dress associated with the gay stereotype. That these mannerisms become so much a part of gay activity that they may be inseparable from the gay's true self, is illustrative of the sort of processes I discussed earlier. While the use/manipulation of stereotypes is more evident perhaps in the case of gays, it is by no means limited to them.)

The situation of gays is also different because there is no legitimate social role for them — unless the comic content of some gay stereotypes lends them some legitimacy. (However, lesbians do not even have this potential). Oddly enough, while the same should be true of criminals, it is a less clear case. There can at least be 'honour among thieves', but not according to stereotypes, among gays. The strong 'group solidarity' of criminal stereotypes is totally lacking from the gay one. Gays are generally portrayed as self-centred bitches — more akin to the negative 'grasser' criminal than any of the more positive criminal stereotypes.

It seems to me probable that this 'unique' illegitimacy of gays, which reflects their almost total powerlessness, will in fact make it very difficult for them to present an effective challenge to this ideology. The change in gays' situation, and stereotypes, will be most likely to come in on the coat-tails of other changes. Furthermore the other three oppressed groups discussed all have important structural (economic) links with their oppressors. Gays do not.

Stereotypes are Structurally Reinforced

There is a risk that in rejecting the oversimplified mechanistic version of ideology as being determined by the infrastructure we will ignore the influence of material conditions altogether. I wish therefore to make it absolutely clear that I believe while ideology is not a mere reflection of the socio-economic structure, material conditions are important determinants of consciousness. For example, the work situation of the housewife is such that she develops the capacity to cope with several things at once and learns not to concentrate on one thing so hard that she is not aware of what else is going on and cannot switch skills instantaneously. It will not encourage the capacity for analytical (critical) thought but will call considerably on the emotional side of her personality and for quick emotional responses. Her organisational skills may be highly developed in a limited area. Similarly, the work situation of a manual worker will encourage a decline in his/her capacity for creative or critical thought, while that of a junior executive will exercise his/her decision making capacity and necessarily develop 'human-relation' skills related to his/her position of authority (that is, leadership skills).

These are gross oversimplifications no doubt, but illustrative of the sort of determining influences material conditions have on consciousness. In each situation there are factors which counteract these tendencies, but they are weaker and tend either to be non-typical features of the work situation, or to be typical but subject to social sanctions thereby weakening their potential influence. These three examples illustrate one of the ways in which stereotypes are structurally reinforced. Part of the stereotype of women concerns their inability to concentrate on one issue at a time, their mental flightiness, scattiness and so on. In the middle of a conversation about one issue they skip to something completely different. This is all part of the 'irrational, illogical, inconsistent' (female logic) stereotype. Now what this seems to me to relate to is a mode of thinking which is essential to the housewife's job. Most other jobs demand concentration on a single issue and the application of one skill at a time; the capacity to keep shifting attention back and forth, and changing skills, is characteristic of a housewife's job. What the stereotype does is to identify this feature of the woman's job situation, place a negative evaluation on it, and then establish it as an innate female characteristic, thus inverting its status so that it becomes a cause rather than an effect. It is these features of stereotypes which explain why stereotypes appear to be false — indeed, *are* false. The point at the moment is to identify their validity, because the strength of stereotypes lies in this combination of validity and distortion.

Whether or not I am correct in identifying this capacity as one which is produced by the housewife's situation is something only research could tell us. Undoubtedly it is a difference which cartoonists recognise, as shown by all those cartoons of father sitting at the breakfast table immersed in the newspaper while all hell lets loose around him. This characterisation of women as incapable of sticking to a single topic is a good example of flexibility — gross exaggerations occur in comedy and cartoons — but a more realistic version is used in everyday life.

Stereotypes: Short-Circuiting as an Ideological Feature

It would of course be naive to argue that the work situation was totally determinant. However if we accept the view that the educational curriculum is so structured as to restrict the development of critical ability to those going on to higher education and to conceal the 'constructed' nature of knowledge until then, then the propensity of most jobs to discourage such intellectual abilities will be greatly increased. (The greater decline in measured intelligence of manual as compared to white collar workers may reflect this. It may also explain the negative correlation between stereotypical thinking and education). The underdevelopment of analytical/critical thought at school is in itself ideologically important but does not concern us here. I simply want to point to this linkage: stereotypes short-circuit critical thinking; their effectiveness depends in part on our willingness to short-circuit. Our willingness derives from two things: firstly, it may simply make life easier, more convenient; the other is that information may be limited and our critical faculties may be underdeveloped, and effectively we. may often have no other choice but to short-circuit. This is true of all of us sometimes. But the more limited our knowledge and training then the greater the area will be where short-circuiting is the only solution. This characteristic of stereotypes appears to locate them firmly in the area of 'common sense', one of whose distinguishing features, according to Gramsci, is its unworked-out character. However, though this may be their main arena, we cannot limit our analysis of stereotypes to this level. Common sense also contains 'scientific ideas' and 'philosophical currents'. So too do stereotypes and our understanding of their location in systematic worked out ideology, in legislation and so on, is essential to an understanding of how they function ideologically.

Accuracy — the Central Problem?

I have already dealt in passing with many of the issues which are related to accuracy. I have said that stereotypes are often 'valid'; that they are often effective in so far as people define themselves in terms of the stereotypes about them; that they are structurally reinforced; that they refer to role performances, and so on. However, having said all this there are important senses in which stereotypes are inaccurate or false. Here I refer to my earlier claim that stereotypes are similar to ideology in that they are both (apparently) true and (really) false at the same time. I will discuss this in the context of differences between stereotypes of dominant and oppressed groups. Two main points about their falsity are to be made: Firstly, stereotypes present interpretations of groups which conceal the 'real' cause of the group's attributes and confirm the legitimacy of the group's oppressed position. Secondly, stereotypes are selective descriptions of particularly significant or problematic areas and to that extent they are exaggerations.

Stereotypes are evaluative concepts about status and role and as such are central to interpreting and evaluating social groups, including one's own. Definition of oneself as a member of a group is essential to the socialisation process, and an important element of social control. Oppressed groups pose particular problems of control and definition. The fact that group membership is a much more salient part of the self-definition of oppressed groups than is membership of high status groups to them, reflects these problems (Holter, 1970 p. 210). This saliency is the effect of the contradiction and is a mechanism of social control. Because one's membership of a group is always present, so too is the stereotype of oneself and so too therefore, is a self-derogatory concept − to be socialised is to be self-oppressed. (Effectiveness of the ideology relies on this as does its 'legitimacy'). But to have adopted this concept will have involved adopting contradictory value orientations as well, which means that the self-definition (self-oppression) is always vulnerable and needs constant reinforcing. Furthermore, the consciousness of oneself as a member of a particular group, which is essential to social control, is also potentially threatening. The continued and persistent class-consciousness of an often apparently a-political and apathetic working class, the feminine consciousness of 'unliberated' and repressed women, are evidence of this consciousness of group membership.

Stereotypes are particulary strong, I have argued, when they have to operate as conceptual (cognitive) resolutions of such contradictions. It is this resolution that is the real location of their inaccuracy. Stereotypes were described earlier as being descriptions of an effect (consciousness) which was then evaluated and inverted, so it becomes a cause, which then explains the differentiation of which it is actually a description. This process (similar in structure to alienation) is typical of ideology. The inversion of effect into cause is the primary means of conceptually resolving the contradiction involved, for example, in the socialisation of oppressed groups. However, it can become a cause only because it makes ideological sense. The content of stereotypes is not arbitrary (nor are they interchangeable). Stereotypes are selective descriptions − they select those features which have particular ideological significance. Hence, remarkably few stereotypes refer to such qualities as kindness, compassion, integrity − or even honesty) nor their opposites). Personality traits can be subdivided into: mental, sexual and personal. However it is the mental attributes which are definitive and which seem to 'dictate' the rest of the content. Other attributes become linked to mental characteristics in a non-reciprocal way. Dumb does not imply dirty; 'dirty' as a social description does imply 'stupidity'. The reason mental characteristics are dominant is that they are ideologically the most significant (and therefore convincing). Briefly, economic differentiation is the most important differentiation. The ideological criterion for economic differentiation in our capitalist society is primarily intelligence; and only secondly 'contribution' to the society and possession of skills which are necessary but 'supposedly' scarce (for example, decision-making, responsibility, leadership qualities). The most important and the *common* feature of the stereotypes of the major structural groups relates to their mental abilities. In each case the oppressed group is characterised as innately less intelligent. It is particularly important for our ideology that attributes should be conceived of as being innate characteristics either of human nature in general (competitiveness) or of women/men/blacks in particular, since this supports the belief that they are not the effect of the socio-economic system (and the order of things appears to be inevitable — the survival of the fittest and may the best man win). The fact that stereotypes do so often present attributes as if they were 'natural' is not a feature of stereotyping *per se*, so much as an indication that they are ideological concepts. The existence of endless research programmes into innate differences and the publicity their results receive, supports the legitimacy of stereotypes (regardless of the actual results) and of the ideological claim that social differentiation arises from innate differences. The notion that we can (do) have any control over social relationships is absent, and its absence confirms its irrelevance. This problem of course has considerable political importance to oppressed groups, and they need to question the efficacy of involving themselves in disputes about innate differences — there is no easy answer, I might add!

What then are the main differences between stereotypes of oppressed and of dominant groups? Stereotypes of oppressed groups are stronger and sometimes more numerous, and more 'present' in the consciousness (and self-definition) of the oppressed group. They will also be more present in the consciousness of the dominant group. A member of an oppressed group will, by definition, have limited access to the 'goods' of society, and the stereotype will confirm this limited access (and its legitimacy) but should not be seen as causing it.

Stereotypes of dominant groups will also confirm the boundaries of their own legitimate activity (as will the stereotypes of oppressed groups, of which dominant groups may be more conscious than their own stereotypes). It is *as* important for them to adopt the value structure and to confirm that the goods of society are 'good' as it is for others to continue to see them as good (if unattainable). (Good here refers to anything defined as socially desirable, not just material goods, for example going *out* to work rather than doing housework). Men who choose (prefer) to stay at home to look after the children while their wives go out to work, challenge the value structure. And a challenge from a dominant group is potentially more threatening (if much less likely) than one from a subordinate group. (The content of gay stereotypes might deserve analysis in this light.) In that respect, a male/white/upper class stereotype is *more* limiting. A challenge from a subordinate group can often be interpreted as a confirmation of the value structure. Stereotypes of oppressed groups will be pejorative, but their pejorativeness is complex and often concealed. Stereotypes of pariah groups may be unambiguously pejorative, but the pejorativeness of female stereotypes is concealed since they must resolve the specific contradictions of women's position. Hence the stereotype presents female characteristics as desirable, for women, and masculine characteristics as undesirable. So the negative female stereotypes 'cunning minx', 'bluestocking', 'career woman' (or the lesbian ones) are stereotypes that essentially acknowledge that women may be intelligent (or aggressive) but define that intelligence as, in *their* case, undesirable (and 'unnatural'). These three stereotypes also reflect another aspect of female stereotypes which *is* more limiting than others – that is, a great many alternative stereotypes have been generated to accommodate this particularly difficult group. The 'bluestocking' or 'career woman' stereotype accommodates women in these categories by excluding them from being sexual beings or mothers. Male stereotypes are rarely so specific. It need hardly be said that this difference reflects 'objective reality' (it *is* extremely difficult to be a career woman and a mother).

There is always a danger in setting oneself tasks at the beginning of a paper however modest those tasks may then seem to be. I was conscious of one particularly serious problem – namely the very few and scattered references to how stereotypes function aesthetically, but I came to the conclusion that we can not begin to answer that without first working out the more general question of how they function ideologically. I am conscious of other omissions and errors of emphasis – and I have no doubt the reader is too. What I hope I have achieved is to provide a theoretical perspective on stereotypes which allows us to investigate them as ideological phenomena, which begins to establish in some detail their ideological role and also which explains the existence of stereotypes, their varied number, content and form, as sociologically significant rather than as random and arbitrary phenomena.

Notes

1. This paper would not have been written had it not been for the encouragement and unfailing confidence of Richard Dyer. I am indebted to him for that. There is little in the paper that has not benefited from his insights and constructive criticisms, and any credit that is given is due equally to him; the blame I will keep for myself.

I must also acknowledge a debt to Terry Lovell, some of whose (currently) unpublished work I found very helpful in clarifying my own ideas and in suggesting new ones.

2. I use the term 'negro' here in order to distinguish between a social group with a specific historical background and the larger group of 'non-whites' which the term 'black' now often includes.

7 TELEVISION AS TEXT: OPEN UNIVERSITY 'CASE-STUDY' PROGRAMMES

Grahame Thompson

I

This paper will review certain aspects of the nature of educational television. It will do this by analysing in detail a particular Open University TV programme. The Open University (OU) is by far the largest user of TV for educational purposes in the UK. It is now using some 35.5 hours of television transmission time weekly (and 26 hours of radio transmission time per week, though this aspect of its broadcasting activity is not considered here). In 1977 there were a total of 1305 separate television programmes being broadcast to the 55,600 registered students of the University (Gallagher, 1977). Of course there are other users of TV for directly educational purposes, for example the Schools Service of the BBC, further education and various language teaching programmes and *ad hoc* series of programmes pitched at particular groups like non-readers, managers, trade-unionists, and so on. The whole range of these programmes has not been looked at in any systematic manner here, and the paper does not claim to offer a comprehensive review of television educational broadcasting in this country. In fact it does the opposite. It concentrates upon one particular programme, but in doing so it is hoped that that some useful general points about such broadcasting can be made.

There is a great diversity of styles employed in these programmes. Indeed, even within the Open University, the range of programme formats is equally diverse. It certainly cannot be said that the Open University has developed its own distinctive style of broadcasting let alone one specifically educational in character. By and large it has merely 'taken over' the already existing practices and conventions of the general service. In this respect it tends to mirror and re-produce already existing and well tried forms of television programme construction. In this it is not always as successful as the general service, since it does not have the resources that are available to general service programme makers. Nor does it have quite the same 'expertise of presentation', since Open University academics are obviously not primarily recruited as television presenters. However, there are great pressures to become as 'professional' as possible and in this regard such 'professionalism' is judged against 'general service standards'. A great deal could be said here about why such pressures arise and the justifications offered for them by both academics and BBC personnel though for reasons of space this paper will not directly address these issues. Nor are these pressures confined just to those responsible for producing the programmes. The ethic or ideology of 'good television' pervades the 'viewer-student' reaction to TV broadcasting as well. This is perhaps not surprising since the viewer-student judges against what she/he 'normally' sees on TV and, indeed, is encouraged to do just that with the adoption and duplication of general service conventions and codes by most Open University TV programmes themselves. Thus this ideology of 'good television' is shared by more or less all those concerned with Open University broadcasting. However, it is here that a problem arises. This becomes apparent when an attempt is made to specify more precisely what is meant by 'good television' and, in particular, what is meant by good television in the context of a university educational objective. This problem has continually arisen in relation to the evaluation of the effectiveness or otherwise of broadcasting that is conducted by the University through its media research group. For certain reasons, which are more fully developed later, the feeling on reading the recent reports of this group is that the issue always just manages to slip through their fingers. It is largely spirited away in the form of a very specific but highly abstract consideration of student reaction to TV broadcasts. This does not get very much further than identifying 'interesting', 'helpful', 'useful', and so on as the main criteria of success (or otherwise) employed by the student-viewer in judging programmes.

It is to this very problem of a more adequate assessment of the effects of particular forms of educational broadcasting that this paper is addressed. The paper looks at the first TV programme of the current Social Sciences Faculty's Foundation Year Course, D101, 'Making sense of society' (approximately 7,400 students per year). This is an example of what might be called the predominant genre 'current' within the social science field of broadcasting. This field does not only include courses within the Social Sciences Faculty but also those of the Educational Faculty and also some of the courses within the Science and Technology Faculties which touch upon 'social' issues'. It must be said that within this field there are very different styles of programme. These include didactic lectures; studio discussions with academics/experts; illustrative film/studio material; case study/mini-documentary, and so on, or any combination of these. However, one of the most strongly represented forms within this area (indeed, the most strongly represented form within the Social Sciences Faculty itself) over the last few years has been the case-study type programme (CS). It would be easy to get into a long discussion of what exactly constitutes a CS programme, and what precisely demarcates it from other forms. It is not intended to pursue this discussion here (for those interested see Bates and Gallagher, 1977; and my comments upon this, Thompson 1977b).

Suffice it to say that what dominates in these types of programmes in one form or another, is the notion of 'recording real events' — the emphasis being upon some 'real-life event' which happens 'in the real world'. In the context of the Open University this has predominantly meant getting the people involved in those events (the real social actors) to express their 'points of view' (experiences) in one way or another. Hence, what is invoked in these programmes is the notion of 'realism' (and sometimes 'naturalism') and with it primacy is afforded to the 'real world of experiences' as the location or generator of knowledge. This 'real world' tends to be given an (unargued) privileged position. It acts as a referent against which the social actors 'speak' and 'work' and against which the camera 'records' and 'reflects'. It is in relation to this concept of 'realism' that I want to examine the teaching message carried in these kinds of programme and the educational effects that they engender. Thus I will ask a series of innocent but difficult questions. 'What can this form of programme teach?' How can the effects of these programmes be assessed?' 'How is meaning constructed in these programmes?' and so on.

Before addressing these questions directly, however, a more immediate problem must be faced. This involves the principles employed in assessing or 'reading' TV programmes of any kind. Here I will briefly review current conceptions of this within the Open University. Fortunately, these are of a more general interest since they largely parallel the predominant conceptions of assessment held also outside of the University. They fall into three major approaches, which I have termed respectively: reduction to 'author' theory, reduction to 'spectator' theory, and the theory of television as 'text'. Each is discussed in turn below.

II

Reduction to 'author' theory involves reducing the programme to the intentions of its authors. Thus, the point of programme assessment becomes one of finding out what the authors really intended to demonstrate in their programme. This leads to the endless interviews conducted with programme/film makers to try and 'track down' this elusive intention. Once such intentions are 'identified', the programme's effects can be read directly as more or less a simple expression of these. In the context of the Open University it is the 'producer/academic alliance' which is held to author such programmes and their intentions can be read from what are called in OU parlance Programme Notes. These accompany the programme, being sent to students and (usually) embody a series of aims and objectives for that programme. It is here that such 'intentions' can be found.

This conception is closely tied up with what might be termed the 'point of view' theory of intellectual effort. The conscious point of view of the author determines what she/he 'sees' and hence the pertinences highlighted in the subject matter of the programme. This 'point of view' determines the concept and form of explanation offered by the programme, and hence any criticism of it is a criticism of the author as such. This leads to great inhibitions about criticising programmes within the Open University context for obvious reasons associated with personal and academic freedoms ('in attacking my programme you are attacking me'). In another context this kind of conception is similar to a certain sociological tradition of cultural explanation based upon 'encoding/decoding' practices. Cultural expression is one forming a chain of (i) encoding with socially determined intentions, (ii) communication by a particular technology or form of enunciation and finally (iii) a 'decoding' by the recipient, again on the basis of the consciously determined view-point of that recipient. With this conception the material factors of life which determine cultural meaning are thought to be produced by distinct classes or groups through the activity of consciousness. There is an inherent capacity in human beings to invest the material forms of existence with a rationality and meaning. In relation to this, television is purely instrumental. It performs a certain function of communication of these 'already' determined meanings (see Coward, 1977a for a critique of this kind of approach).

The problems with this conception are that what is intended may not be what is actually executed. What might be actually 'present' in the programme can be very different to what was intended by the author or even what was thought was being done by that author (as is the case with the programme analysed below, I would suggest). Of course, all programmes are 'authored' in one sense, in as much as there is some *position* (whether political or theoretical) represented in the signifying practices of the programme as such. It is important to point out, however, that this 'authorship' is neither the result of a conscious intention — it is objectified by a position which is itself the result of a field of determinations, these being supported by human subjects — nor can this position be read 'prior' to the programme's execution of it. Any non-subjective, authored position of this character can only be read from the programme as such; in and from the signifying practice embodied in that programme, these being actually 'constitutive' of that programme as a programme.

Reduction to 'spectator' theory is much more strongly represented in the social sciences generally, and particularly within the Open University Media Research Group. The approach has been well formalised into a series of statistical gathering and processing practices. It is particularly concerned with identifying the characteristics and circumstances of the audience. These can be more or less detailed, more or less significant, more or less personal, but they take as their starting point an already constituted and 'pre-given' individual viewer with certain such characteristics. The programme only has meaning in relation to these already given characteristics and circumstances, hence the importance of 'finding them out'. The programme is decoded by, and in relation to these, by the viewer. The viewer 'sees' what she/he 'wants' to find in the programme, and this depends upon a proliferation of personal, family and social characteristics and circumstances. The individual can freely accept or reject whichever 'message' she/he likes in as much that these characteristics and circumstances impart the individual with a consciousness that enable that individual to make just such a choice. An implication of this approach is that, in a fundamental sense, nothing general can be said about any programme because the way it is received and the message 'abstracted' from it will all depend upon the subjective characteristics and circumstances of the viewer and these are as diverse as the individuals themselves.

This leads to the approach of questionnaire and data collection in order to establish the audience's 'reaction' to the programme (Gallagher, 1977; Audio Visual Media Research Group Broadcast Evaluating Report No. 22, 1977a and No. 23, 1977b). Such an approach is of course not confined to the Open University as a look at the proceedings of a recent international conference held at the Open University should demonstrate (Bates and Robinson, 1977). The main problem with this kind of approach is that it can never penetrate to the issue that it is, ostensibly at least, trying to pose. This issue is the effectiveness, or otherwise, of the programmes as a teaching vehicle. Attitudes and reactions to broadcasting are assessed in the abstract and not in relation to the content of the programme and its effects but in relation to whether or not it was 'interesting', 'useful', 'helpful', 'stimulating', and so on. The problem of what is meant by these vague and abstract terms is never posed (they just represent the characteristics associated with 'good television'). *Effectiveness is equated with 'interesting', 'useful', and so on, not with the effectivity of the programme as such.* But to pose the problem of the effectivity of a programme means to abandon the notion of an already-given, 'average' viewer who just happens to be a student and who reacts to a programme; that is, the notion of 'student' must itself be problematised. This means it is necessary to recognise that programmes of themselves are constitutive of the viewer in a particular way, and not vice versa. This means that the audience is created 'student' in relation to the programme, and is not pre-given as students but only as 'general viewer/observer'. 'Students' are constituted only in their articulation into a process of teaching and learning. Hence, this alternative approach requires a recognition (amongst other things) that students can be constituted in different ways in relation to different programme types and formats (different forms of representation and signification). However, before this is pursued, it is important to point out that the argument effectively being made here against the Media Research Group and the like is not meant to be entirely negative. The kind of studies referred to above can fulfil a very useful initial function (and indeed have done just that), in as much as they provide a 'raw material' which signals a problem and to some extent situates this problem accurately. Hence, it can highlight the problems with particular programmes but fundamentally it cannot, within its own terms, tie the problem down sufficiently to effect a 'solution'.

In addition here, it is important to point out that this is the site of a real theoretical problem which has not been entirely solved. This problem is that of the constitution of the subject in discourse (Ellis, 1976; Caughie, 1977; Nowell-Smith, 1976). A few comments on this are in order at this stage.

It is not being suggested here that the viewer is a *tabula rasa* when she/he comes to Open University television programmes. Indeed, at a very minimum, it is recognised that three important aspects are present at such an encounter. These are, in the first place, that the viewer-observer has already been partly constituted as student in relation to other aspects of the course and in relation to prior forms of teaching and learning both within the University and outside it. Hence, some 'attitude' towards what is involved in and required of learning (or not, as the case may be), is present at the moment of that encounter. Secondly, such students have their own 'experiences' which partly guide them in their relationship to what is being taught (this aspect is discussed in much greater detail below). Thirdly, viewers already expect something of television, given that they are general viewer-observers articulated within normal TV watching activities. This may be summed up by saying that there is an aspect of intertextual determination to the viewing subject.

What is both necessary but difficult is to specify theoretically the nature of this audience in its relationship to the television teaching-learning process. It is argued below that it is the representations, the practices of signification, which make up television that constitute the space in which the relationship between the viewer and the viewed can be posed. Within this space, the viewing subject is not simply a passive support but is inscribed by being caught within a particular configuration of discursive and non-discursive practices. The viewer (audience) and the viewed programme) provide the mutual conditions of each other's existence and the intertextual character of this relationship enables, in principle, a 'negotiation with meaning' to be made on the part of the viewing subject. However, certain forms of this configuration tend merely to condense and confirm the action of the already constitut-*ing* and subject-*ing* determinations mentioned above and as a consequence effectively silence such negotiation, whilst others tend to displace and dissolve these determinations and in so doing, it is argued, precisely open up the possibility of such negotiation. It is hoped that these points can be made more concrete in relation to the actual programme analysed below.

Both the reduction to authorship and the reduction to the spectator tend to locate the meaning of television in something other than itself — they either reduce it to the circumstances and characteristics of the 'author' or alternatively to those of the 'spectator'. Thus the constitution of the message it carries is outside of itself, and the programme's meaning of itself must effectively 'disappear'. However, if we are to get around the problems highlighted above, it is necessary to treat TV as a form of discourse in its own right, with its own effects, that is to treat it as text. TV must be 'read' like any other text to discern what its content or message is, and this content or message is actually in the programme. It is in the codes and representations and their signification (meaning) — it is these that produce its effects. The programme produces nothing but effects, which are the result of the articulation of its discourses and this is actually what the programme is — an articulation of discursive practices and spaces which give meaning to what the programme 'says' (definite practices of signification). Here it is important to recognise that what is signified is not independent of (a) the chain of signifiers and their order, and (b) the very process of significa- tion itself; that is the determinations of the practices entailed in the action of those means of representation — the action of that chain. This is in distinction to the notion of encoding/decoding, where the signifying practices are attributed a neutrality (they are a function) which 'meaning' can merely appropriate, i.e. the subject and object are already given prior to the action of the means of representation.

What is involved in 'reading' a programme in this manner? In fact, what is involved in any 'reading' of this character? It is the result of assessing its 'arguments'; reading its 'presences' and 'absences', its strengths and weaknesses, its 'silences' and the points of its lacunae and 'slippages', the adequacy and inadequacy of its demonstration in rela- tion to what it purports to show and so on. In relation to the teaching function what is required is to make this argument apparent, pointing out its nuances, weaknesses, strengths, and so on and trying to assess the reasons for these, that is, to give some meaning to the form of the argument. Clearly, this is not an easy thing to do, and I make no claim for comprehensiveness in my own attempt to undertake such a reading below. This is doubly difficult when one recognises that no text dis- plays a homogeneous argument, but always a set of sometimes disparate and contradictory arguments (though there tends always to be a resolu- tion of any such contradiction in the text in the form of a metadis- course). We are now in a position to turn to some of the problems associated with case study type programmes as such.

III

The effect of the way in which most case studies have been conducted within Open University educational broadcasting is to afford the 'real world' a privileged position in relationship to knowledge. The ideology associated with these kinds of programmes is to let real social actors speak for themselves and to intervene (as an academic) as little as is possible. Even where such intervention is active, by and large, the privileged position of the immediate conception made by social actors of their own position or their perception of their own, or others', social predicament, is hardly challenged. The intervention is only made to link or to facilitate the development of the 'story' as told by such actors. Indeed, it is seen as one of the strengths of these programmes that such actors are given the opportunity to 'speak' as such, and that Open University students are privileged to learn something from this. But the question is, what do they learn? As soon as this question is asked, a further and crucial issue is raised. 'What conception of knowledge informs the format and structure of the programme itself?' The teaching process is one which, at its very minimum, must engender the conditions under which genuine knowledge can be both taught and constituted or produced. In a very general sense such a process requires the breaking of any seeming continuity there might be between experiences and knowledge. Experiences need to be utterly transformed if the real processes and mechanisms which determine just those experiences are to be made apparent and known.

The appeal to 'realism' made in these programmes, and the conception of the programme as merely reflective of such a real situation is a particular appeal and one that severely constrains and confines programmes. In so doing it imparts them with a particular epistemological structure. This produces certain by now well known but problematical effects in the viewer (McCabe, 1974; McCabe, 1976b).

Traditionally, 'realism' has been associated with fictional texts, most notably with the novel, though more recently with film and other aesthetic forms. Recent theoretical developments have begun to link these aesthetic considerations with the 'order of the unconscious' through the use of the Freudian (or Lacanian) conceptions of 'pleasure' and 'paranoia'. Certain directions within these developments have gone further to address explicitly the issue of the encounter between psychoanalysis and historical materialism which has been made possible by these theoretical developments. In so doing, it has become possible (I would argue) at least to borrow certain of the theoretical results of the analysis of realism undertaken in relation to fictional texts for the analysis of non-fictional forms. Now it is clear that there is no one thing called realism but many 'realisms', with different conditions of existence which secure their definite forms. Without being able in this paper to explore this borrowing systematically, I shall simply invoke certain aspects of it. It is clear, for instance, that the absence of a narrator, but the presence of a (silent) narration, is one of the specific features of fictional realist texts. Of course, in non-fiction forms of a documentary type such a narrator is usually present. However, as will be argued below, there can also be silent narrations, even where the narrator is present. In addition, nor must the distinction between 'fictional' and 'non-fictional' texts be taken for granted. Both of these are constructed by certain definite signifying practices. With this respect, it needs to be said at once that there are obviously some properties of realism that are specific to non-fictional documentary forms like those articulated around such notions as 'observation', 'truth within visibility' and verification through camera as neutral recorder, and so on. This is not denied, but what is being attempted here is rather to secure for such further exploration the encounter between psychoanalysis and historical materialism specifically in relation to a particular use of realism within a teaching/learning context.

The reason for the strength of realism is that it is ultimately 'pleasurable' in a comforting, familiar sort of way (rather like a hot bath), and this is precisely its problem from a teaching point of view. It engenders an unconscious relaxation because it is familiar. It does not distance one from anything but in fact encourages the reverse, an emotional, accepting type of response, which tends to 'put students to sleep' intellectually. The reasons for this are fundamentally the way the real is constituted in these kinds of texts. The real is presented as always-already pre-given and unproblematic; it is never the result of a process of production, nor the result of an intellectual effort, but purely the result of an experiential effect. The real world is mirrored as closely as is possible; reflected in the 'eye' of the camera. These kinds of programmes are entertaining and fascinating precisely because they engender an (unconscious) pleasurable effect (in both 'producer' and 'consumer'). The classic realist situations are the 'work' situation and the 'home' situation (mirrored almost completely in Open University case-study programmes). We are all familiar with these situations, we 'know' from experience the problems we face in them, and hence the allegiance of both producers and consumers to them. These kinds of programme are ones that do not demand anything of us as viewers. They transform nothing but simply reinforce existing, experiential notions of what 'life is really like' (albeit sometimes in an exaggerated and even 'fantastic' form). This non-transformation of the immediate conditions of social existence engenders a non-understanding of these conditions by the viewer. She/he is hardly constituted as 'student' at all, but is merely confirmed as general 'observer-viewer'. It may well engender anger, concern, interest, involvement, and so on, but in purely emotional terms — which in relation to an educational objective, remain abstract and transitory. Hence the kinds of response just mentioned to questionnaires: no understanding of the *'why'* is engendered on the part of the student. No knowledge is imparted. In this respect, the low viewing figures that have been recorded for OU programmes are not surprising even when judged against the pleasurable fascination of the realist situation. Since these kinds of situations are much more effectively handled by the general service, why should students bother to watch Open University attempts to duplicate them?

The knowledge producing process associated with the transformation of experiences and the 'real world' generally requires the intervention of concepts, and it is precisely the function of teaching to 'carry' this intervention. What is more, these concepts cannot be the 'same thing' as the concrete reality that they are supposed to signify. They operate in a different space, a conceptual, thought space which can never be either reduced into that so-called concrete reality nor deduced from it. They are a knowledge of 'it', not actually 'it ' itself.

This is not to deny that 'real' people do not go about doing 'real' chores and engaging in 'real' conflicts, but it is to postulate that a knowledge of the determinants of those actions are located in a theoretical/conceptual space which is a real enough space (it is a space characterised and constituted by real processes of signification, construction and transformation) but it is not the philosophically constituted space of the 'absolute', 'concrete', 'ever-present' homogeneous reality which empiricists and positivists alike are continually trying to embrace with their hypothesis-testing procedures. The one can never be conflated with the other. The process is one involving the constitution of these individuals as 'real people' acting in a particular manner, through conceptual intervention and appropriation which in so doing creates the 'facts' adequate to its explanation. Hence that 'real world' is a creation in discourse. Real world is put in inverted commas here to signify that it is constructed, or 'spoken,' through representation in discourse — there is no other discoverable 'really' real world behind those representations. This 'real concrete world' only exists as a constituted thought object. It is the result of a discursive transformation and the 'site' of a further such conceptual transformation. It is important to note here that because of this, 'realism' is not a 'natural attitude' but a practice of signification in its own right (Coward and Ellis, 1977). Within the reflections of the camera are embodied certain forms of representation which construct that other as 'reality' itself.

It should be made clear here that this critique of realism is made from the point of view of its educational effects in relation to a certain form of its deployment. It is not meant to imply that realism has no place in cultural activity. That would be absurd. Nor is it meant to imply that it does not have any use in terms of purely educational activity. It is vital to tap the strengths of realism but in a different manner to that generally adopted in CS type educational programmes. The word 'generally' is employed advisedly here, since no programme as yet produced within the OU has been entirely negative in respect of the argument above. Some, in fact, have been very positive. They always operate in combination with some (however inadequate) intervention of a 'knowledgeable' discourse, which 'orders' these programmes in particular ways (Thompson, 1977a).

IV

Many of these general points may be illuminated and elaborated by means of a detailed consideration of the operation of a particular CS text. For this purpose I have chosen to look at the first TV programme transmitted as part of the OU Foundation Course in Social Sciences, D101. (A shot sequence breakdown appears at the end of this paper.) The choice of this programme for analysis is purely fortuitous. It was one picked upon, within a group discussion context, more or less at random without knowing very much about either its content or its structure: it was thought to be typical of the CS TV products of the Social Sciences Faculty. The programme is about unemployment, or more precisely about the experience of being unemployed. At this early stage, it would be in order to make a number of points about the context in which this programme is analysed.

The first point to note is that analyses and criticisms similar to those made of this particular programme could be made of a large number of other programmes which adopt a similar style. The programme below is employed for illustrative purposes, though clearly the specific analysis (and criticism) can be made only in relation to this particular programme.

Second, it might be objected that this programme is not a true realist case-study in the terms discussed above in as much as it embodies a style more akin to an illustrated lecture. However, the point that will be made here is that this 'illustrated lecture' is predicated upon interview sequences which of themselves embody the features of a CS approach. This is not to suggest that 'something else' could not be made of this interview material — it certainly could, as is indicated in the discussion of the analysis. But as it stands the programme is constructed around these sequences and the conception of unemployment that they articulate/signify is only made more apparent in the structure and comments that seem to provide the very rationale of their existence within the programme. In this sense, the programme is doubly articulated; once in relation to the questions asked, and what the real social actors 'spontaneously' say in relation to these questions in the interview sequence, and secondly in relation to the use made of this material within the general construction of the programme. This double articulation is a specific feature of documentary type programmes of this character.

Third, it should be made clear that there is no attempt here to provide a formal dissection of the discourses of this film/programme. In undertaking the analysis, the main question is the 'teaching message' carried by the programme. An attempt is made to discern what is taught about the nature of unemployment through this programme. This means that a lot of emphasis is put upon what is actually spoken by the participants. Less emphasis is given to what is 'said' by the visual part of the construction, though this aspect is not ignored. This makes it rather different from a recent analysis of a 'World in Action' TV programme conducted along similar lines (Heath and Skirrow, 1977). Clearly, the total signification of any programme is made up of the articulation of the visual and the verbal so that neither can be given priority. However, an interview programme of which both of these are examples, demands that the spoken aspect be afforded its due weight. The fact that it is largely ignored in their analysis seems to me to be the main shortcoming of the Heath-Skirrow paper (bearing in mind even that the objective of the following analysis is to discern directly the educational message carried by the programme, which is not the same as the objective of the other analysis). One final preliminary remark: in conducting this analysis, points at which the programme could have been interrupted and 'improved' are signalled and some comments made. In other words, a critique is made along with the analysis. The final section of this paper will draw together these and other strands to suggest a style of programme somewhat different to that so far attempted systematically within the OU.

The programme can be roughly divided into five parts: an introductory first part which lays the foundation for the idea of the programme (shots 1-5); a second part which mainly involves an interview with Dave Hunt and his wife about their experience whilst Dave has been out of work (shots 6-52); a short third part in which the presenter links the previous interview with the one to follow (shots 53-55); a second longish interview with John Lockyer, an electrician, about his experiences whilst unemployed forms the fourth part (shots 56-77); and finally a closing sequence in which the main presenter sums up the points brought out in the programme (shots 78-90) — this is done with the interjection of a small piece of additional interview material with Dave Hunt (shots 82-83). The total length of the programme is approximately 25 minutes. There are two presenters of this programme, designated as 1 and 2 in the shot sequence breakdown. The main presenter (1) is the academic with overall responsibility for the programme, and the other presenter, who only undertakes interviews with the Hunts, is the producer of the programme.

The idea of the programme, as already pointed out, is the experiences of the two main interviewees and their families during periods of unemployment. There is also another idea, however, and this is a past/present one (Heath and Skirrow, 1977). The programme contrasts the 'past' (1971) situation with the 'present' (1974) situation for both characters. In fact, this is facilitated by the use of an already filmed sequence taken from an older BBC documentary which involved both participants: this material is used in shots 6-25 and in shot 56. The other subsequent interview material was shot specially for the OU programme. This is a particular feature of OU TV programmes, in that they tend to make use of a lot of already existing material and 'organise' this around the decided programme topics. It is mainly because of lack of resources that more film material is not specially shot, but the existing material does offer a real constraint (though one that can be exaggerated by BBC personnel). In particular it means that re-editing is difficult, but also, and more important, the material is shot in the 'general service' style, with all the usual filmic codes that this embodies. (This aspect of the problem is usually ignored by OU BBC personnel.) In fact, in the major sequence taken from the earlier documentary (shots 6-24) a more 'ambitious' style can be seen to operate than the material shot specifically for the OU. This involves a 'little story,' partly filmed with a hand held camera, of Dave Hunt arriving home and confronting his wife with the fact of his continued unemployment, and ending with her breaking down over the sink. It seems to be impossible to attach any particular significance to the use of this material, other than to record the fact of its existence. This is in fact signalled both by the presenter in the programme and with a caption over the film. As it is, it forms part of the overall programme as constructed and must be assessed in that light. The classic practices of film editing for narrative continuity are in evidence throughout the whole film, as are the simplest kind of cutting on word/image relations.

The programme takes up the classic realist situations of home, work (or lack of it in this case) and family. This has added significance for OU students who are mostly 'mature' and hence are in a real sense placed in just these situations. It is explicitly stated in the presenter's introductory remarks that abstract statistics and discussion cannot give one the real 'feel' of unemployment (shot 5). The experience of unemployment and the effects this has upon the individuals concerned ostensibly, at least, provide the rationale and substance of the programme, but, as is argued later, a completely abstract and formalistic conception really structures the mode of argument of the programme ('authors' it and gives it a coherence), and this appears in the open more clearly in the final sequences of the programme.

The programme opens with Dave Hunt saying that unemployment is above all else degrading and that doctors may know about childbirth, but they do not really know about it until they have actually experienced it (shot 4). The implication here is that knowledge (in the deep sense) can only be gained by experiencing things. In fact, knowledge is reduced to experience. Now this would have been a good place to interrogate Dave's argument, to stop the programme and examine in what sense Dave was correct in his characterisation. Clearly, there is an important point here for social science which should have been brought out in an early programme of this character and indeed could have been at this very point. However, the actual programme begins at exactly the same 'level' that Dave himself is at — his personal perceptions of his own predicament — and never really leaves this level. All the way through the programme, unemployment is represented as the result of personal or subjective characteristics and experience: little else is explicitly provided in the actual format, though there is a very clear silent discourse (the meta-discourse) which actually gives this a coherence.

The real point and strength of experiences is that they do always provide an immediate rationalising mechanism for the individuals concerned. One could quite easily have pointed out here, in relation to Dave's analogy about doctors and childbirth: 'Well, what about a woman doctor who has been through childbirth?' Knowledge of the physiological and emotional determinants and reactions on the childbirth experience are of a different order than the actual experience itself. They are just two completely different fields or spaces which cannot simply be conflated one with the other. This is not meant to be a criticism of Dave or anyone else, but it is an obvious point that should and could have been made. Clearly, many women go through the experience of childbirth without knowing (in the scientific sense) what it is all about and, indeed, why should they? Similarly, people may experience unemployment without knowing its real determinants and effects, as I would argue is the case with Dave in this instance.

The beginning of the second part of the programme involves part of the 1971 documentary sequence (shots 5-19). As pointed out above, this involves a 'little story' of Dave's homecoming after a day at a government re-establishment centre. The discussion that takes place concerns his (non) prospects of getting a job after five years without work. Two things can be said about this.

In the first place, the question of employment/unemployment is utilised here to open up and develop the tensions such a situation engenders within the family structure, and this is something that is carried very strongly throughout the rest of the programme. In fact, this is the most obvious manner in which the employment/unemployment discourse is made manifest in the programme — unemployment affects family relations foremost — it *disrupts and threatens them and hence it is threatening in itself.* The discourse of family relations, the ideologies associated with male and female roles, is the most obvious sub-discourse operative in this programme. By and large, this sub-discourse is not developed any further in this paper, other than to use it in constructing the different representations of the main (male) characters.

The second point to make here concerns the manner in which this sequence is handled. It is handled in a very manipulative fashion. The sequence looks contrived, involving as it does some supposedly 'spontaneous' and 'natural' discussion in the kitchen culminating in the breakdown of Pat (Dave's wife) over the sink. It is difficult to see why this is done other than to engender an emotional response from the viewer. The effect of this manipulation of Pat is that the viewer is also manipulated in a manner which degrades both Pat and the viewer. It is difficult to see for what reasons this sequence is included in a film of this character, other than to engender such effects. This sequence is followed by another from the 1971 documentary which involves a scene that is of central importance to the film (shots 20-24). Dave and Pat sit down to write letters of application for jobs. Pat is represented as having given up hope when she asks 'Do you think it's worth writing to these?' (shot 23). Dave answers 'Have you seen any people who give up, love? Well, I have, up there in the queue' (shot 24). 'They just go right down and that's it' (shot 25). This is important, because the effect of this (regardless of the intentions of the programme makers) is to make the couple look pathetic, and this is reinforced later in the programme where Dave is 'shown' to have precisely given up in this manner (shots 33-5). This is despite Dave's own verbal procrastination on just this issue when directly asked about it at the end of his interview (shot 52). The dialogue that precedes this demonstrates that he has 'given up.'

As far as the programme's representation of Dave and his family is concerned, Dave himself appears as a sympathetic and sincere character but he is also rather an inadequate one. He is a nice enough fellow and manages well, given his problems, but he hasn't really got the drive to get work. If only he would move, get his stomach complaint sorted out, be prepared to take on shift work again, and so on he could 'find' a job. This representation of Dave is reinforced later when the presenter asks the audience whether Dave has eliminated himself from the job market, made himself unemployable, by setting certain (restrictive) conditions to be met before he will work (shots 53-4). Thus the 'message' here is that unemployment is the result of the volition of Dave and his setting 'unreasonable' conditions to be met before he will work. There is nothing about the kind of systemic conditions that might contribute to the creation of unemployment, the form that work takes in our society, the organisation of labour markets, the existence of employers, and so on. Basically, unemployment appears to be the result of individual inadequacies, lack of initiative or even 'bloody-mindedness' (a refusal to live elsewhere).

This negative representation of the Dave character can be seen particularly clearly in the 1974 interview material (shots 33-52). What does he do with his time now that he has 'given up'? He potters around with local history (shot 48), and makes toys for the children (shot 49) amongst other things, the sort of activity retired people are supposed to do. He has rows with his wife and only just restrained himself from taking out his frustrations on his children (shot 33). Dave's wife Pat is also rather pathetically (but sympathetically) represented here (shots 36-43) though this sympathetic representation is very much in terms of her qualities as a good wife and mother. For instance — she does wonders with mince (shot 39). The overall effect of this interview is to build up a picture of Dave as having lost his pride and being completely despondent about finding work.

The form of interview is also important here. Dave and his wife are always asked what they can do about their situation — move? — wife get a job? When it is clearly represented by their responses that they can do very little, it 'looks' both as though it is their own fault, and as if there is nothing that can be done fundamentally to prevent unemployment. It is a fact of life. This leads to and explains the despondency and passivity of the Dave character. Of course this also constitutes the viewer in a particular manner as well, since this reaction is represented to him/her in this manner. Since the causes of unemployment other than in these terms are nowhere raised, the viewer also perceives unemployment in this manner. It would again seem reasonable at this point to interrogate this kind of explanation implicitly offered by Dave himself via his own experience and crystal-lised in the form that the programme itself takes. This is not to suggest that the answer given by the programme might not be a valid one. It may well be, but there are other explanations so why not raise these and interrogate them as well?

We now come to the second character, John Lockyer. The represent-ation here is significantly different (shots 56-77). This is partly the result of the different employment situations in which the two main interviewees find themselves *vis à vis* the past/present narrative.

In the three years between the two interviews Dave Hunt did not find a job, but John Lockyer did. This imparts the form of interview with a very different significance. To begin with, the questioning here is more positive. Is work an end in itself (shot 66)? Is he concerned about (his family's) security (shot 72)? No questions here about his being worried about what the neighbours might think of his being unemployed (see shot 35 of the Hunt interview). At the same time, the response to these questions is more positive.

John found a job soon after the 1971 interview and has kept it since then. Although he is not such a sympathetic character as Dave he is a thoughtful, happy family man who is more decisive. He has overcome the dreadful internal doubts that still haunt Dave Hunt. He wanted work and sees work positively (something worth doing – shot 60). He is not withdrawn or despondent –sitting about in his kitchen or living room – he is out and about in the countryside with his family (the opening shots of the 1974 Lockyer sequence, shots 58-59). He has not been 'put out to pasture' (a phrase actually used by John accompanied by a panning shot of open pasture-land – shot 63). John has a new perspective on work, though this is articulated in a slightly contra-dictory manner. On the one hand he thinks work is not such an important aspect of his life after being unemployed (shot 67) but on the other hand he has made more sacrifices in terms of leisure and pay to get and retain a job (shot 71). He took lower pay to get the work (shot 71) and would even have moved, if pressured, to get a job (shot 75) or, as a last resort, allowed his wife to work (shot 77).

In fact, John really 'benefited' from his period of unemployment – he certainly came back refreshed and with a new perspective on life and a more vigorous attitude towards work. The implication (unconsciously) is drawn from this later in the programme, where it is suggested that we should all have this experience (redistributed unemployment). Pre-sumably, we would all benefit and reform ourselves to be more fit for work, to accept the routine of work (shot 64). After all, it is only a holiday anyway — a maldistribution of leisure. John Lockyer also 'had more to lose' than Dave Hunt because he was a skilled man (shots 78-79).

This representation adds up to the following: because John values work we value John, and he has been successful because of it. If we were all like him unemployment would disappear. Or would it? Again this question is not raised. There is no interrogation of the 'self-representation' of John's position. Instead there is a summing up which, if in a slightly different manner, simply reinforces it.

Before we proceed it is important to point out here that this summing up in the programme is done with a genuine concern for the problems (as conceived in the terms of the programme format) that unemployment creates. This obvious sincerity is not being challenged here. What is being suggested is that it is ultimately misplaced since the representation it is based upon and constructs is predicated upon an abstract series of 'remedial' suggestions which cannot form an effective basis for a solution to those problems. The reasons for this are elaborated below.

The summing up (shots 78-84, but also to some extent the linking sequence, shots 53-8) draws on the previous material to make its points. These are articulated around the notion that the 'solution' to unemployment is a matter of its *redistribution* in various forms. It has nothing to do with the forms of production in a particular society but can be addressed in terms of some abstract suggestions about redistribution. In one sense they are formal and actually divorced from any 'real' solution, but, on the other hand, they parallel the kind of representation of the problems as conceived in the programme itself:

(a) Unemployment is the result of lack of personal mobility. This is represented through the notion of its being largely a regional problem (shot 53). If only Dave (or John even) would move around the problem could be solved. Thus, if only labour would move to where capital wants it (redistribute itself) then there would be no problem. It is this lack of labour mobility which 'creates' unemployment.

(b) The 'problem' with unemployment is its uncertainty (shot 81). Uncertainty is the constraining factor. Unemployment as such is acceptable, but it is the uncertainty associated with it which creates the personal problems. This leads to the final suggestion; why should it not be spread out amongst us all?

(c) The 'problem of unemployment' could be solved if we were to 'spread it out'. This is represented both to Dave, and by him, in the discussion of overtime (shots 82-83). He is annoyed that some people are doing overtime while he is unemployed. Unemployment is unfair (shot 81) and it is basically Dave's bad luck (shot 81) that he is un-employed while others are (greedily — shot 83) doing overtime. Hence the suggestion about two million being unemployed for two weeks each year being equivalent to 80,000 people permanently un-employed (shot 84). Thus if we all took two more weeks holiday a year 'unemployment' would presumably be solved. But would it?

This abstract representation is confounded when the implication is drawn from this that _unemployment equals maldistribution of leisure_ (shot 84). Hence the implication is that if leisure were to be redistri-buted, unemployment could be solved. It is at this point that 'unem-ployment' as such quietly dissolves as a concept (it is actually some-thing else) and is also effectively spirited away as a social problem.

How is it that unemployment can be represented in this manner and dissolved so conveniently? What is the theoretical support for this? Despite the explicit absence of this question in the actual programme it is there implicitly all the way through. Why can't Dave (we) do anything about it other than through his (our) own initiative in trying to 'find' a job — as John did? The answer to this is characterised by an 'absent presence' in the programme. _The metadiscourse of the programme, which gives a coherence to its absent (but actual) narrative is that of neo-classical economics._ This conceives employment and unemployment as being based upon the subjective decisions of individuals about their work/leisure trade-offs. Hence, unemployment is fundamentally a matter of individual decision, the decision whether or not to substitute work for leisure. Clearly the question that this programme asks of this trade-off decision is: 'What are the personal characteristics of the individuals which determine such a decision?' The answers are given in the forms suggested above. In addition, there is another aspect of the neo-classical conception which (silently) supports the argument advanced in this programme. This concerns the nature of markets in general and particularly the operation of the labour market. Since un-employment exists it must be a consequence of this market, but the market itself is never brought into question. Hence, once established all that can be done about unemployment is to try to ameliorate it and its more 'unpleasant' effects (such as its 'uncertainty'). Given that the market is not called into question, unemployment will always exist and cannot be fundamentally altered. It is a fact of life which is whisked away, in this instance, on a flight of fancy (the redistribution of leisure (It is interesting to note here that, although absent from this TV programme, the theoretical support of this position is more openly addressed in the written unit which accompanies this part of the course. The neo-classical framework also constitutes the sole basis for the explanation of unemployment offered in the course unit (Open University, 1976)).

The way in which the discourse of neo-classical economics intervenes in the programme through the agency of the presenter and the way in which the interview material and other parts of the programme are marshalled in relation to this raises once again the double articulation of programmes of this character. Clearly, a lot of this very same interview material could be marshalled in relationship to quite a different programme and project. However, the unity of this articulation is secured in this programme via a form of positivism/empiricism which characterises the use of both 'realism' as a mode of representation and neo-classical economics as an academic discourse, enabling the traces of the one to be neatly folded and blended into those of the other.

So far the representations of the two main characters in the film have been largely constructed from the dialogue of the programme, although in doing this, the visual aspect has also been invoked. In fact, the directly visual elements are central to those very constructions, since it is through them that the dialogue is registered. It now remains to treat these visual representations and their meanings more systematically.

First, the interview sequences make much of the technique of cutting backwards and forwards from interviewer to interviewee. A particular feature here is the 'concerned look' of the interviewer which adds to the gravity and seriousness afforded the response from the interviewee. On a number of occasions in the film this 'concerned look' is accompanied by a 'grave nod' of the head which adds to the overall effect of sincerity and the authority afforded the answers to the questions.

Second, this question of the look and its significance also arises with the visual mode of intervention of the main presenter. He 'looks on' at the interview sequences as well as being 'looked on' by the audience. Within the programme, however, his mastery and authority is stamped on it by him being the only subject who 'looks on' the programme from within it, by his addressing the audience directly ('looking at it'), and in addition, his academic authority is secured by the fact of his address being conducted 'neutrally' from a clearly represented academic's office (books lining the wall in the background, and so on). This general question of the various looks of filmic discourse and their meaning – the way they (unconsciously) impart particular forms of authority and power – has recently been the subject of work by Mulvey (1976) and Willemen (1976).

Third, we can return to the point at which Pat breaks down over the sink. The way the visual images are handled here is particularly important in engendering certain effects (directly 'emotional' in character, in this instance). At the point of her breakdown, when she clasps her face in her hands, the camera first moves in closely and then just 'backs off' slightly. It acts as if it were a 'real person' in this situation (surrogate-subject) who would tend to hesitate slightly, particularly in a situation of not knowing well the person crying. This use of the camera in this manner itself generates 'emotion', 'concern', and so on in the real viewer since it 'acts' for this viewer (becomes the surrogate viewer and represents the reaction of the viewer), but this is done at the expense of 'displaying' Pat. She becomes pure spectacle here.

Fourth, there are two instances of a more general use of visual time and space possibilities in this film which are worth mentioning. These relate particularly to the visual representations of the two main interviewees. The sequences involving the first family, the Hunts, are shot mainly indoors and are confined to a rather claustrophobic home environment. There are two sequences when the main character, Dave Hunt, is shown not at home. The first of these is a short sequence (shots 6 and 7) in which he is shown returning home and the second involves two separated shots (54 and 81) in which Dave is shown walking alone by the dockside in Sunderland. In both these his manner is one of dejection. These shots are relatively 'atmospheric' in character – the lonely man image, reminiscent of that well-known TV advertisement, You're never alone with a Strand – and on these occasions the shots are juxtaposed with the presenter talking about the conditions Dave himself has put on finding a suitable job – why he 'seems to have settled down to living with unemployment' (shot 54); and the fact of the uncertainty associated with unemployment being one of its main problems (shot 81). In this case, both of the shots/dialogue juxtapositions reinforce each other in their particular 'negative' representation and signification of the subject. The whole manner is one of 'closing-in', both in personal terms and in terms of the family relationship ('inward looking').

A similar comment can be made about the other character in the case study, though here the representation is quite different. It concerns John Lockyer: in a slightly longer and more developed sequence, John is shown first with his family walking in fields near their home (shots 58 and 59). What is significant here is the fact that he is established from the very start with his family outside in the countryside, enjoying an active family life. It is only later that John is shown being interviewed in what is presumably his home — though as opposed to the case of the Hunts, there is little indication that it actually is his home. In the second sequence John is shown by himself leaning on a fence in a field looking over the countryside. His manner is reflective and thoughtful but positive, and this is juxtaposed with his own dialogue about his 'positive' attitude to work (shots 61-3). At one point in this sequence there is an identification of word and image when John talks about being put out to pasture, with a panning shot of his view from the fence of pasture land. In this case then a positive characterisation is represented and signified with these juxtapositions. The whole manner with these sequences is one of 'outward looking' in terms of personal and family relations.

Fifth, it is significant in relation to the overall programme construction that the interview with Dave Hunt precedes the interview with John Lockyer. We first have the 'failure' followed by the 'success'. This temporal separation within the time of the programme is itself partly constitutive of the message of the programme — the reasons for the failure are 'forgotten' but the reasons for the success are 'remembered' in the time of its construction — within the 'memory' of the film and its past/present support. In fact it is precisely within this difference between the two main characters that the meaning of the film is inscribed and, in this case, this difference is also inscribed temporally within the film. This basic structure and meaning of the film, revolving as it does around the *difference* between the two main character representations, also serves to secure a re-establishment of 'order' in the programme. The existence of unemployment is 'disordering' to the routine of work and family and hence also threatening to social and personal life. This is clearly the case with the Hunts and this disorder is retained in their case because the re-ordering mechanism of finding work is not established over the past/present temporal dimension to the film. This is so despite the fact that Dave has now 'grown to live with unemployment', established a kind of order within the more general disorder associated with unemployment. Here a contradiction within the process of signification is operative. On the other hand, John Lockyer did find work. The initial disorder here is no longer present (there is no contradiction). Order is re-established and an equilibrium restored

which confirms the more general re-establishment of order within the
time of the actual film and re-secures its own equilibrium. The presenters' remarks also work to re-establish this equilibrating mechanism
by drawing out a series of 'remedial' suggestions for unemployment.
One of the more general operations of television as a medium is its
tendency to secure equilibrium within difference. By demonstrating
'both sides' of an argument it eliminates difference and secures a hegemony for one reading or meaning, that represented by the fulcrum
around which the balance is secured: the 'absent' centre (which is, of
course, actually present).

V

It now remains to pull some of these criticisms together and make positive suggestions about more adequate forms of educational broadcasting.
What is said in this section will by its very nature be rather speculative
in character since a programme needs to be first produced before an
effective assessment of its effects can be adequately undertaken.

I would suggest that the main weaknesses of the programme
analysed here (and of others) is that it does not interrogate or challenge
any of the observations offered by the participants on the programme.
This tends to be a feature of the CS type programmes where 'real social
actors' are given a more or less free hand in terms of their explanations
of the conditions of social existence. Clearly, there is nothing wrong in
'beginning' at this level of experience, indeed it has real strengths in
terms of an initial engagement of interest, but what is required is an
interrogative questioning of the rationalisation offered by experience
(and such rationalisation can always be offered and indeed will always
be offered). It is the 'obviousness' of such rationalisations which is their
major strength because they require little or no thought. But paradoxi-
cally this is also their major weakness in terms of teaching. Within the
context of television teaching, what is required to break the continuity
between experience and knowledge is the dissolution of the
'pleasurable/comfortable' effects of watching. These must be displaced
by demanding of the viewer an intellectual effort and rigour which is
satisfying in a different sense to that of a 'pleasurable' (emotional) satisfaction, that is one which is 'demanding', 'stimulating', and so on in the
sense of a knowledgeable achievement. How can such an objective be
realised both verbally and visually in TV programmes?

At a very general level this requires an 'interrogative' mode of programme construction. Whatever is 'said' (verbally and visually) in the
programme needs interrogating, and this interrogation needs to take

place within the programme itself. Whether arguments are enunciated by 'real social actors' in terms of their spontaneous assessment of social conditions of existence, or by expert or academic opinion, these arguments need to be assessed and an attempt at giving them a meaning made. If such a rigorous method of proceeding within the programme itself is adopted, this will encourage students to do the same of the programme themselves, that is treat the programme as a text *and not take what the programme or its presenter says as in any way given or necessarily privileged.* This kind of approach would create the conditions or environment under which 'students' would become genuinely students and begin to think (enquire) for themselves. This cannot come about spontaneously but requires a very active intervention/demonstration on the part of the teacher, to 'do' what she/he 'expects' the pupil to 'do'. Thus it is for the teacher to engage with the different conceptions of the constitution and determination of social existence, to encourage the student to do the same of the programme itself, to encourage the student to first disassemble and then to re-assemble the text; to deconstitute the text and then to re-constitute it; at one and the same time to produce it within its consumption and consume it within its production, to negotiate with it so that finally the student becomes the producer of that text and not simply its consumer.

There are also a number of fairly well known *techniques* which can be employed in terms of the general visual style of programme construction which could be introduced into this interrogative framework. It seems particularly appropriate to try at least to show that real social actors are being filmed 'saying what they think' at the time that they are actually saying these things. As it is, a lot of so-called 'spontaneous' dialogue in documentary type films is in fact re-constructed. The intrusions that the filming process makes can never be entirely eliminated so, as far as possible, why not let these effects be shown, so that it can be made clear under what conditions the social actors were being filmed and interviewed? Such a style would at least have the virtue of authenticity.

Secondly, the OU uses a lot of film that has already been shot to make its programmes. This is then 'organised' for the purposes of the programme. Three points can be made here. This process of organisation could be made clearer to the viewer by being demonstrated. Programmes are 'put together' usually in a studio, so why not make this process of construction part of the programme itself? It perhaps needs to be made clearer than at present that there is an organising role (person) operating here, and instead of trying to integrate this material into a smooth flowing filmic progression, the inevitable disjunctures might be accepted or even emphasised.

Thirdly, programmes themselves need to be consciously interrupted more often. It is interesting for instance that the 're-play' technique has only been systematically employed in sports programmes (but also, though less often, in instances like language teaching programmes). However, this technique would seem particularly appropriate in attempting to seriously question and assess what is enunciated by social actors in response to interview situations.

No doubt there are many other such technical devices that could be adopted or experimented with. The general aim, however, must be to get students to actively 'look' at programmes instead of simply passively 'watching' them. It should always be borne in mind that this 'interrogative' process of teaching/learning is one involving an ever-presentness and at the same time an ever-absentness on the part of the teacher. The teacher always has to be there and not there at the same time, to 'speak' and not to 'speak' at the same time, to demonstrate and not to demonstrate at the same time. This is difficult because the teacher must be able to cut through this process to know the right moment to actually 'say' something and when to remain 'silent' and let the student 'speak' for him/herself and to him/herself in relation to an unspoken problem that may arise for him/her in 'another place' and/or at 'another time'.

In this respect it is important to remember that there will always be a number of explanations offered for any problem and these should be engaged with and interrogated by the programme. For instance, it should be obvious that there is no absolute already given thing called 'unemployment'. What unemployment is depends upon the meaning given to it by the conceptual apparatus used to construct it. The concept of unemployment is constituted differently by different social theories and hence means different things to those theories, and similarly it may be measured differently by those theories. These theories or problematics are not talking about the same thing when they use the same word 'unemployment'; because this only has a meaning, as a concept, in relation to the discourse or field of related concepts that are employed to think that 'thing' called unemployment. In the case of the programme analysed above, a particular conception of unemployment is constructed in such a manner (which has a legitimation in the sense that it is widely held within economics) but this conception is nowhere challenged in the programme. Thus, despite a rhetoric of opening issues up for an analysis in this early part of the course, the issue is effectively immediately closed off. The film itself offers an immediate closure in its narrative.

Shot No.	Time	Credits	Action and Shots	Dialogue
1	5"	Making Sense of Society: a foundation course in social science	Caption sheet	
2	10"		Fade to people moving about at random. Shot in partial colour negative.	
3	10"	Unemployment	Music: closes into 35mm photo surround.	
4	20"		Dave Hunt speaking in his home: camera slowly closes in on him.	Hunt: It's the most degrading feeling I think that man could ever go through. You go down the office, you get these people there telling you they know all about work — there's plenty of work you know, I suppose a doctor knows all about childbirth but he doesn't know what it's like to go through birth himself. And this is what it's like going through unemployment yourself.
5	30"	Professor Derrick Brooman	Presenter at desk in academic room. Holds single shot of presenter as he directly addresses camera.	Presenter 1: What is it really like to be unemployed? Well the correspondence unit says quite a lot about this in an abstract way, but it obviously can't convey the experience of being unemployed. So in this programme we're going to be talking to two people who've actually experienced it, one for a long time, the other for a rather shorter spell. You'll see that this brings up a number of rather important further questions, particularly about the definition of unemployment.
6	15"		Dave walking in housing estate: long shot, slowly pans.	This is Dave Hunt as he appeared in 1971. He'd been out of work for five years.
7	6"		Shot looking down stairs of flats: pans up as Dave passes	He was attending a government re-establishment centre. These centres are meant to give people who've been unemployed some time a chance to get back into the routine of daily work.
8	5'		Interior of flat. Wife (Pat) and child at sewing machine making clothes. 'knock, knock' heard.	Dave Hunt lives in Sunderland with his wife and young family. Pat: Come in. There's your dad, let him in sweetheart.
9	5"		Child opens door and in walks Dave. Turns to close door.	
10	8"		Shot from interior of Dave closing door. Moves into other room preceded by camera.	Presenter 1: Dave's spell at the centre was due to end. He still had no prospect of a job.
11	3"		Shot of children playing at table.	Pat: Be quiet you two.
12	19"		Pat at sink filling up kettle. (close up) swings and pans	Dave: I don't know what's going to

Shot No.	Time	Credits	Action and Shots	Dialogue
			out to show Dave in kitchen/room.	happen love, you know, I wonder if I go back on the dole again like that, you know — what will happen. It could be another five years, I suppose Pat.
13	5″		Pat at sink with back to camera pouring water.	Pat: Oh dear, don't say that.
14	6″		Shot of room and Dave. Pat moves into frame, united with Dave.	Dave: It could be — one thing, it couldn't get any worse. What worries me is you hear of people getting their money stopped.
15	4″		Pat back at sink.	Pat: Well you haven't done anything to get the money stopped, so . . . well what are you going to do?
16	4″		Close up of Dave: bows head (looks down despondently).	
17	6″		Pat at sink.	Dave: Hope it's not just a continuation of before you know, sitting about, nothing to do, no money to go anywhere
18	5″		Dave sitting down.	
19	15″		Close in on Pat at sink; she breaks down, hands to face — cries. Camera moves out a little.	Pat: Oh God . . . (cries)
20	12″		Scene in living room. Dave draws up a table and sits down on sofa. Camera faces this scene.	Presenter 1: Every evening the Hunts would get down to writing applications for jobs. At that time they felt it kept their hopes up even though Dave had already gone a long time without working.
21	8″		Pat joins him. Camera side on.	
22	4″		Close up of Dave's head looking down.	Dave: Did you get them to bed love? Could you write the envelopes out for us? Pat: Do you think its worth writing to these?
23	8″		Close in on Pat's hand-writing — wedding ring predominant. Writing application for job.	Dave: What do you mean, worth it? Pat: Well, keep trying I mean. Dave: Well, what happens if you give up? Have you seen any people who give up love? Well I have up there in the queue.
24	18″		Medium close in on Dave.	Pat: Just seems a bit silly. Dave: They just go right down and that's it.
25	4″		Presenter in room directly addressing camera.	Presenter 1: Three years later Dave Hunt still hadn't got a job.
26	44″		Dave and Pat sitting on sofa together.	Hunt: I've been out of work since autumn 1966.
27	4″		Interviewer (speaking).	Presenter 2: How did this come about?
28	40″		Dave speaking (holds single shot).	Dave: I was on shift work er quick change-over shifts three on and one off and er for three or four years and this

Shot No.	Time	Credits	Action and Shots	Dialogue
				started affecting me stomach like you know and er I used to go to the doctor with stomach complaints, and I was on the sick quite a while and in the end he told us I'd have to either find a permanent day shift job or pack in the — altogether.
29	2″		Pat looking to left (at Dave off frame).	I looked in the factory for a day shift job for about a year and nothing turned up and I was slowly, you know, getting worse, and in the end I went to see the doctor again and he told us to get out of the factory altogether.
30	5″		Interviewer.	Presenter 2: Well what kinds of jobs would you be willing to take, if they were offered to you?
31	1′11″		Dave — holds single head shot.	Dave: Well, be willing to take on anything you know, er preferably day shift for obvious reasons you know. I don't want me health affected again and of course er they'd have to pay out more than I'm getting at the moment — because we just couldn't manage on less — or even at the same amount you know, put bus fares on and lunch and things like this — it wouldn't be worth working for less than I get now, or the same. I'd have to have near about five to ten pounds more — especially with bus fares in Sunderland now 'cos they went up, practically doubled, and they're going up again.
				Presenter 2: So what in fact do you get now, financially?
				Hunt: Er Twenty-five sixty-five.
				Presenter 2: You must have faced the problem of what to do with your time, being unemployed how did you fill your day?
32	3″		Pat — moves head round left.	Hunt: Well at first it wasn't so bad, I mean when I was first made unemployed I was, you know, financially reasonably well off, and it was er just a sort of holiday, you know, at first. I thought a couple of months and I'd be back at
33	1′7″		Dave (to interviewer).	work. But as the money ran out and um I started really looking for jobs. At first I thought as I say it'd be a couple of months but I kept trying, wrote round, travelled round. I used to spend two or three pounds a week on letters and bus fares looking round. And I kept on trying oh for about a year and a half solid you know, spending two or three pounds a week on bus fares and meals. I used to travel about a ten mile, twelve mile radius round Sunderland you know, looking in telephone directories, all the factories I had to look up you know, and this kind of thing and then, that was the

Shot No.	Time	Credits	Action and Shots	Dialogue
				most of me time was spent writing letters. I didn't have any social life, you know, and then I um as nothing turned up I became more and more worried. And I got depressed and in the end I just sort of thought to meself Oh to hell with the lot of them, you know. It's not worth carrying on. After about six months to a year the novelty of having freedom sort of wore off, you know, and then I'd nothing to do with me time. And Pat and I always used to be having rows and I used to snap at the kiddies and that you know, and . . . this really got us down you know. 'Cos I knew what was happening but I didn't seem to . . . stop meself. Never actually struck them physically, control of meself better than that, but . . . I could see what was happening, you know.
34	5"		Interviewer.	Presenter 2: Why did you feel bad about not having a job?
35	1.4"		Dave. Camera moves out when Pat starts speaking to include Pat in frame: sitting next to Dave on sofa.	Hunt: Pride? But I've grew to accept it now. I think most people do. But at first . . . it was pride, you know what I mean? I'm the breadwinner and you know . . . and er I think that's what was getting at us. Plus boredom. Presenter 2: Were you worried about what the neighbours thought? Hunt: No. Not up here because unemployment I mean in the North East is accepted as a way of life. Fullstops, you know. I mean every two or three doors you can walk down you'll find somebody who's unemployed. They're either making damn good money up here, or they're making nothing at all you know. Presenter 2: Are you surviving on social security? How do you manage financially? Hunt: Well I have nothing to do with the finances, you know. I leave that all up to Pat. Presenter 2: Pat, how do you manage with the housekeeping?
36	4"		Dave looking at Pat.	Pat: (laughs) No actually. When I . . . when we first went unemployed it was damned hard 'cos . . . you're that used to the big wage and when you get a small
37	19"		Pat looking at off frame interviewer.	wage, by the time you've got your weekly payments done you find that you've got next to nothing left. But um mind most of the firms were pretty good, they took half the payments, you know till things were finished and of course after that I just couldn't afford to buy sort of furniture and that. And er I found it pretty easy after that

Shot No.	Time	Credits	Action and Shots	Dialogue
38	4"		Dave looking at Pat.	because you got into a sort of routine of what to buy and what not to buy. Um joints of meat of course are completely off and er . . . Mince is pretty cheap, I use a lot of mince you know make me own beefburgers and things like that. And er I make a lot of me own bread, which we call stutty-cake. And er well that's about half easy, of what I get — goes towards food, quite easy. And what I tend to do actually is um I don't buy potatoes by quarters and things, I buy the big four-stone bag and it lasts us - about — nearly three weeks, and I find it's cheaper, it runs out cheaper that way. But er it works out that if you buy sort of bulk for your main things, flour and stuff like that it, it works out better. Of course I do a lot of cooking, which helps out a lot. But I never go in for these um frozen things and er things like that and the pre-packed stuff — just couldn't afford it, it's far too expensive, that stuff. I go in for the more down to earth plain cooking.
40	4"		Interviewer.	Presenter: Have you yourself, Pat, ever thought of getting a job?
41	50"		Pat: move out to include Dave in frame.	Pat: I did, but um of course I have a slipped disc which puts us right out. I'm not supposed to do heavy housework so of course working's completely out — it's out of the question: not that Dave'd allow me to work anyway.
42	30"		Dave: shot held.	Presenter 2: Is that right Dave? Hunt: No. Not up here you know that's one thing you know . . . I . . . the man if anything is the breadwinner and the woman working, you know, I mean that would sort of really knock my pride that. If I thought I had to stop in and do the housework and she was out keeping me. Be sort of immoral earnings as far as I'm concerned. Wouldn't be so bad if I was working and she got a part time job, you know. I wouldn't mind that. But I'm a strong believer — maybe old fashioned — but I think the woman's place is in the
43	4"		Interviewer: nodding looking concerned.	home with the kiddies you know. Presenter 2: Would you say that you're now adjusted to being out of work?
44	5"		Dave: shot held.	Hunt: Not fully, you know. I still have bad nights you know now and then when
45	3"		Pat looking left at (out of frame) Dave.	I'm sort of worrying meself sick you know, wondering what I'll be doing this time next year, you know. But on the
46	35"		Close in of Dave — gradually moves out.	whole you know I accept it as a way of life, but I couldn't honestly say I fully accept it — I'll be walking down the street and suddenly I'll get a pang of con-

Shot No.	Time	Credits	Action and Shots	Dialogue
				science and I start worrying about it you know. You hear the older people talking about the means-test and this kind of thing, and the horrors of social security, and you know the pang's still there you know, and you still tend to worry about it you know.
47	4"		Interviewer.	Present 2: Dave, what sort of pressures have there been on you to actually get a job?
48	56"		Dave held in shot.	Hunt: Er none really, you know er. At first they used to ask us where I'd been and what I'd done, you know, about getting a job but there wasn't actually any, you know specific pressure on us. Used to ask for proof, you know, never used to ask outright but I used to give them proof that I had been trying you know, plenty of proof you know. But now, well, they come up and ask us if I'm still trying . . . yes — or no, you know whatever I did — and er that's it.

Presenter 2: Did you ever consider moving away from the North East in order to get a job?

Hunt: No I didn't wish to move from this area. Not at all, you know. All me friends and relatives are up here. Me family's up here — I love the North East you know. One of me hobbies is local history so . . . I'd hate to shift. And I'd hate to shift down south. The housing situation down there — I mean I'd have to get a flat and then look for a house and it's already crowded down there, you know. And I've been down there just visiting and to me it's the most inhuman place I've ever been to. I'd rather go to the African jungle than live down south. |
49	3"		Interviewer (concerned look).	Presenter 2: You mention one of your hobbies is local history, but what else do you do to fill in your time?
50	7"		Dave.	Hunt: Well, I've got quite a few hobbies I er I enjoy music, folk music, classical music, at the moment I'm trying to . . . trying to learn to play the guitar er I enjoy playing backgammon and chess, billiards but on the whole you know I lead a pretty full life you know. I enjoy woodwork, I do quite a bit of woodwork I make toys for the kiddies at Xmas things like that, you know.
51	6"		Pat looks left and then round to the interviewer.	Presenter 2: In 1971 you were both interviewed about being out of work. Dave, you said then that the one thing you mustn't do was to give up. How do you feel about that now?

Shot No.	Time	Credits	Action and Shots	Dialogue
52	55'		Dave.	Hunt: It's very difficult that, I . . . I'm not sure meself whether I've given up or not you know I'm not . . . really certain. I don't think I have, you know. I still try you know if I see something I fancy . . . I really fancy, I'll try for it, you know, but I tend to pick and choose now. I'm a bit nervous about starting work actually. I don't know why. It's probably 'cos . . . I I've never worked for a long time. I mean meeting new people, strange people. The actual work doesn't frighten us you know, because I do, well I do quite a bit now, you know in me hobbies you know I do quite a bit of work. So actual work doesn't frighten us, you know, more than anything else, starting afresh, you know, breaking me routine.
53	16"		Presenter in office addressing camera.	Presenter 1: Clearly it's harder for Dave Hunt to get a job in Sunderland than it would be if he were to move further south. What do you make of his experience? He's imposed a number of fairly strict conditions that make it rather unlikely he'll ever get quite the job he wants . . .
54	31"		Dave walking by dockside wild soundtrack.	First of all it has to be in Sunderland, and then it mustn't be shift work or the kind of job that could damage his health. It looks as though he's pretty well settled down to living with unemployment. He has a way of life that's very well adapted to it. You may wonder in fact whether he really still counts as being part of the labour force, or whether for practical purposes he's really withdrawn from it . . .
55	19"		Presenter in office addressing camera.	Now let's turn to our second individual. He's Mr John Lockyer, an electrician who lives in Watford with his wife and four children. He's in employment now but back in 1971 he had a spell of unemployment that lasted for three months. He too was interviewed in the BBC documentary.
56	24"		John Lockyer sitting at bottom of stairs in house.	John Lockyer: I think without realising it over the weeks it chinks away at your confidence you know, your confidence in many ways. You probably don't realise it at first then as you sit back and assess it in your mind um your whole way of living has been changed and I would say that it even affects the way you approach your sport. It affects your confidence in every way.
57	13"		Presenter in office.	Presenter 1: Not long after that programme was made he got a job as maintenance electrician in a local hospital and he's kept it ever since. All the same he looks back on his experience of unem-

Shot No.	Time	Credits	Action and Shots	Dialogue
				ployment as something bad that he wouldn't like to repeat.
58	18″		John with family walking in fields, wife, two kids; gradually move off frame.	Mrs Lockyer: Did you see where they put that, that well they shut that off to the . . .
59	8″		Boy climbing over stile followed by John and daughter.	John Lockyer: Yes, that's the local school now the new swimming pool and the builders' hut. They're going to do the dressing room soon. Over there Martin, you'll be able to swim over in the er when they get the pool going.
				Mrs Lockyer: He won't because he doesn't go.
				Mr Lockyer: Well he might be able to use it. Right, that's it, we're nearly home Sue . . .
60	28″		John at home speaking to just off camera.	I want work — I wanted something worth doing, this was the problem you know, did you just kind of take anything that came along irrespective of whether it paid good money or not, or did you do something that you'd get satisfaction from. This is the question that always crops up, you know, you've kind of got
61	9″			to choose really and and, er, I did hang on long enough to get something that er you know I do enjoy doing. In general, it
62	6″		Close in on John.	er I didn't realise but it did gradually have its effects on me in lots of ways and
63	14″		Panning shot of fields/ countryside.	er, as I say, I was glad to get back you know, its kind of er getting from under a cloud. You're out of work and you know it in your own mind, and you can kind of kick it around and er do different thi: gs, go different places, but basically you've been put out to pasture. As I say,
64	39″		John in room.	work is only a routine and if you break routine for any length of time the new routine that you er grow into becomes quite forceful, er not having to get up at the time that you usually — and if you
65	21″		Moves out on John.	do this for a number of weeks, er it takes some time getting back on the rails to do what you're used to doing, you can wander from the line which is in between working and if it's too long sometimes it's you know, to pick up the pieces again can be difficult.
66	4″		Presenter/interviewer.	Presenter 1: Do you feel that work is a kind of end in itself?
67	36″		John.	John Lockyer: Well I think my attitude to work is er changed. I see it as a necessity to — to take part of your life — but I often wonder to what extent work should play in your life as against the other things. I don't take it as seriously as I used to, let's put it that way.

Shot No.	Time	Credits	Action and Shots	Dialogue
68	2"		Presenter/interviewer.	Presenter 1: It's a thing you do for money in fact.
69	39"		John.	John Lockyer: Well, everybody likes to think that they've earned their money. I don't think many people want their money given to them, but on the other hand er, I think that your leisure is very important. So you know er work it wouldn't to me be the overriding factor: the one thing now, that would govern my life, because I realised that the work front can change so quickly, that it isn't really worth taking that seriously any more.
70	2"		Presenter/interviewer.	Present 1: Would you have been willing to take work at lower wages?
71	25"		John.	John Lockyer: Well er I have gone below what I was earning previously and er I knew this would be you know on the cards because my other job was fairly well paid, and er you know this didn't surprise me that I had to settle for a lower paid job, so I just adjusted to this and as a — plus the fact that I work extra hours to compensate which I'm lucky to be able to do, but er, and this obviously affects the fact that I don't have the amount of leisure time, and this is the one big thing I notice. But as I say you know, er I did drop on money, yes.
72	11"		Presenter/interviewer back to John.	Presenter 1: Would you say you now had more security in your job?
73	28"		John (closer in).	John Lockyer: Well, as I'm getting older you know this is the fact that you know. I don't want to rush around, I want to do a job and it's near for me, and that's another great thing, and er I would say the security er does mean a lot because one — you know, I don't want to be in and out of jobs er I'm happy to be set in a routine that suits me so you know in this way this job is you know to me is of value.
74	5"		Presenter/interviewer.	Presenter 1: Suppose you'd been asked to move you know, you'd been offered a job in, say, Birmingham or Newcastle or even South London, would you have been willing to do?
75	39"		John.	John Lockyer: Er this was put to me, this was obviously when I was out of work but er you know seeking fresh pastures and that you know, moving, it wasn't really on. Obviously if I'd have had to have moved, well that would have been it, but I'd have been very reluctant to have moved from this area which, you know, I enjoy living here, this is the thing so that was er, that would have been the

Shot No.	Time	Credits	Action and Shots	Dialogue
				last move.
76	5″		Presenter/inverviewer.	Presenter 1: If it had been necessary and your wife could have found a job, outside would you have been willing for her to go and work while you were unemployed?
77	20″		John Lockyer:	John Lockyer: Well I, I think it rather kind of er it's a bit humiliating I suppose it's happened before to other people but I wouldn't have been happy. Obviously the man probably thinks he should be er the main source of income, it doesn't always work out that way, but er when you've got children, think it's expected that the man must do the you know the major share of earning the money, so I wouldn't have been happy, but I say if it had come to that desperate, then obviously it would have happened, but you know, I wouldn't have liked it.
78	16″		Presenter in office addressing camera.	Presenter 1: John Lockyer's case contrasts with Dave Hunt in a number of
79	16″		Closer in on presenter.	obvious ways, he wasn't out of work, for anything like so long, and as a skilled man he'd more to lose while being unem-
80	28″		Out on presenter.	ployed. All the same there are a number of interesting points they have in common. For one thing, neither of them was willing to move to another part of the country, in order to get work. Well that doesn't seem unreasonable. Still it does reinforce the point that quite a lot of Britain's unemployment problem is a regional problem rather than a national one. Secondly it brings out the duration aspect, the factor that really creates anxiety for — to a man losing his job is that he doesn't know how long it's going to last. Dave Hunt couldn't know when he fell out of work that he was going to be unemployed for eight years. John Lockyer couldn't know he was going to get another job in three months' time, and it's this uncertainty that's one of the most distressing things about unemployment.
81	24″		Dave Hunt on dockside moves round and walks along quay and moves out of frame.	If a man could know in advance that his unemployment would last say, two, three or four months exactly, then he could plan to do something about it. As it is he's out on a limb. The fact that certain individuals with various kinds of bad luck can go on being out of work for a long time, while other people are continuously employed and even do over-time, seems rather unfair.
82	8″		Interviewer.	Presenter 2: There's quite a lot of over-time being worked in certain industries in Sunderland, Dave, what do you think of that, given that you've been unemployed

Shot No.	Time	Credits	Action and Shots	Dialogue
				for such a long time?
83	43″		Dave and Pat on sofa moves in to focus on Dave.	Hunt: I'm completely against it. I'd like to see them sort of work ordinary time and employ men. It would cost about the same. I mean it would give them the . . . the people who work overtime . . . know whether they do it because they need the money or just greed . . . I'm not sure which it is, you know because I reckon most of them are making about 45-50 pounds a week which to me is quite sufficient to live on. And to work overtime and bring in sixty and seventy pounds a week you know that's greed as far as I'm concerned, when people are unemployed. You know, I can't understand it at all — they see this and they do nothing about it.
84			Presenter in office.	Presenter 1: There are a lot of practical difficulties in spreading work out among individuals, but it would surely be better if something of the kind could be done. To have two million people unemployed for just two weeks each year is arithmetically the same as having 80,000 people permanently unemployed. Now, that, you might say, is a real example of the maldistribution of leisure. When you come to look at the figures of unemployment, indeed, you should remember that it's not just the total number out of work at any given time, but the average duration of the unemployment that's also important.
85	4″	Programme presented by Professor F.S. Brooman		
86	5″	Taking Part: Dave and Pat Hunt, John Lockyer		
87	4″	Film Editor: Ron de Mattos		
88	4″	Executive Producer Michael Philps		
89	4″	Producer Grahame Turner		
90	5″	A production for the Open University BBC TV (c) Open University 1974		

BBC TV ©

8   IDEOLOGY AND THE MASS MEDIA: THE QUESTION OF DETERMINATION

Peter Golding and Graham Murdock

Our central argument in this paper is that sociologists interested in contemporary mass communications need to pay careful and detailed attention to the ways in which the economic organisation and dynamics of
mass media production determine the range and nature of the resulting
output. In proposing this we are not arguing that economic forces are
the only factors shaping cultural production, or that they are always
and everywhere the most significant. Nor are we assuming 'a tight and
necessary correspondence between market forces and decisions on the
one hand, and the nature of the media's ideological output on the
other' (Connell, 1978, p. 71). We do not deny the importance of the
controls and constraints imposed by the state and the political sphere,
or the significance of the inertia exerted by dominant cultural codes
and traditions. Nor do we deny the 'relative autonomy' of
production personnel and the pertinent effects of professional
ideologies and practices. Nevertheless, for us the crucial term in
this couplet is 'relative'. Hence, while we fully endorse Stuart Hall's
view that 'the level of economic determination is the necessary but
not sufficient condition for an adequate analysis' (Hall, 1978a,
p. 239), we would underline the term 'necessary'. In our view,
any sociological analysis of the ways in which the mass media
operate as ideological agencies which fails to pay serious attention to
the economic determinants framing production is bound to be
partial. However, despite the considerable upsurge of academic
interest in the mass media in Britain over the last decade or so, it is
precisely this 'necessary' element that has most obviously been missing
from much recent work. The significance of this absence for a more
adequate analysis has been made both more conspicuous and more
damaging by recent developments in the structure of the British mass
media.

The last two decades have seen a massive expansion of the mass
media in Britain. The great bulk of this growth has taken place within
the private sector, firstly through the development of new products and
markets (as in the rapid expansion of the record industry), and secondly
through the penetration of advanced capitalist operations into pub-

lishing where older styles of enterprise had previously predominated, and into the hitherto entirely public, broadcast sector (initially through the introduction of independent television and latterly with the take-off of local commercial radio). By contrast, the countervailing developments within the public sector — the initiation of BBC2, the establishment of BBC local radio, and the experiments with municipal cable networks — have been nowhere near sufficient to re-establish parity between the two sectors. As we have pointed out elsewhere (Murdock and Golding 1977b) this expansion of the private sector has been headed and dominated by a relatively small number of large corporations, with significant interests in a range of core communications sectors and in the cognate areas of leisure and information provision, operating on an increasingly international scale. Far from weakening or dispersing the control that the major communications corporations are able to exercise over cultural production therefore, recent developments have consolidated and strengthened it. The BBC remains the single significant exception to this emerging pattern of conglomerate dominance. It is however an exception. It is not paradigmatic. Indeed there is evidence that in key areas of its operations the Corporation's activities are increasingly governed by essentially capitalistic criteria.

Taking the field of mass communications in contemporary Britain as a whole then, the centre of gravity lies decisively with the communications conglomerates. Consequently, we would argue, sociological analysis must begin by confronting this emerging economic structure and exploring the ways in which its organisation and underlying dynamics shape the range and forms of media production. Ironically however, at the same time that this process of conglomerate domination has accelerated and extended, so the question of economic determinations has been displaced from the centre of academic analysis, and in much recent writing on the media in Britain has disappeared altogether.

One influential justification for this displacement is provided by the various versions of pluralism. Here the links between the cultural and the economic are dissolved, by arguing that possession of the means of production has become a progressively less important source of cultural control in contemporary capitalism, and by emphasising the significance of alternative and countervailing sources of power. In pursuing this argument pluralists usually draw on some version of the 'managerial revolution' thesis. In the case of the mass media this takes the form of emphasising the relative autonomy of production personnel, their monopoly of operational control and the resulting ideological plurality of media output. External constraints on production are seen to stem primarily from the various controls imposed by the state. Despite the consistent barrage of criticism aimed at it by radical commentators, versions of pluralism retain a considerable currency within discussions of the mass media in Britain. In its popular variants it furnishes the basic concepts with which owners and practitioners legitimate the present structure of the communications industry (see for example Whale, 1977). In more sophisticated forms it is strongly entrenched in academic studies of mass communications. It underpins the work of one of the most distinguished mass communications researchers in Britain, Professor Jay Blumler (see for example, Blumler, 1977). Here the displacement takes the form of a concentration on the relations between the mass media and political and state institutions, both domains being regarded as independent power blocs essentially separate from the economic structure. Hence for Blumler, pertinent questions about the political and cultural role of the mass media can be adequately examined without reference to the economic structures and dynamics underpinning them (see Gurevitch and Blumler, 1977). A separate but related mode of displacement is offered by the recent work of Daniel Bell with its powerful argument that the economic, political and cultural spheres of modern capitalism now constitute distinctive realms, separated from one another and governed by different and increasingly antagonistic axial principles (Bell, 1976). These assertions of dissociation are not particularly surprising. Indeed they are an integral and necessary element in liberal and conservative critiques of Marxist sociology. What is surprising however, is the appearance of analogous arguments within the Marxist sociology of culture itself.

As Stuart Hall has recently pointed out, the insistence on the importance of economic determinations is 'the cardinal principle of Marxism without which it is theoretically indistinguishable from any other "sociology" ' (Hall, 1977d, p. 23). 'When we leave the terrain of "determinations" ' he argues, 'we desert not just this or that stage in Marx's thought, but his whole problematic' (Hall, 1977b, p. 52). And yet, the dominant British currents of Marxist work on the sociology of culture, Hall's included, have persistently failed to explore this question of economic determinations with any degree of thoroughness.

To a large extent, this deletion of determination as a significant focus of analysis is rooted in a reaction to the crudities of the reductionist position which presented the mass media as instruments of the capitalist class, and saw their products as a more or less unproblematic relay system for capitalist interest and ideologies. This position had its hey-day in the inter-war years and in the early 1950s. Even so it lingers on and continues to find powerful academic supporters. Ralph Miliband's presentation of the role of the media, for example, is often strongly tinged with reductionism, as in this extract from his recent book, *Marxism and Politics*:

> Whatever else the immense output of the mass media is intended to achieve, it is also intended to help prevent the development of class consciousness in the working class . . . the fact remains that 'the class which has the means of material production at its disposal' does have 'control at the same time of the means of mental production'; and that it does seek to use them for the weakening of opposition to the established order [Miliband, 1977, p. 50].

Over and against the limitations of this kind of reductionism, contemporary Marxist sociologists of culture have emphasised the relative autonomy and specificity of the cultural sphere, and its irreducibility to class interests and class control, and have looked for the central connections binding the mass media to the power structure, not in its relations to monopoly capital but in its relations to the capitalist state. Both these thrusts have been immensely valuable in that they have addressed crucial but underdeveloped areas in Marxist sociology. The decisive rejection of crude reductionism which they represent was both important and necessary, and continues to be so. However, in its attempts to purge itself of economism, much contemporary work, we would argue, has been 'led to what can be seen as an increasingly debilitating neglect within ideological analysis of precisely the economic level' (Garnham, 1977, p. 345). The result is a curious paradox. On the one hand sociologists of communications working from within a Marxist framework are obliged to evoke economic determination, since this is what distinguishes their position from others. At the same time, the fact that they fail to investigate how these determinants operate in practice severely weakens both the power and the distinctiveness of their analysis. Determination becomes a kind of ritual incantation rather than a necessary starting point for concrete analysis.

In the next section we will look more closely at this paradox in action in the work of the two most important and influential Marxist theorists of communications currently working in Britain — Raymond Williams and Stuart Hall.

The members of the Birmingham Centre for Contemporary Cultural Studies have recently described their main aim as 'developing theories of cultural and ideological formations within the broad framework of a Marxist problematic, without resorting either to economism or idealism' (Chambers *et al.*, 1977, p. 109). This aptly characterises not only their own work, but the principal thrust of Marxist cultural studies in Britain more generally. The battle against economism has had various outcomes. It has led Edward Thompson, for example, to reject the central metaphor of base and superstructure altogether and to replace it with a conception of the economy and culture as adjacent domains interacting dialectically. As he put it in a recent interview, 'There are certain value systems that are consonant with certain modes of production, and certain modes of production which are inconceivable without consonant value systems. There is not one which is dependent on the other . . . these two things are different sides of the same coin' (quoted in Mason, 1977, p. 229).

A similar position underpins the argument which Raymond Williams developed in one of the seminal books of modern communications studies, *The Long Revolution* (1965). He presents the 'long revolution' in culture, initiated by the extension of the education and communications systems, as a third current of change alongside the industrial revolution in the economy and the democratic revolution in the political sphere. These three processes together, he argues, define the texture and tempo of contemporary experience. They interact continuously, dialectically, with no one sphere exercising a determining influence over the others. Consequently he argues, it is necessary to study the complex interactions between the spheres of culture, polity and economy 'without any concession of priority to any one of them we may choose to abstract' (Williams, 1965, p. 62). However, in the concrete and polemical analysis of mass communications in contemporary Britain which he published the following year, he is constantly tugged back towards acknowledging the pivotal position of the economic structure and the determinations it exerts on cultural production. He concedes that the growing concentration of control in the hands of the large communications corporations is the key defining characteristic of the emerging situation, and that as a result 'the methods and attitudes of capitalist business' have penetrated more deeply into more and more areas and 'have established themselves near the centre of communication' (Williams, 1968, p. 31). Confronted with these facts his solution is to propose an extension of public ownership as the single most significant lever for change (Williams, 1968, p. 155).

The tension between Williams' general theoretical stance and his concrete analysis of contemporary mass communications systems has been further sharpened in his later work. Consider these extracts from two of his recent writings:

> The insertion of economic determinations into cultural studies is of course the special contribution of Marxism, and there are times when its simple insertion is an evident advance. But in the end it can never be a simple insertion, since what is really required, beyond the limiting formulas, is restoration of the whole social material process, and specifically of cultural production as social and material [Williams, 1977a].

> It was impossible, looking at new forms of broadcasting (especially television) and at formal changes in advertising and the press, to see cultural questions as practicably separable from political and econ-omic questions, or to posit either second-order or dependent relations between them [Williams 1976b, p. 90].

Here is the paradox in action. On the one hand he argues forcefully that a close attention to economic determinations is indispensable to a thoroughgoing Marxist sociology of culture. On the other he insists that it is impossible to posit 'second-order or dependent relations' between cultural production and economic dynamics.

Once again, however, when it comes to the concrete analysis of the contemporary mass media he is obliged to concede the centrality of expanding corporate economic control and to recognise its enormous potential for determining the range and form of the coming mass communications system. As he forcefully points out in his book, *Television: Technology and Cultural Form* (1974), the new electronic technologies of data processing, video, satellite communications and cable television.

> can be used to affect, to alter, and in some cases control our whole social process . . . These are the contemporary tools of the long revolution towards an educated and participatory democracy, of the recovery of effective communication . . . But they are also the tools of what would be, in context, a short and successful counter-revolution, in which a few para-national corporations could reach further into our lives, at every level from news to psycho-drama, until individual and collective response to many different kinds of

experience and problem became almost limited to choice between
their programmed possibilities [Williams, 1974, p. 151].

In that last sentence particularly, determination returns with a
vengeance albeit through the back door of polemics and in a form
which is never systematically explored in Williams' more theoretical
work.

As we have already noted, Stuart Hall, like Williams, maintains that
questions of economic determination are central to a Marxist sociology
of culture. However, unlike Williams they make no significant appearance in his substantive analysis of the contemporary mass media. They
are announced and placed in a theoretical bracket. This is principally
because he locates his central problematic elsewhere, drawing extensively on Gramsci and Althusser, whom he argues, 'constitute the really
significant contribution, post Marx, Engels and Lenin, to the development of a Marxist "theory of the superstructures" and of the base/
superstructure relation' (Hall, 1977b, p. 64). Both thinkers have
exerted a complex and continuing influence on the course of British
cultural studies and it would require at least another paper to do
justice to this process of assimilation. For the present though, we simply
wish to indicate some very basic points of influence.

Both Gramsci and Althusser present the sphere of culture and
ideology as increasingly central to the maintenance of modern
capitalism's relations of production, but both are at pains to emphasise
that the domain of ideology is relatively autonomous and has its own
specific dynamics and its own unique effectiveness. Within this definition of the situation, therefore, the field of ideological analysis can be
seen not only as a crucial area for analysis in its own right, but as an
area whose internal dynamics can be uncovered independently of a
consideration of the economic contexts in which it is embedded. In one
of his recent articles, for example, Stuart Hall has forcefully argued
that the growth of the modern mass media 'coincides with and is
decisively connected with everything that we now understand as
characterising "monopoly capitalism" ' and that in their latest phase of
development 'the media have penetrated right into the heart of the
modern labour and productive process itself'. Nevertheless, he argues
'these aspects of the growth and expansion of the media historically
*have to be left to one side by the exclusive attention given here to media
as ideological apparatuses*' (Hall, 1977a, p. 340; our italics). We would
argue to the contrary, that the ways in which the mass media function
as 'ideological apparatuses' can only be adequately understood when

they are systematically related to their position as large scale commercial enterprises in a capitalist economic system, and if these relations are examined historically. Given the way in which Hall defines his central problematic, however, this separation of the ideological and the economic dimensions of media operations is entirely understandable. Nevertheless, we would argue that it necessarily results in a partial and truncated explanation of ideological production.

Althusser's influence is also very evident in the phrase 'ideological apparatuses'. Indeed, the extension of what was to be included under the conceptual umbrella of 'ideology' constitutes Althusser's second great contribution to cultural sociology. Within this widened definition, ideology 'was not only a description of a system of relatively formal beliefs; it was rather a description of a body of practices, relationships and institutions' (Williams, 1977b, p. 13). Consequently, as Pierre Macherey has pointed out, 'to study the ideology of a society is not to analyse the systems of ideas, thoughts and representations. It is to study the material operation of ideological apparatuses to which correspond a certain number of specific practices' (quoted in Mercer and Radford, 1977, p. 5). In point of fact, however, most work on the media conducted under this rubric has not examined the 'material operations of ideological apparatuses' and the practices corresponding to them. At least, it has not done so directly. Rather it has approached them obliquely, as they are refracted through the forms of particular media products. Here the decisive influences have come from the various styles of semiological analysis. Semiology has been, in Althusser's phrase, the 'pup' that has consistently slipped 'between the legs' of contemporary Marxist analyses of ideology (Hall, 1977c, p. 30).

Starting from the very reasonable assumption that 'every text in some sense internalises its social relations of production' (Eagleton, 1976, p. 48), this approach takes the argument a stage further and suggests that these relations can be retrieved and explicated through a reading of the text. In order to become cultural goods for public consumption, the raw materials of media output — the events, sets of relations and general ideologies — have to be translated into cultural forms — soap opera, news items, documentary programmes — each of which is governed by particular processes of signification employing a range of codes and sub-codes. Hence media products are messages in code, messages about the nature of society, about the nature of productive relations within the media themselves, and about the nature of the relations between media organisations and other institutional domains and social processes (see Hall, 1973 and 1975).

The analysis of media products is therefore essentially an act of decoding, an attempt to excavate the various levels of social and ideological relations which are embedded in the form. It is a kind of archaeology of social knowledge. One of the best examples of this technique applied to the contemporary media is Stuart Hall's analysis of the centre piece political discussion in the special edition of *Panorama* before the crucial election of October 1974.

As Raymond Williams has pointed out, 'the television discussion is not only a political event but also a cultural form, and that form indicates many overt and covert relationships' (Williams, 1976a, p. 38). Hall extends this point and uncovers the way in which the programme form contains and reproduces both the structure of the legitimate political domain pivoted upon parliament, and the structure of the relations between broadcasting organisations and the sphere of politics and the state (see Hall *et al.*, 1976 and Hall 1976).

Despite its fertility the analysis is, however, ultimately unsatisfactory. In the first place the programme chosen is atypical of television output in general in at least two important respects. The fact that the final processes of production take place 'live' in the studio means that they are much more clearly visible than in the case of say plays, series or documentaries, where production is fully accomplished before transmission and where the underlying relations of production are concealed rather than revealed by the form. Secondly, the fact that the programme is embedded in a set of public and highly formalised relations, between broadcasters and the political and state apparatuses, makes the reproduction of these relations within the form of the programme relatively easy to detect. More often than not, however, the crucial relations between production personnel and other significant sources of determination and constraint, particularly those in the economic domain, lack this degree of codification and tend to work more covertly and surreptitiously. Consequently it is not just a question of devising more adequate modes of textural analysis and applying them to a comprehensive range of media output. In addition to the problems of typicality common to any case study there is a fundamental methodological difficulty in approaching social and structural relations through the analysis of texts. However well conceived and executed, textural readings remain a variety of content analysis and as such they suffer from the familiar but intractable problem of inference. It is one thing to argue that all cultural forms contain traces of the relations of production underlying their construction, and of the structural relations which surround them. It is quite another to go on to argue that an analysis of form can deliver an adequate and satisfactory account of these sets of relations and of the determinations they exert on the production process. They can't. In our view the sociology of culture and communications has been seriously incapacitated by the tendency to over-privilege texts as objects of analysis. Textural analysis will remain important and necessary, but it cannot stand in for the sociological analysis of cultural production. Indeed, if sociology is to make an important contribution to contemporary cultural analysis, then it is primarily in the analysis of social relations and social structures that its strongest claim to significance can and should be staked.

In addition to highlighting problems of methodology, the *Panorama* piece also exemplifies the key conceptual focus of much contemporary British work — namely its concern with the relationship between the media and the state. Here again the twin influences of Gramsci and Althusser have been seminal. Hall and his colleagues follow Gramsci in arguing that, 'in capitalist social formations, the state is the site where the "unity" of the dominant ideology, under the dominance of a leading faction of capital, is *constructed*, and thus where hegemony is secured' (Chambers *et al.*, 1977, p. 114). This emphasis on the pivotal role of the state in organising and orchestrating legitimation processes is further reinforced by Althusser's very influential conception of the 'ideological state apparatuses'. There is no space here to debate the adequacy of these formulations or to explore the important and complex differences between them. We simply wish to indicate their general influence.

Firstly and most obviously, they have concentrated attention on that sector of the media which is most closely and formally bound to the state and to the political sphere — broadcasting. With the exception of the news coverage in the press, the exclusively commercial sectors of the media have been largely ignored. Secondly, the areas of content singled out for sustained analysis are primarily those concerned with presenting aspects of the political system or state apparatuses — the coverage of parliamentary politics, the legal and judicial systems, the role of the state in industrial relations. Thirdly, within these chosen areas, analysis has concentrated predominantly on actuality presentations — news, current affairs and editorials, and documentaries — and neglected the wealth of pertinent fiction. Once more these skews in attention raise important questions of typicality and generalisability, and these questions are touched in turn by a central problem of conceptualisation.

By displacing economic dynamics from the centre of analysis and concentrating so centrally on the relations between the media and the state, this general thrust necessarily results in a partial account of the contemporary situation. Firstly it ignores or glosses over several very important developments. It fails to analyse the growing economic inter-penetration of the different media sectors and the consequences of this movement for the structure of control and for the range and forms of the resulting products. Similarly, it ignores the growing internationalisation of the British mass media and the concomitant theoretical problems raised by their position in the global economic system of communications. Despite the theoretical overtures to continental Europe, in its concrete practice the Marxist sociology of culture in Britain remains remarkably parochial. This is a logical but nonetheless regrettable consequence of taking the relations between the media and the nation state, rather than those between the media and trans-national corporate capitalism as the central focus of analysis. However, it is not simply that the prevailing perspective contains important imbalances and hiatuses; it is also that it is unable to produce a convincing account of those areas and processes that it chooses to concentrate on. As we shall suggest with the case of news production, the failure to explore the nature and consequences of economic determinations has produced a partial and truncated explanation. It is not that the role of the state is not a significant dimension of analysis. Clearly it is. However, as we shall argue in more detail in our discussion of cultural imperialism, its role and significance can only be adequately grasped and incorporated into analysis when it is systematically related to the structure and operations of the economic system, both nationally and internationally.

Despite the gaps and problems with their analyses, both Hall and Williams attempt to combine an emphasis on the specific dynamics and effectivity of cultural production with at least an insistence on 'determination in the last instance by the (economic) mode of producton'. Recently however, this general project has come under fire from two opposed directions, represented by Barry Hindess and his colleagues on the one side, and Dallas Smythe on the other.

According to Hindess and his collaborators, the attempt to retain both 'determination in the last instance' and the relative autonomy of the cultural sphere is irredeemably flawed at root. Ultimately, they argue, there are only two choices; either you take determinations seriously in which case you are inevitably involved in some variant of reductionism, or you take the tenet of relative autonomy a stage further and treat the cultural sphere as genuinely autonomous. As Barry Hindess has recently put it, 'Either we effectively reduce ideological phenomena to class interests determined elsewhere (basically in the economy) . . . Or we face up to the real autonomy of ideological phenomena and their irreducibility to manifestations of interests determined by the structure of the economy' (Hindess, 1977, p. 104). According to this view then, anyone who continues to hold to the tenet of economic determination is inevitably tugged back towards forms of analysis which, however disguised, are fundamentally economistic and reductionist.[1] In order to avoid this undertow it is therefore necessary to reconceptualise the connections between relations of production, and ideological and cultural forms, and to conceive them 'not in terms of any relations of determination "in the last instance" or otherwise, but rather in terms of conditions of existence' (Cutler *et al.*, 1977, p. 314). Consequently, they argue, while certain ideological and cultural forms provide some of the necessary conditions of existence for the continued reproduction of capitalist relations of production, these forms are in no way determined by the economic mode of production. Rather they are generated from within the sphere of culture and ideology itself. Although arrived at by a very different route, this formulation is strikingly similar to Edward Thompson's position outlined earlier. Both are based on a decisive rejection of economic determinations.

A diametrically opposed criticism of the position exemplified by Hall and Williams has come from Dallas Smythe. For him the problem is not that they retain a notion of economic determination, but that they do not follow its implications through in their concrete analysis. According to Smythe, the 'first question that historical materialism should ask about mass communications systems is what economic function for capital do they serve' (Smythe, 1977, p. 1). His answer is that the media's primary function is to create stable audience blocs for sale to monopoly capitalist advertisers, thereby generating the propensities to consume which complete the circuit of production. For Smythe then, the media's role in reproducing ideology is essentially secondary:

> What is the nature of the content of the mass media in economic terms under monopoly capitalism? The information, entertainment and 'educational' material transmitted to the audience is an inducement (gift, bribe or 'free lunch') to recruit potential members of the audience and to maintain their loyal attention. [Smythe, 1977, p. 5].

While we endorse Smythe's general project of restoring economic dynamics to a central position in the analysis of mass communications, the way he develops his argument is seriously flawed in several crucial respects (see Murdock, 1978). Firstly his analysis is skewed. It concentrates exclusively on the American press and commercial television, both of which have a clear and obvious articulation to consumer advertising. It entirely ignores a number of very important media sectors with a minimal dependence on advertising revenue — notably, paperback publishing, the cinema and the popular music industry. This is no accident. It is symptomatic of Smythe's severely truncated conception of the relations between economic dynamics and cultural production. Ironically, despite his emphasis on the centrality of the economic, his presentation succeeds in severing the crucial links between the economic and ideological dimensions of media production. In his concern to highlight the role that the media plays in the circulation of economic commodities he completely ignores their independent role in reproducing ideologies, and consequently fails to explore the ways in which economic determinations shape the range and forms of media production and its resulting products. He reduces the media entirely to their economic function.

We do not accept that the effective choice is between economism and reductionism on the one hand, and the 'necessary non-correspondence' proposed by Hirst and his colleagues on the other. Rather, we wish to argue for a position that retains the necessary stress on the relative autonomy of cultural production which characterises the work of Williams and Hall, but which takes the question of economic determinations as a central category and focus of analysis.

When Ian Connell argues that 'the media belong first and foremost to the region of ideology' (Connell, 1978, p. 75), he is speaking not only for himself, but out of the dominant tendency of Marxist cultural theory examined above. Clearly the mass media do play a central ideological role in that their products are a key source of images, accounts and legitimations of British capitalism and of the structured inequalities in wealth and power which it generates. Our quarrel, however, is with the phrase 'first and foremost'. For us the mass media are 'first and foremost industrial and commercial organisations which produce and distribute commodities' within a Late Capitalist economic order (Murdock and Golding, 1974a, pp. 205-6) Consequently, we would argue, the production of ideology cannot be separated from or adequately understood, without grasping the general economic dynamics of media production and the determinations they exert.

These economic dynamics operate at a variety of levels and with varying degrees of intensity within different media sectors and different divisions within them. At the most general level the distribution of economic resources plays a decisive role in determining the range of available media. For example, as we have argued elsewhere, the absence of a mass circulation radical daily newspaper in Britain is primarily due to the prohibitive costs of market entry and to the maldistribution of advertising revenue (Golding and Murdock, 1978). Economic imperatives also help to determine the general form of available media. The lack of fit between the media systems of many Third World countries and the social needs of their populations — the institutionalisation of domestic, studio-based television in communally oriented outdoor cultures for example — is due in large measure to the historical and economic dominance of the major multi-national corporations. Similarly, dispersed rural populations are not particularly well served by urban-based daily newspapers. Within individual media organisations economic imperatives may play an important role in determining the allocation of productive resources between divisions with varying ratios of costs to audience appeal, as between sports coverage and educational broadcasting, or between foreign and crime news for example. And lastly, as two recent studies of television fiction production have clearly shown, economic considerations may penetrate and frame the forms of particular productions (see Alvarado and Buscombe, 1978, Murdock and Halloran, forthcoming).

How these various levels of determination, either singly or in combination, impinge on particular production situations is a matter for empirical investigation. However it is our contention that such investigations should form a focus of future sociological work on the contemporary media. To illustrate the contrast between the approaches we have been describing and our own perspective we will look briefly at two particular areas. The first is news, and particularly broadcast journalism, which has attracted the attention of analysts working from a variety of theoretical and methodological positions. The second example is cultural imperialism, which by contrast to news, has been largely neglected by sociologists of culture and communications. This oversight seems to us symptomatic of the limitations of approaches which divorce cultural analysis from political economy.

News is an account of events in the world produced for public consumption, and as such is bound to attract analysts interested in the ideological nature of media output. There is certainly no originality in displaying the partial view of affairs included in the news, whatever the medium. It is over fifty years since Walter Lippmann's brilliant essays showed how and why 'news is not a mirror of social conditions but the report of an aspect that has obtruded itself' (Lippmann, 1965, p. 216). But more recent research has attempted to show that this partiality is ideological in the sense that it creates a coherent view of reality, and furthermore a view that is derived from and functional for prevailing structures of power.

There are many problems in demonstrating the links between news, ideology, and power structures, and we cannot review all of them in this paper. We do wish, however, to suggest one or two gaps in recent discussions and briefly indicate an alternative approach. It is interesting that many writers have focused their attention on the BBC, and have sought explanations for its output in terms of the complex relationship of the corporation to the state. This is to be expected since much of this work derives from a concern with the theory of the state. It does present problems, however, when examining the news media as a whole, the majority of course being in the private sector.

One recurrent theme in recent analysis of news is the detection of frameworks of understanding within which news is constructed. These are discovered in the analysis of texts by a circumspect reading of the assumptions and nuances of routine journalism. This work is often brilliant and insightful. It does not, however, tell us anything of the social derivation of such frameworks; by whom are they shared and how do they come to be part of the very rhetoric and character of news? It only begs the question to invoke the refrain that news media are part of a system which is 'structured in dominance'.

A common instance of such textual inspection is that of industrial relations news. But the structures discerned in such news, the meticulous balancing of CBI and TUC, the emphasis on disruption and the disturbing effects of strikes on the public, the avoidance of rank and file spokesmen, all add up to a partiality which is not so easily displayed in other areas of news as the implication that such analysis is generalisable would suggest. Far from being a paradigm instance, industrial relations news is exceptional in the clarity with which the limitations of news can be discerned. This clarity invites far too easy an explanation of the sources of news structures. In *Bad News*,[2] the most important of recently published accounts of industrial relations news, the authors are anxious to get beyond economic explanations of media behaviour. They see such explanations as simply based on a view of the influence of commercialism.

Thus far theoretical analysis of the mass communications industry has revealed that critiques which simply stress commercialism are in themselves too limited . . . Although for instance in the buying of receivers and the paying of licences it can be admitted that the mass media or the consciousness industry is in many areas highly profitable and is generally subject to the logic of commercialism, it does serve another and no less important function at the cultural level, a function which is unaltered by the private or public ownership of the medium. This second function, the cultural legitimation of the consensus and the status quo is not subject to the narrow confines of commercialism. It is the role of television as a front-runner medium of cultural legitimation that is served by institutions of broadcasting however funded, whether privately or state owned [Ibid., pp. 13-15].

There are many problems with this view. Not least it is a very constricted view of the realm of the economic, which is rather more than the incidental matter of funding. Second, it is an oddly essentialist view which seems to attribute the ideological character of television culture to something in the nature of the medium. Third, and related to this, it blanks out any discussion of practice in and control of the production process, ruling out, apparently, any voluntarism in the work place.

Most importantly, where do these roles and functions come from? For Stuart Hall the immediate explanation is the power of 'accredited spokesmen', elite sources who provide news in a form acceptable to the dominant view of social order. 'In short the media reproduce the event, already presignified, and they do this because they obey the requirement on them to report 'impartially' what the decision makers say and do, and because the structure of news values orients them in certain predictable and practised ways to these privileged sources of action and information' (Hall, 1975, p. 131). This is the exercise of cultural power, which consists of: '(a) the power to define which issues will enter the circuit of public communications; (b) the power to define the terms in which the issue will be debated; (c) the power to define who will speak to the issues and the terms; (d) the power to manage the debate itself in the media' (Ibid., p. 143). In this account the link between the news and ruling ideologies is explained in two ways, by the shared perspectives of journalists and sources, and the institutional connections between their social milieux, most crucially broadcasting and the state. For a sociologist this begs many questions. Significantly a recent examination of BBC news, based on a study of actual newsroom practice, returns to a position akin to our own. In this study Philip Schlesinger argues for the importance of 'the context within which television news is itself produced. This is, despite genuine public service features, a pre-eminently commercial one, . . . Nor can such news be divorced from the political economy of the society and state in which it is produced' (Schlesinger, 1978, p. 245). Another study, even more concerned with the politics of the BBC's interaction with the state, nonetheless emerges from studying production with a focus on the congruence between pro-gramme making routines and the needs and interests of ruling groups, and on the way in which commercial imperatives provide a framework which 'underpins the programme-making process and the premises upon which political television rests' (Tracey, 1977, p. 245).

A displacement of analysis to the purely political results in a view of the state as the arena of critical struggle in the search for cultural democracy. Command and control of both the means and the practice of cultural production disappear from view as critical points of conflict. Oddly, this is an approach which is forced to see the media as inert, passive, neutral transmission belts for ideological distribution. Not surprisingly the structures of ownership, control, production, and indeed the complex interplay between the media and other blocs in the power structure all have to be abandoned. By implication any media, in any configuration, would play this role. Power is reduced to influence. This view says that 'it is in politics and the state, not in the media, that power is skewed' (Hall *et al.*, 1976, p. 92). But how then does this skew occur? This limited account of control is a recurrent problem. Thus Hall is left arguing that the media 'install themselves' as dominant in the production and distribution of culture, so that, as we have noted, the historical and economic explanation for this process can be 'left to one side'. He poses the crucial question 'what are the actual mechanisms which enable the mass media to perform this "ideological work"?'. Yet the answer he suggests merely poses the question in a different form.

> The selection of codes . . . casts these problematic events, con-sensually, somewhere within the repertoire of the dominant ideo-logies . . . Hence though events will not be systematically encoded in a single way, they will tend systematically to draw on a very limited ideological or explanatory repertoire, and that repertoire . . . will have the overall tendency of making things 'mean' within the sphere of the dominant ideology [Hall, 1977a, pp. 343-5].

In other words, the news is in the mode of the dominant ideology because it draws on the ideology that is dominant for its framework.

To begin to account for these links between ruling ideas and news demands an explanation of the actual processes of production, and of the control of resources which are in the last instance the ultimate boundary of those processes. The relationship of occupational beliefs and practices in journalism is a complex one, but it is only discoverable by reference to the history and political economy of news production.

Broadcast journalism draws many of its assumptions and practices from the press. In the early days of newspapers, after an initial period when publisher-printers seek freedom from licensing or other forms of control, growing commercial prosperity secures the independence of the press and eventually some form of constitutional guarantee of its autonomy. The transformation of a 'political' press, particularly a party-based press, to a mass circulation popular press, is a complex process and it would be misleading to present it as a clear process common to all countries. But there are essentially similar features that can be abstracted. The major change is in the economic base of the press. The 'retail revolution' results in competitive selling of branded products and an advertising industry to promote them. Newspapers are the ideal medium to convey such advertising to their consumer-readers, and advertising gradually replaces sales to a greater or lesser extent as a source of revenue. Consequently, newspaper prices can be reduced and the seeds of the popular mass circulation press are sown. The political party-based press often persists through this 'revolution', though normally forced to concede to the economic logic of the process. Where advertising is limited, political parties may be the only source of subsidy, thus sustaining a party-based press.

The journalistic consequences of this process are important. The search for readers draws newspapers away from a strident factionalism and towards a central neutrality of comparative inoffensiveness. Fact and opinion are distinguished. Their new relative value is captured in the famous 1921 dictum of C.P. Scott, editor of the English *Manchester Guardian*, that 'Comment is free, facts are sacred'. Opinions are caged in editorial columns, facts command the news pages. The distinction is institutionalised in the contrast between the reporter and the journalist, correspondent, or columnist.

Broadcasting began as a technical novelty, and only later was it developed commercially by the more opportunist members of the radio and telecommunications industry, until finally it became the major entertainment form of the twentieth century. It became a news medium at the same time, and news broadcasting was universally advanced to the front line in the scheduling considerations of broadcasting executives. Normally television news is the fixed point in a kaleidoscopic world of dramas, quizzes, soap operas, documentaries, and education. Three problems face broadcast journalism in its evolution as a distinct form of programming.

Firstly, broadcasting organisations are normally sanctioned by law and have their operations and structures defined by statute. Legal requirements have to be translated into routine practice, and it is in the consequent attempts to operationalise the generalities of the law that broadcast journalism falls back on the conventions of the press. Secondly, broadcast journalism has to establish a degree of autonomy from the press. Initially it is seen as a competitive threat, particularly to evening newspapers, and it is common for the press to demand limitations on the timing and extent of news broadcasting. Broadcast journalists were usually dependent on the press as a source of news in the early years, and it was only gradually recognised that broadcast news was potentially other than newspaper news distributed in a new way. For many journalists the trend to autonomy became too advanced and threw up a conflict of identity between the role of broadcaster and of journalist. Thirdly, broadcast journalism had to come to terms with the highly regulated distinction between fact and comment which it was constrained to observe by its centrality, close relationships with government, and constitutional position. Newspaper journalism had produced the creed of objectivity. Broadcast journalism had to be more than honest about the debate; it had to be above it. Gradually new creeds of impartiality and balance were developed while the distinction between fact and comment was institutionalised in organisational form by the separation of 'news' and 'current affairs'.

Broadcasting was involved with government from its inception. What was thought to be a technical necessity for national monopoly control of the new medium brought it to the attention of licensing authorities almost as soon as it was weaned from its inventors. This emphasis on the distribution system of the new medium displaced concern with its content. What was licensed was the reception and dissemination technology. As a result the controls seen as suitable for broadcasting were derived, by default, from the understanding and ideologies already evolved by earlier media, especially the press. Broadcasting was different in two vital respects; its output was heterogeneous — both information and entertainment — and it was almost universally organised in a monopoly service closely wedded in one form of relationship to the state. Yet the difficulties and fundamental problems these differences were to create went unforeseen in the early years of broadcasting.

Among the many complexities these origins generated was frequently a confused set of regulations governing the production of news. A variety of constitutional, legislative, and administrative strictures circumscribe not merely what news operations may be conducted, but what form news may take. What becomes apparent very often in a careful examination of these, is their studied vagueness, forcing television journalists back on their own definitions of correct professional practice and standards.

Journalistic notions of what is and is not news have been forged in the workshops of a commercial press serving historically particular needs and interests. It is in this process that news values are created. Discussions of news values usually suggest they are surrounded by a mystique, an impenetrable cloud of verbal imprecision and conceptual obscurity. Many academic reports concentrate on this nebulous aspect of news values and imbue them with far greater importance and allure than they merit. News production is rarely the active application of decisions of rejection and promotion to highly varied and extensive material. On the contrary, it is for the most part the passive exercise of routine and highly regulated procedures in the task of selecting from already limited supplies of information. News values exist and are, of course, significant. But they are as much the resultant explanation or justification of necessary procedures as their source.

News values are used in two ways. They are the criteria of selection from material available to the newsroom of those items worthy of inclusion in the final product. Second, they are guidelines for the presentation of items, suggesting what to emphasise, what to omit, and where to give priority in the preparation of the items for presentation to the audience. News values are thus working rules, comprising a corpus of occupational lore which implicitly and often expressly explains and guides newsroom practice. It is not as true as often suggested that they are beyond the ken of the newsman, himself unable and unwilling to articulate them. Indeed, they pepper the daily exchanges between journalists in collaborative production procedures. Far more, they are terse shorthand references to shared understandings about the nature and purpose of news which can be used to ease the rapid and difficult manufacture of bulletins and news programmes. News values are qualities of events or of their journalistic construction, whose relative absence or presence recommends them for inclusion in the news product. The more of such qualities a story exhibits, the greater its chances of inclusion. Alternatively, the more different news values a story contains, the greater its chances of inclusion.

We cannot here describe in detail the linkages between social values, news values, and news itself. Research into broadcast news (see Golding and Elliott, forthcoming), based on the approach we are advocating, suggests that the resultant product lacks two crucial dimensions, power and process, and is thus structurally incapable of providing other than an uncritical and consensual view of the world. The invisibility of power, both within and between nations, is caused by many factors; the geography of news gathering, the simplification of the *dramatis personae* of news and the limited arenas which news can survey, which leads to an emphasis on formal political events. Social process similarly disappears as the exigencies of production mould a view of reality which is fragmented and ahistorical.

Analyses which see news as necessarily a product of powerful groups in society, designed to provide a view of the world consonant with the interests of those groups, simplify the situation too far to be helpful. The occupational routines and beliefs of journalists do not allow a simple conduit between the ruling ideas of the powerful and their distribution via the air-waves. Yet the absence of power and process clearly precludes the development of views which might question the prevailing distribution of power, or its roots in the evolution of economic distribution and control. A world which appears fundamentally unchanging, subject to the genius or caprice of myriad powerful individuals, is not a world which appears susceptible to radical change or challenge.

There are three ways in which broadcast news is ideological. First it focuses our attention on those institutions and events in which social conflict is managed and resolved. It is precisely the arenas of consensus formation which provide both access and appropriate material for making the news. Second, broadcast news, in studiously following statutory demands to eschew partiality or controversy, and professional demands for objectivity and neutrality, is left to draw on the values and beliefs of the broadest social consensus. The prevailing beliefs in any society will rarely be those which question existing social organisation or values. News will itself merely reinforce scepticism about such divergent, dissident,or deviant beliefs. Thirdly broadcast news is, for historical and organisational reasons, inherently incapable of providing a portrayal of social change or of displaying the operation of power in and between societies. It thus portrays a world which is unchanging and unchangeable. The key elements of any ruling ideology are the undesirability of change, and its impossibility; all is for the best and change would do more harm than good, even if it were possible. Broadcast news substantiates this philosophy because of the interplay of the three processes we have just described.

News evolves then in response to a range of imperatives in its market situation which become incorporated in the working routines and beliefs involved in its production. Occupational ideologies make a virtue of necessity, and such necessities are born of the markets for which news was and is designed. There is, in effect, an evolutionary coincidence between the conventions which define what we mean by news and the ruling ideology. Cultural stratification is thus a function of the emerging structure of ownership and control over the means of cultural production. This is very much more obvious in the case of the press, as we have described at length elsewhere (see Murdock and Golding, 1974a and Golding and Murdock, 1978). Much remains to be done in charting the relationship between news, ideology and the reproduction of social order. Such work cannot progress, however, by confining the analysis of ideology to its determination by the state.

To display the history and economic infrastructures of news media is not to explain the form and function of the ideology they produce. It is quite obviously true, for example, that if British television news is ideological, it is equally so, and in similar ways, on both the commercial and public networks. However to understand the form news takes it *is* essential to account for its origins as a commodity both within a production process and in history. In an earlier article we have suggested some ways in which the form of ideological statements within news is constructed, and outlined the kinds of factors which may explain these forms (Murdock and Golding, 1974a, pp. 228-230). It is important, too, to understand which news media are available for the articulation of particular ideologies. It is a major task of a media political economy to explain the constricted range of communication outlets and the systematic relationship between this range and prevailing distributions of power and economic control. It is both politically defeatist, and methodologically essentialist, to assume that news is inherently composed of a particular set of ideological formulae. Why are some witnesses 'accredited' and others less so? The operation of the market and its response to changing forces in the organisation and control of production are the crucial mechanisms to explore if we wish to explain the unavailability of particular channels of communication to radical or politically dissident views. It is this task that a political economy of news media can attempt.

The international diffusion of media companies and their products has become a major feature of mass communications in recent years. In fact this is only an exaggeration of an aspect of the culture industries which has always been present, most notably in publishing. This international growth should be central to the sociology of the media for two reasons. First, contemporary capitalism is characterised by the emergence of multinational companies and the variety of economic relations loosely labelled neo-colonialism. If we are interested in the relationship between the media and structures of power and dominance it is essential to examine the multinational media in this context. Second, if we are concerned to locate the media in an overarching structure of cultural production it is important to make the linkages with language and education. These linkages are starkest in the history of colonial relations and the subsequent development of these relations in the current period.

To focus on texts as ideology is to remain blind to the forces which lie behind the production of these texts. It is interesting that many of the writers discussed earlier in this paper were concerned with language. Yet cultural dependency is a critical arena in which to examine the ties between media, language, culture, and structures of domination (see, *inter alia*, Tunstall, 1977, Mazrui, 1975, and Cardona *et al.*). This would require both an historical and economic approach, analysing the role of indigenous elites in dependent societies, the education industry, as well as news and culture as export commodities.

Similarly a limited concern with the link between culture and the state relies on a sociology of the state which is unable to relate the nation-state to the international economy. It is symptomatic of the misplaced concern of many in the recent rediscovery of cultural sociology that their discussions of the media have totally ignored this international dimension. We suggest this is not merely a question of priorities or interests, but a missing dimension which is bound to result from extracting cultural sociology from the context of political economy.

Most major cultural producers are related to multi-national corporations. Several writers, most notably Schiller (1976), Mattelart (1976), Hamelink (1977) and Varis (1976) have demonstrated the acceleration of this trend in recent years. Yet their work is largely ignored by analysts of the media and the state. It is not that the state is irrelevant. But the relationship of the state to the international economy is a complex question to be explored not ignored, even if one's initial concern is with the state. It is not possible, for example, to analyse the role

of American media in the American state without discussing the place
of the electronics and telecommunications industries in twentieth century American expansionism. Nor is it realistic to relate the British
media to the production of class ideologies without an understanding
of the changing role of British capital in the post-imperial period. The
context of the ebb and flow of state power is its relation to the international economy, particularly flows of capital controlled by international firms; this is precisely what has been referred to as the crisis
of incorporation faced by British capitalism in the last thirty years. It is
ironic that the priority given to analysis of the state by some writers on
the left mirrors an outmoded liberal vision of a global web of nation-
states in perpetual political balancing acts. Murray has summarised this
development as follows:

> Certainly there is a tendency in twentieth century Marxist writing
> on the world economy to infuse the nation-state with an independ-
> ence set apart from the range and power of its own national capital.
> Nation-states become an entity without substance. This, in part,
> reflects the predominantly political treatment which the state has
> received in Marxist literature. Until recently it was primarily the
> repressive role of the state in capitalism which has been emphasised:
> two recent works by Miliband and Poulantzas have brought out its
> ideological function. What is remarkable is how little attention has
> been given to the economic role of the state in capitalism, and it is
> this which seems to me to be central to any discussion on the robust-
> ness of the nation-state in an era of interpenetration of national
> capitals . . . [Murray, 1975, p. 61].

Even if one wishes to concentrate on the political rather than the
economic as a context for the study of ideology, the growth of cultural
imperialism should be a particular concern. For many Third World
countries the attempt to construct a 'new information order' has become not merely a complement to, but an intrinsic part of the struggle
toward a new economic order. Beginning with minor rumblings in the
forum of UNESCO in the late 1960s, cultural decolonisation has
become a major theme in the 'north-south' dialogue. In important
statements at the Algiers non-aligned countries conference in 1973, at
the UNESCO General Assemblies in 1974 and 1978, and at major
gatherings in Quito, Lima, Tunis, and most controversially Nairobi and
New Delhi, the demand for a 'new international order for information'
has emerged as a focal point of struggle.[3]

The objection is to the flow of cultural goods, such as news and television programmes,[4] and to the flow of practices and institutions,[5] which act as a 'Trojan horse' for economic domination, or which in themselves constitute a threat to cultural autonomy or authenticity. None of this debate surfaces in recent work on the politics of the media, even by those writers apparently concerned to exhume the state as a central issue. One of the most interesting lines of inquiry to follow is the role of culture in securing the power of the 'new bourgeoisie' in dependent countries. The link between this group and the wider structure of dependence is very much bound in to the international structure of cultural flows. Their role as cultural brokers, using their membership of a cosmopolitan and mobile elite to lubricate the diffusion of cultural goods and values, is a key function in the international spread of the culture industries. The link between education and publishing exemplifies this.

Publishing, though traditionally a small-scale, even cottage industry, has followed the paths of the other media into diversified conglomerate industries (see Golding, 1978). The largest producers of educational books and materials include such firms as Xerox, CBS, ITT, Westinghouse and so on. Publishing is an international business. In 1977 exports accounted for 36 per cent of British book sales, and increasingly profits are further derived from sales of local subsidiaries in Third World countries. Most books in the Third World are college or school texts. The education and publishing industries are thus inextricably entwined, and both are central to the structure of cultural dependency. To fully explain the relationship of the capitalist state to dependency such links have to be explored. Cultural dependency is itself, however, an aspect of a more fundamental system of economic domination, and only comprehensible as such.

A political economy of cultural dependency is thus best developed by working from theories of imperialism or dependency. Many of these links have been explored by Latin American theorists. Their prime concern is with the historical evolution of capitalism from colonial to imperialistic, to neo-imperialistic phases, and with the corresponding structures of mercantilism, industrial laissez-faire and monopoly capitalism. By concentrating on the conquest and colonisation of Latin America, these writers reject approaches to development in terms of necessary and ubiquitous stages, and concentrate on the role of foreign investment and finance in creating a global structure in which development and underdevelopment are two sides of the same coin. In looking at the cultural components of this process such theorists, even those with a particular interest in the media, have kept the economic context in close focus. Faraone notes that

> . . . in Latin America the press and other media support the hier-archical power structure of society, the ideology of the ruling class. This kind of role of the mass media is a consequence of capitalist class society and the function of international imperialism [Faraone, 1974, p. 23].

Corradi similarly argues that

> the task is to analyse the social structures of Latin America and their processes in terms of changes that have taken place in the more inclusive system of international stratification. Social structures and idea-structures can then be studied as substructures of this more inclusive system. In other words what is being developed is a theory of dependent capitalism [Corradi, 1971, p. 40].

Other theorists in the field have stressed similarly the ultimate deter-mining role of economic relations, seeing their own work as dealing

> . . . with questions concerning the nature and dynamics of a super-structure that is the expression of a dependent economic system . . . It is in this context that the cultural and ideological system assumes major importance. For it must fulfil a strong need for holding together a system that is heavily divided by inequalities in the distri-bution of resources [Dagnino, 1973, pp. 129-31].

Duner, similarly, in looking at cultural dependency in the light of his studies of Colombian education, concludes that:

> the ideological factor, however, is not a totally independent variable but can well be understood in the light of the prevalent dependency structure. The latter can be seen as expressing the interests on which ideologies rest [Duner, 1973, p. 10].

As yet, work on cultural imperialism has been inconsistent and theoretically uncertain. But enough has been done to suggest that even, in fact particularly, if one's initial concern is with the state or with language, then the international culture industries are a crucial domain to explore. To ignore this area is more than a mistake of emphasis or a choice of interests. It is only possible if the links between ideology and power are sought outside the structures of material control, structures whose uncovering must now be an urgent priority for any serious sociology of culture.

Conclusion

The media make a major contribution to the legitimation of continuing inequalities both within and between nations. It is for this reason that we see the study of mass communications as occupying a central position in the heartland of traditional sociological inquiry into the maintenance of social order. We have suggested two weaknesses in recent attempts to analyse this question. The first derives from an undue emphasis on the links between the media and the state, an emphasis which leaves aside the massive evidence for the historical and political importance of capitalist ownership and control of the means of communication throughout the range of the cultural industries. The second weakness derives from the classic difficulty of inference from content analysis, which in recent guise has led to too much authority being given to the circumstantial evidence provided by qualitative textual analysis.

The new emphasis being given to the study of culture and ideology within sociology is a welcome one. We have suggested in this paper, however, that to make the most of this revival such studies must start by developing a political economy of the culture producing industries. Only then will we have the scaffolding on which a secure account of the relationship between the media and ideology can be built.

Notes

1. The general case has been argued by Paul Hirst in (Hirst, 1977, 131) and it has been applied to the work of the Birmingham Centre by Rosalind Coward (Coward, 1977a, p. 90).

2. Glasgow University Media Group (1976). For a more extensive study, as yet unpublished, see P. Hartmann (1976). We are not able here, obviously, to enter into a general discussion of either of these studies.

3. Behind the growing debate about 'communications policies' lies a whole complex of issues relating the state to the media multinationals. For a brief critical look at this debate see Schiller (1976, ch. 4.)

4. There is a massive amount of literature on news flows. For a summary and discussion see Harris (1974, 1976). On the flow of TV programmes see Varis (1973).

5. See Cruise O'Brien (1976), Golding (1977), and Pilsworth's paper at the 1978 British Sociological Conference on Culture, at which the papers in this volume were presented.

BIBLIOGRAPHY

Note: Unless specified otherwise place of publication is London.

Albrecht, M.C. (1956), 'Does literature reflect common values?'
American Sociological Review, vol. 21
—— (1968), 'Art as an institution', *American Sociological Review*,
vol. 33, no. 3
—— Barnett, J.H., Griff, M., eds., (1970), *The sociology of art and
literature*, Duckworth
Althusser, L. (1969), *For Marx*, Penguin
—— (1970), *Reading Capital*, New Left Books
—— (1971), 'Ideology and ideological State apparatuses' in *Lenin and
philosophy*, New Left Books
—— (1972) 'Marx's relation to Hegel' in *Politics and history,* New Left
Books
—— (1976) *Essays in self criticism,*New Left Books
Alvarado, M. and Buscombe, E. (1978), *Hazell: the making of a tv series*,
Latimer New Dimensions
Anderson, P. (1964), 'Origins of the present crisis', *New Left Review*,
no. 23
—— (1966), 'Socialism and pseudo-empiricism', *New Left Review*,
no. 35
—— (1968), 'Components of the national culture', in A. Cockburn and
R. Blackburn, eds., *Student power*, Penguin
Antal, F. (1947), *Florentine painting and its social background*, Kegan
Paul
Audio Visual Research Group Broadcasting Evaluating Report 22 (1977a),
Patterns of inequality – 'A Woman's work', *D302 TVI*, Open
University, Milton Keynes
—— Report 23 (1977b), *Patterns of inequality – 'Looking at inequality'*,
D302 TV2, Open University, Milton Keynes
Barnett, J.H. (1958), 'Research areas in the sociology of art', *Sociology
and social research*, vol. 62, no. 6
—— (1959), 'The sociology of art', in R.K. Merton, L. Broom and
L.S. Cottrell, eds., *Sociology today*, Basic Books, New York
Barr, C. (1974), 'Projecting Britain and the British character: Ealing
studios', *Screen*, vol. 15, nos. 1 and 2
—— (1977), *Ealing studios*, Cameron and Tayleur

Barthes, R. (1957), *Mythologies*, Seuil, Paris
—— (1975), *S/Z*, Jonathan Cape
—— (1977), *Image, music, text: essays*, Fontana
Bates, T., and Gallagher, M. (1977), *Improving the effectiveness of Open University television case studies and documentaries*, Institute of Educational Studies, Papers on Broadcasting, no. 77, Open University, Milton Keynes
Bates, T., and Robinson, J. (1977), *Evaluating educational television and radio*, Open University, Milton Keynes
Beechey, V. (1977), 'Some notes on female wage labour', *Capital and class*, no. 3
—— (1978), 'Women and production: a critical analysis of some sociological theories of women's work', in A. Kuhn and A.M. Wolpe, eds.
Bell, D. (1976), *The Post industrial society*, Penguin
Benveniste, E. (1971), *Problems of general linguistics*, University of Miami Press, Florida
Beveridge, W. (1942), *Social insurance and allied services*, reprinted HMSO, 1974 (*The Beveridge Report*)
—— (1943), *Pillars of security and other wartime essays*, Allen and Unwin
Bland, L., and others (1978), 'Woman "inside and outside" the relations of production' in CCCS Women's Studies Group, 1978
Bloomfield, J., ed. (1977), *Class, hegemony and party*. Lawrence and Wishart
Blumler, J.G. (1977), *The social purposes of mass communication research: a transatlantic perspective*, first Founders' lecture, Annual conference of the Association for Education in Journalism, Wisconsin
Bogdanor, V., and Skidelsky, R., eds. (1970), *The age of affluence*, Macmillan
Bonilla, F., and Girling, R., eds. (1973), *Struggle of dependency*, Stanford University, California
Bowlby, J. (1953), *Child care and the growth of love*, Penguin
Brewster, B. (1973), 'Notes on the text "Young Mr. Lincoln" by the editors of *Cahiers du cinéma*', *Screen*, vol. 14, no. 3
Brighton, A. (1977), 'Official art and the Tate Gallery', *Studio International*, vol. 193
Bromley, R. (1977), 'Natural boundaries: the social function of popular fiction', *Red Letters*, no. 7
Brown, G.B. (1908), *The Glasgow School of painters*, James McLehose,

Glasgow

Burch, N. (1976), 'Avant garde or vanguard?' *Afterimage*, no. 6

—— and Dana, J. (1974), 'Propositions', *Afterimage*, no. 5

Burke, P. (1974), *Tradition and innovation in Renaissance Italy: a sociological approach*, Fontana

Cahiers du cinéma editorial collective (1972), 'John Ford's "Young Mr. Lincoln" ', *Screen*, vol. 13, no. 3

Campbell, R. (1977), 'The fugitive kind', *Jumpcut*, no. 15

Cardona, G.R., and others (n.d.), *Power relation between Europe and other continents in the language and cultural field*, Stichtung voor Internationale Kommunkatie, Amsterdam

Caughie, J. (1977), 'The "world" of television', *Edinburgh Magazine*, no. 2

—— (1977/78), 'The television festival', *Screen*, vol. 18, no. 4

Caw, J. (1908), *Scottish painting past and present, 1620-1908*, T.C. and E.C. Black, Edinburgh

Centre for Contemporary Cultural Studies, Women's Studies Group (1978), *Women take issue*, Hutchinson

Chambers, L. and others (1977), 'Marxism and culture', *Screen*, vol. 18, no. 4

Clark, T.J. (1973a), *The absolute bourgeois: art and politics in France 1848-1851*, Thames and Hudson

—— (1973b), *Image of the people: Gustave Courbet and the 1848 Revolution*, Thames and Hudson

Clarke, S. (1977a), 'Marxism, sociology and Poulantzas' theory of the State', *Capital and class*, no. 2

—— (1977b), *Althusserian Marxism: a bourgeois disorder*. Mimeo

Cohen, S. (1972), *Folk devils and moral panics*, MacGibbon and Kee

Connell, I. (1978), 'Monopoly capitalism and the media: definitions and struggles', in S. Hibbin, ed., *Politics, ideology and the State*, Lawrence and Wishart

Corradi, I. (1971), 'Cultural dependence and the sociology of knowledge: the Latin American case', *International journal of comparative sociology*, vol. 8, no. 1

Coward, R. (1977a), 'Class, "culture" and the social formation', *Screen*, vol. 18, no. 1

—— (1977b), 'Response', *Screen*, vol. 18, no. 4

—— (1978), ' "Sexual liberation" and the family', *m/f*, no. 1

—— and Ellis, J. (1977) *Language and materialism*, Routledge and Kegan Paul

Cruise O'Brien, R. (1976), *Professionalism in broadcasting: issues of international dependence*, Institute of Development Studies, Discussion papers, DP 100, University of Sussex

Curran, J. ed. (1978), *The British press: a manifesto*. Macmillan

—— and others, eds. (1977), *Mass communication and society*, Edward Arnold

Cutler, A., Hindess, B., Hirst, P., and Hussain, A. (1977) *Marx's 'Capital' and capitalism today, Vol. I*, Routledge and Kegan Paul

—— (1978) *Vol. II*, Routledge and Kegan Paul

Dagnino, E. (1973), 'Cultural and ideological dependence: building a theoretical framework', in F. Bonilla and R. Girling, eds.

Davies, M. (1978), *Maternity: letters from working women*, Virago

Davin, A. (1978), 'Imperialism and motherhood', *History workshop*, no. 5

Dobb, M. (1945), *Studies in the development of capitalism*, Routledge and Kegan Paul

Duner, B. (1973), *Cultural dimensions of dependency*, University of Uppsala, mimeo

Durgnat, R. (1970), *A mirror for England*, Faber and Faber

—— (1976) 'Britannia rules the waves', *Film Comment*, July-August

Duvignaud, J. (1965), *Sociologie du théâtre*, PUF, Paris

—— (1967), *Sociologie de l'art*, PUF, Paris

Dyer, R. (1977a), 'Stereotyping' in *Gays and film*, British Film Institute

—— (1977b), 'Victim: hermeneutic project', *Film form*, vol. 1, no. 2

Eagleton, T. (1976), *Criticism and ideology: a study in Marxist literary theory*, New Left Books

Edholm, F., Harris, O., and Young, K. (1977), 'Conceptualising women', *Critique of anthropology*, vol. 3, no. 9/10

Ellis, J. (1976), 'Ideology and subjectivity', *Working papers in cultural studies*, no. 9

—— (1977), 'The institution of cinema', *Edinburgh Magazine*, no. 2

Elsaesser, T. (1972), 'Between style and ideology', *Monogram*, no. 3

Engels, F. (1973), 'The origin of the family, private property and the State', in K. Marx and F. Engels, *Selected works in one volume*, Lawrence and Wishart

Erben, M., and Gleeson, D. (1977), 'Education as reproduction' in M. Young and G. Whitty, eds., *Society, state and schooling*, Falmer Press, Brighton

Family Planning Association (1957), *The human sum*, FPA

Faraone, R. (1974), *The function of mass media in capitalism: Latin American experience*, University of Paris, mimeo

Fargier, J. (1971), 'Parenthesis or indirect route', *Screen*, vol. 12, no. 2

Fishman, J. (1956), 'An examination of the process of social stereotyping', *Journal of social psychology*, vol. 43

Foucault, M. (1976), *La volonté de savoir*, Gallimard, Paris
—— (1977), *Discipline and punish*, Allen Lane

Francastel, P. (1940-48), 'Art et sociologies', *Année sociologique*
troisième série, vol. 2
—— (1965), *Peinture et société*, Gallimard, Paris
—— (1970), *Etudes de sociologie de l'art*, Denoel, Paris

Freund, J. (1968), *The sociology of Max Weber*, Allen Lane

Gagnon, J., and Simon, W. (1973), *Sexual conduct: the social sources
of human sexuality*, Hutchinson, 1974

Gallagher, M. (1977), *Broadcasting and the Open University student*,
Institute of Educational Technology, Papers on Broadcasting, no. 80,
Open University, Milton Keynes

Gamble, A. (1974), *The conservative nation*, Routledge and Kegan Paul

Garnham, N. (1977), 'Towards a political economy of culture', *New
universities quarterly*, Summer

Genovese, E. (1974), *Roll Jordan Roll*, Pantheon, New York

Geras, N. (1972), 'Marx and the critique of political economy', in
R. Blackburn, ed., *Ideology in social science*, Fontana

Gittins, D. (1977), 'Women's work and family size between the wars',
Oral history, vol. 5, no. 2

Glasgow University Media Group (1976), *Bad News, Vol. 1*, Routledge
and Kegan Paul

Golding, P. (1977), 'Media professionalism in the Third World: the
transfer of an ideology', in J. Curran and others, eds.
—— (1978), 'The international media and the political economy of
publishing', *Library Trends*, vol. 26, no. 4
—— and Elliott, P. (forthcoming), *Making the news*, Longman
—— and Murdock, G. (1978), 'Confronting the market: public intervention and press diversity', in J. Curran, ed.

Goldmann, L. (1964), *The hidden god*, Routledge and Kegan Paul
—— (1967), 'The sociology of literature: status and problems of
method', *International social science journal*, vol. 19, no. 4

Gombrich, E. (1963), 'The social history of art', in *Meditations on a
hobby horse*, Phaidon

Gouldner, A. (1976), *The dialectic of ideology and technology*,
Macmillan

Gramsci, A. (1971), *Prison notebooks; selections*, Lawrence and
Wishart

Gray, R.Q. (1976), *The labour aristocracy in Victorian Edinburgh*,

Oxford University Press, Oxford
Griff, M. (1970), 'The recruitment and socialisation of artists' in
M. Albrecht and others, eds.
Gurevitch, M., and Blumler, J.G. (1977), 'Mass media and political
institutions: the systems approach', in G. Gerbner, ed., *Mass media
in changing cultures*, John Wiley, New York
Gurvitch, G. (1956), 'Sociologie du théâtre', in *Les lettres nouvelles*,
Paris
Hadjinicolaou, N. (1978), *Art history and class struggle*, Pluto
Hall, C. (1977), 'Married women at home in Birmingham in the 1920s
and 1930s', *Oral history*, vol. 5, no. 2
Hall, S. (1971), 'Introduction', *Working papers in cultural studies*
(hereafter, *WPCS*), no. 1
—— (1972a), 'The social eye of the *Picture Post*', *WPCS*, no. 2
—— (1972b), 'The determination of news photographs', *WPCS*, no. 3
—— (1973) *Encoding and decoding in the television discourse*, CCCS,
Birmingham, mimeo
—— (1975), 'The "structured communication" of events', in *Getting
the message across*, Unesco Press, Paris
—— (1976), *Broadcasting, politics and the State: the independent-
impartiality couplet*, Paper, Tenth biennial conference of the International Association for Mass Communication Research, University
of Leicester
—— (1977a), 'Culture, the media and the "ideological effect" ', in
J. Curran and others, eds.
—— (1977b), 'Rethinking the "base-and-superstructure" metaphor', in
J. Bloomfield, ed.
—— (1977c), 'The hinterland of science: ideology and the "sociology of
knowledge" ', *WPCS*, no. 10
—— (1977d), 'The "political" and the "economic" in Marx's theory of
class', in A. Hunt, ed.
—— (1977e), 'Some problems with the ideology/subject couple',
Ideology and consciousness, no. 3
—— (1978a), 'The tv feuilleton and the domestication of the world:
some preliminary critical notes', in *The feuilleton in television,
Vol 1*, Edizione RAI, Turin
—— (1978b), *Reformism and the legislation of consent*, CCCS,
Birmingham, mimeo
—— Connell, I., and Curti, L. (1976), 'The "unity" of current affairs
television', *WPCS*, no. 9
Hamelink, C. (1977), *The corporate village*, IDOC, Rome

Harding, J. (1968), 'Stereotypes', *International Encyclopedia of Social Sciences*

Harris, J. (1977), *William Beveridge: a biography*, Clarendon Press, Oxford

Harris, P. (1974), 'Hierarchy and concentration in international news flow', *Politics*, vol. 9, no. 2

— (1976), 'International news media authority and dependence', *Instant research on peace and violence*, vol. 6, no. 4

Hartmann, P. (1976), *The media and industrial relations*, Centre for Mass Communications Research, Leicester, mimeo

Hauser, A. (1962), *The social history of art*, 2 volumes, Routledge and Kegan Paul

Heath, S. (1976), 'On screen, in frame: film and ideology', *Quarterly review of film studies*, vol. 1, no. 3

— and Skirrow, G. (1977), 'Television: a "world in action" ', *Screen*, vol. 18, no. 2

Henderson, B. (1973/4), 'Critique of ciné-structuralism, part 1', *Film quarterly*, vol. 28, no. 21

— (1975), 'Metz *Essais I* and film theory', *Film quarterly*, vol. 28, no. 3

Henning, E.B. (1960), 'Patronage and style in the arts: a suggestion concerning their relations', *Journal of aesthetics and art criticism*, vol. 18

Hill, C. (1972), *The world turned upside down*, Penguin

Hindess, B. (1977), 'The concept of class in Marxist theory and Marxist politics', in J. Bloomfield, ed.

— and Hirst, P.Q. (1975), *Pre capitalist modes of production*, Routledge and Kegan Paul

— (1977) *Mode of production and social formation*, Macmillan

Hirst, P.Q. (1975), 'The uniqueness of the West', *Economy and society*, vol. 4, no. 4

— (1976a), *Social evolution and sociological categories*, Allen and Unwin

— (1976b), 'Althusser and the theory of ideology', *Economy and society*, vol. 5, no. 4

— (1977), 'Economic classes and politics', in A. Hunt, ed.

Hobsbawm, E.J. (1959), *Primitive rebels*, Manchester UP, Manchester

— (1964) *Labouring men*, Weidenfeld and Nicolson

Hoggart, R. (1957), *The uses of literacy*, Chatto and Windus

Hohendahl, P.U. (1977), 'Introduction to reception aesthetics', *New German critique*, no. 10

Holter, H. (1970), *Sex roles and social structure*, Universitetsforlaget, Oslo

Hunt, A., ed. (1977), *Class and class structure*, Lawrence and Wishart

Husra, B. (1964), 'Patterns of power', *Films and filming*, April
Ideology and consciousness editorial collective (1977), 'Psychology, ideology and the human subject', *Ideology and consciousness*, no. 1

Jakobson, R. (1972), 'Linguistics and poetics' in R. and F. de George, eds., *The structuralists*, Anchor Books, New York

Jameson, F. (1977), 'Conclusion' in *Aesthetics and politics*, New Left Books

Jauss, H.R. (1970), 'Literary history as a challenge to literary theory', *New Literary History*, vol. 2, no. 1

Johnson, R. (1978), *Culturalism and structuralism*, CCCS, Birmingham, mimeo

——— McLennan, G., and Schwarz, B. (1978), *Economy, culture and concept: three approaches to Marxist history*, CCCS, Birmingham, Stencilled papers, no. 50

Johnston, C., ed. (1975), *The work of Dorothy Azner*, British Film Institute

Kael, P. (1966), *I lost it at the movies*, Jonathan Cape

Kavolis, V. (1968), *Artistic expression: a sociological analysis*, Cornell University Press, Ithaca

Klapp, O.E. (1962), *Heroes, villains and fools*, Prentice-Hall, Englewood Cliffs, NJ

Kuhn, A. (1975), 'Women's cinema and feminist film criticsm', *Screen*, vol. 16, no. 3

——— and Wolpe, A.M. eds., (1978), *Feminism and materialism*, Routledge and Kegal Paul

Lacan, J. (1968), 'The mirror phase as formative of the function of the "I" ', *New Left Review*, no. 51

Laclau, E. (1977), *Politics and ideology in Marxist theory*, New Left Books

Land, H. (1976), 'Women — supporters or supported?' in D.L. Barker and S. Allen, eds., *Sexual divisions and society*, Longman

Leavis, F.R. (1962), *The common pursuit*, Penguin

Lippmann, W. (1965), *Public opinion*, Free Press, New York (orig. 1922)

Lovell, A., and Hillier, J. (1972), *Studies in documentary*, Secker and Warburg

MacArthur, C. (1977) '*Crossfire* and the Anglo-American critical tradition', *Film form*, vol. 1, no. 2

McCabe, C. (1974), 'Realism and the cinema: notes on some Brechtian theses', *Screen*, vol. 15, no. 2

—— (1975/6), 'The politics of separation', *Screen*, vol. 16, no. 4

—— (1976a), '*Days of Hope* — a response to Colin McArthur', *Screen*, vol. 17, no. 1

—— (1976b), 'Principles of realism and pleasure', *Screen*, vol. 17, no. 3

——(1977), 'Memory, phantasy, identity: *Days of Hope* and the politics of the past', *Edinburgh Magazine*, no. 2

McIntosh, M. (1978a), 'Who needs prostitutes?' in B. and C. Smart, eds., *Women, sexuality and social control*, Routledge and Kegan Paul

—— (1978b), 'The State and the oppression of women', in A. Kuhn and A.M. Wolpe, eds.

Mackintosh, M. (1977), 'Reproduction and patriarchy: a critique of Claude Meillassoux *Femmes, greniers et capitaux*', *Capital and Class*, no. 2

McLaren, A. (1978), *Birth control in the nineteenth century*, Croom Helm

MacNicol, J. (1978), 'Family allowances and less eligibility' in P. Thane, ed., *The origins of British social policy*, Croom Helm

MacRobbie, A. (1977), 'Working class girls and the culture of femininity', in CCCS Women's Studies Group, 1978

Martin, D. (1897), *The Glasgow school of painting*, Bell, Edinburgh

Marx, K. (1863a, b, c), *Capital, Vol. IV: Theories of Surplus Value, Vols. I, II, III*, Progress, Moscow, 1969-1972

—— (1973), *The Grundrisse*, Penguin

—— (1974), *Capital, Vol. I*, Lawrence and Wishart

—— (1976), *Capital, Vol. I*, rev. ed., Penguin

—— and Engels, F. (1846), *The German Ideology*, full version, Collected Works, Vol. 5

—— (1970), *The German Ideology*, Lawrence and Wishart

—— (1975), *Selected correspondence*, Lawrence and Wishart

Mason, T. (1977), 'Enthusiasms: *Radical History Review*', *History Workshop*, no. 4. (Cf. Thompson, E.P., 1976)

Mattelart, A. (1976), *Multinationales et systémes de communications,* Paris

Mazrui, A. (1975), *The political sociology of the English language: an African perspective*, Mouton, The Hague

Mepham, J. (1974), 'The theory of ideology in *Capital*', *Working papers in cultural studies*, no. 6

Mercer, C. and Radford, J. (1977), 'An interview with Pierre Macherey',

Red Letters, no. 5

Miliband, R. (1972), *Parliamentary socialism*, Merlin Press

— (1977), *Marxism and politics*, Oxford University Press

Mitchell, H. (1977), *The hard way up*, Virago

Montagu, I. (1964), *Film world*, Penguin

Montgomery Hyde, H. (1970), *The other love*, Heinemann

Mulhern, F. (1975), 'Ideology and literary form – a comment', *New Left Review*, No. 91

Mulvey, L. (1976), 'Visual pleasure and narrative cinema', *Screen*, vol. 16, no. 3

Murdock, G. (1978), 'Blindspots about Western Marxism: a rejoinder to Dallas Smythe', *Canadian journal of political and social theory*, vol. 2, no. 2

— and Golding, P. (1974a), 'For a political economy of mass communication', *Socialist Register* 1973, Merlin Press, 1974

— (1974b), 'Communications: the continuing crisis', *New Society*, no. 603

— (1977a), 'Capitalism, communication and class relations', in J. Curran and others, eds.

— (1977b), 'Beyond monopoly: mass communications in an age of conglomerates', in P. Beharrell and G. Philo, eds., *Trade unions and the media*, Macmillan

Murdock, G., and Halloran, J.D. (forthcoming), 'Contexts of creativity in television drama', in H.D. Fischer, ed., *Entertainment communication*, Hastings House, New York

Murray, R. (1975), *Multinational companies and nation states*, Spokesman Books, Nottingham

Nairn, T. (1964a), 'Anatomy of the Labour Party, I', *New Left Review*, no. 27

— (1964b), 'Anatomy of the Labour Party II', *New Left Review*, no. 28

Neale, S. (1977), 'Propaganda', *Screen*, vol. 18, no. 3

Newsom, J. (1948), *The education of girls*, Faber

Nowell-Smith, G. (1976), 'Six authors in pursuit of *The Searchers*', *Screen*, vol. 17, no. 1

O'Laughlin, B. (1974), 'Mediation of contradiction: why Mbum women do not eat chicken', in M.Z. Rosaldo and L. Lamphere, eds., *Women, culture and society*, Stanford University Press, California

Open University (1976), *Making sense of society: Unit 1, unemployment*, Open University, Milton Keynes, Course D101

Our Towns: a close-up (1943), Oxford University Press

Pinto-Duschinsky, M. (1970), 'Bread and circuses? The Conservatives in office, 1951-1964', in A. Bogdanor and R. Skildelsky, eds. 1970

Plummer, K. (1975), *Sexual stigma*, Routledge and Kegan Paul Political Economy of Women Group (1975), *Pamphlet, no. 2*, Conference of Socialist Economists, Brighton

Poulantzas, N. (1973), *Political power and social classes*, New Left Books

—— (1976), *Classes in contemporary capitalism*, New Left Books

Rancière, J. (1974), 'The concept of "critique" and the "critique of political economy" ', *Theoretical Practice*, nos. 1-3

Read, H. (1936), *Art and society*, Faber and Faber

Report of the consultative committee on differentiation of the curriculum for boys and girls respectively in secondary schools, (1923), HMSO (*The Hadow Report*)

Report of the committee of the secondary schools examination council, Curriculum and examinations in secondary schools (1943), HMSO (*The Norwood Report*)

Richardson, T. (1959), 'The man behind an "angry young man" ' *Films and filming*, February

Royal Commission on Population (1949), *Report*, HMSO

Saussure, F. de (1974), *Course in general linguistics*, Fontana

Saville, J., ed. (1954), *Democracy and the labour movement*, Lawrence and Wishart

Sayer, D. (1979a), 'Science as critique', in J. Mepham and D. Reuben, eds., *Issues in marxist philosophy*, Harvester Press

—— (1979b), *Marx's method* Harvester Press

Schiller, H. (1976), *Communication and cultural domination*, International Arts and Sciences Press, New York

Schlesinger, P. (1978), *Putting 'reality' together: BBC news*, Constable

Scott James, A.H. (1943), *Picture Post*, 13 November

Scottish Arts Council (1968), *The Glasgow boys*, 2 volumes, Exhibition Catalogue

Sewter, A.C. (1935), 'The possibilities of a sociology of art', *Sociological Review*, vol. 27

Silbermann, A. (1968), 'Introductory definitions of the sociology of art', *International social science journal*, vol. 20, no. 4

Slater, E., and Woodside, M. (1951), *Patterns of marriage*, Cassell

Smythe, D. (1977), 'Communications: blindspot of Western Marxism', *Canadian journal of political and social theory*, vol. 1, no. 3

Sorokin, P.A. (1937), *Social and cultural dynamics*, 4 volumes, American Book Company, New York

Summerfield, P. (1977), 'Women workers in wartime', *Capital and class*, no. 1

Swingewood, A. (1977), *The myth of mass culture*, Macmillan

Thomas, G. (1944), *Women at work*, HMSO

Thompson, E.P. (1963), *The making of the English working class*, Gollancz

—— (1965), 'Peculiarities of the English', *Socialist Register*

—— (1967), 'Time, work-discipline and industrial capitalism', *Past and present*, no. 38

—— (1971), 'The moral economy of the English crowd in the eighteenth century', *Past and present*, no. 50

—— (1973), 'Open letter to Leszek Kolakowski', *Socialist Register*, 1973, Merlin Press, 1974

Thompson, E.P. (1974), 'Patrician society; plebian culture', *Journal of Social History*, vol. 7, no. 4

—— (1975), *Whigs and hunters*, Allen Lane

—— (1976), 'An interview with E.P. Thompson', *Radical History Review*, vol. 3, no. 4

—— (1978), *The poverty of theory*, Merlin Press

Thompson, G. (1977a), *Interdisciplinary case study programmes*, Open University, Milton Keynes, mimeo

—— (1977b), *A response to Tony Bates and Margaret Gallagher*, Open University, Milton Keynes, mimeo

Tomars, A.S. (1940), *Introduction to the sociology of art*, Mexico City

Torr, D. (1956), *Tom Mann and his times*, Lawrence and Wishart

Tracey, M. (1977), *The production of political television*, Routledge and K. Paul

Tribe, K. (1976), 'Appropriation/recuperation', *Screen*, vol. 17, no. 1

—— (1977/78), 'History and the production of memories', *Screen*, vol. 18, no. 4

Tudor, A. (1974), *Theories of film*, Secker and Warburg

Tunstall, J. (1977), *The media are American*, Constable

Varis, T. (1973), *International inventory of tv programme structure and the flow of tv programmes between nations*, Institute of Mass Communications, University of Tampere

—— (1976), 'Aspects of the impact of transnational corporations on communication', *International social science journal*, vol. 28

Vinacke, W.E. (1957), 'Stereotypes as social concepts', *Journal of social psychology*, vol. 46

Watson, B. (1968), 'On the nature of art publics', *International social science journal*, vol. 20, no. 4

Weber, M. (1958), *The rational and social foundations of music*,

Southern Illinois University Press, Urbana

Weeks, J. (1977), *Coming out*, Quartet

Wells, A.F. (1970), *Social institutions*, Heinemann

Whale, J. (1977), *The politics of the media*, Fontana

White H.C., and C. (1965), *Canvases and careers: institutional change in the French painting world*, John Wiley, New York

Willeman, P. (1971), 'Distanciation and Douglas Sirk', *Screen*, vol. 12, no. 2

—— (1972/73), 'Towards an analysis of the Sirkian system', *Screen*, vol. 13, no. 4

——(1976), 'Voyeurism, the look and Dwoskin', *Afterimage*, no. 6

Williams, R. (1958), *Culture and society*, Chatto and Windus

—— (1965), *The Long revolution*, Penguin

——(1968), *Communications,* rev. ed., Penguin

——(1973), 'Base and superstructure in Marxist cultural theory', *New Left Review,* no. 82

——(1974), *Television: technology and cultural form*, Fontana

——(1976a), 'Communications as cultural science', in C.W.E. Bigsby, ed., *Approaches to popular culture*, Edward Arnold

——(1976b), 'Notes on British Marxism since the war', *New Left Review*, no. 100

——(1976c), 'Developments in the sociology of culture', *Sociology*, vol. 10, no. 2

——(1977a), *Marxism and literature*, Oxford University Press

——(1977b), 'The paths and pitfalls of ideology as an ideology', *Times Higher Educational Supplement*, 10 June

——(1977c), 'Two interviews with Raymond Williams', *Red Shift* (Cambridge), nos. 2 and 3

Willis, P. (1977) *Learning to labour: why working class kids get working class jobs*, Saxon House

Wilson, E. (1977), *Women and the welfare state*, Tavistock

Wolfenden, J. (1957) *Homosexual offences and prostitution*, HMSO (*The Wolfenden Report*)

——(1976), *Turning points*, Bodley Head

Wolff, J. (1977), 'The interpretation of literature in society: the hermeneutic approach', in J. Routh and J. Wolff, eds., *Sociology of literature: theoretical approaches*, Sociological Review Monograph, no. 25, Keele

Wollen, P. (1972), *Signs and meanings in the cinema*, Secker and Warburg

Wolpe, A.M. (1974), 'The official ideology of education for girls', in

M. Flude and J. Ahiers, eds., *Educability, schools and ideology*, Croom Helm

Women's Studies Group, CCCS *see* CCCS, Women's Studies Group

Young, M., and Willmott, P. (1957) *Family and kinship in East London*, Routledge and Kegan Paul

Zaretsky, E. (1976), *Capitalism, the family and personal life,* Pluto

NOTES ON CONTRIBUTORS

Michèle Barrett. Lecturer in sociology, the City University, London and member of the editorial collective of *Feminist Review*. Currently editing a selection of Virginia Woolf's essays on women writers (The Women's Press, 1979) and writing *Marxist Feminist Theory and the Oppression of Women Today* (New Left Books).

Elizabeth Bird. Currently staff tutor in sociology in the Department of Extra-Mural Studies at the University of Bristol. Her research and teaching interests are in the sociology of art and literature and women's studies.

Lucy Bland. Research student at the Centre for Contemporary Cultural Studies, Birmingham University, and contributor to *Women Take Issue* (Hutchinson, 1978).

Philip R.D. Corrigan. Principal lecturer, Complementary Studies Unit, London College of Printing. Main publications (with Derek Sayer and Harvie Ramsay): *Socialist Construction and Marxist Theory* (1978); *For Mao* (1979); and editor of *State Formation and Capitalism in England: Historical Investigations* (1979). Author, alone and in collaboration with Derek Sayer, of various articles.

Peter Golding. Research Associate at the Centre for Mass Communications Research, University of Leicester. Author of *The Mass Media* (1974) and (with Philip Elliott) of a forthcoming book on news production, *Making the News.* Currently preparing books on the mass media and the Welfare State and (with Graham Murdock) on the political economy of communications.

John Hill. Currently lecturer in Film Studies, New University of Ulster. Holds an MA in Sociology and Drama, University of Glasgow and has undertaken doctoral research in the Sociology Department, University of York. Author of articles on the Glasgow Unity Theatre in *Theatre Quarterly* and *New Edinburgh Review.*

Richard Johnson. Senior lecturer in Social History at the Centre for

Contemporary Cultural Studies, Birmingham University. Publications include essays and articles on popular education in early nineteenth-century Britain and contributions to CCCS publications (some forthcoming) on working-class culture, on contemporary educational policies and ideologies, and on historical writing in Britain.

Annette Kuhn. Lecturer in Film Studies at the Polytechnic of Central London and member of the editorial boards of *Feminist Review* and *Screen.* Editor (with Ann Marie Wolpe) of *Feminism and Materialism* (Routledge, 1978) and author of a number of articles on film.

Trisha McCabe. Research student at the Centre for Contemporary Cultural Studies, Birmingham University and contributor to *Women Take Issue* (Hutchinson, 1978).

Frank Mort. Research student at the Centre for Contemporary Cultural Studies, Birmingham University and contributor to *Women Take Issue* (Hutchinson, 1978).

Graham Murdock. Research Associate at the Centre for Mass Communications Research, University of Leicester. Co-author of *Demonstrations and Communication* (1970) and *Mass Media and the Secondary School* (1973) and author of a number of articles on the sociology of communications, youth and education. Currently preparing books on Youth Culture and (jointly with Peter Golding) on the political economy of the mass media.

Teresa Perkins. Has worked as a stage manager, then as a secretary. Overwhelmed by boredom and by boss's prejudice, made a belated bid for university, and read sociology at Essex. Subsequently a research assistant at North London Polytechnic, and temporary lecturer at Reading University, and is currently doing a PhD at the London School of Economics. She is married and has two children.

Grahame Thompson. Lecturer in Economics at the Open University and member of the editorial board of *Economy and Society*. He has written on the financial aspects of the economy and is particularly interested in forms of economic financial calculation.

Janet Wolff. Currently lecturer in sociology at the University of Leeds. Author of *Hermeneutic Philosophy and the Sociology of Art* (1975).

Current research interests include the sociology of art, and in particular the development of the city of Manchester and the growth of the arts in that city.

INDEX

DATE DUE